W9-CYB-037

Advance Praise for
Putting Government In Its Place: The Case for a New Deal 3.0

"To read David Riemer's bold and provocative *Putting Government In Its Place*, which I strongly urge every citizen to do before Election Day 2020, is to understand the difference between an ideologue — a believer in a defined ideology — and a pragmatist — someone who instead is concerned with practical results. An ideologue believes that which is right works; the pragmatist believes instead that what works is right.

"David Riemer is a knowledgeable, insightful, and honest pragmatist whom I have known for 45 years and who, himself, knows first-hand from his unique experiences in the United States Senate, in the State Capitol, and in City Hall, and as an original public thinker and doer, just what works and what doesn't. Because he has personally written budgets and public laws and made sure a program works for people the way it is supposed to, he gives us in *Putting Government In Its Place* a convincing and clear map forward for making our country healthier, stronger, more prosperous, and more just.

"David Riemer provides the reader a challenging diagnosis of our public condition today and then offers his fresh and his original vision for a better tomorrow. A book every candidate and every citizen should read before the 2020 election."
— **Mark Shields**, PBS NewsHour "Shields and Brooks,"
Syndicated Columnist

"David Riemer does an excellent job identifying the challenges America faces in crafting a New Deal 3.0. And he takes an important step further, by presenting solutions, sometimes provocative ones, to move our nation forward. An engaging read."
— **Tom Barrett**, Mayor of Milwaukee, Wisconsin

"David Riemer is brilliant and is a rare bird. Very few people argue for an economy that includes everyone and uses the word 'justice.' David pulls it all together, from FDR to right now. He gives a map for economic justice and tells us how to get it done. This book is smart and wide. Read it."
— **Peter Edelman**, Carmack Waterhouse Professor of Law
and Public Policy, Georgetown Law Center

"Rooted in the New Deal and intervening decades, Riemer gives us history, detail, and a 'Change of Concept' for the functions of government in the years ahead. An essential, enjoyable read whatever your politics."
— **Jim Tallon**, President Emeritus, United Hospital Fund of New York

"David Riemer draws on his decades in progressive government to offer a sophisticated plan to Make American Government Great Again. This would be the agenda if we elected a new Franklin Roosevelt in 2020. The book is persuasive that these ideas would work."
— **Lance M. Liebman**, William S. Beinecke Professor of Law Emeritus
and Dean Emeritus, Columbia Law School

"Brilliant. David Riemer has written an original, historically grounded and thoughtful book which analyses the achievements, failures and potential of government in the contemporary United States. By shining a light on the 'house that FDR built,' he shows how the New Deal legacy has shaped both contemporary thinking about the role of government and the detail of so many policy programs. Only by understanding that inheritance can today's policy makers begin to construct a new strategy for coping with the pressing agenda of social and economic policy problems. The book deserves to be read by everyone with any interest in or responsibility for governance in the United States."
— **Gillian Peele**, Emeritus Fellow of Lady Margaret Hall, Oxford
and Emeritus Professor of Politics, University of Oxford

"David Riemer understands through long experience almost better than anyone the intricacies, opportunities, and warts in designing policies to promote work, strengthen human capacity, advance health care and budget for it at the same time. At a time when many elected officials claim they want major change but so far don't seem to have any vision for what that entails, he offers a New Deal 3.0. It provides clear ways to provide greater economic security for unemployed, working, disabled, and retired seniors, along with more effective regulation of the market to prevent damage to the environment, workers, consumers, and investors alike."
— **Eugene Steuerle**, co-founder of the Urban Brookings
Tax Policy Center and author of *Dead Men Ruling*

"Anyone who cares about the state of US democracy, economic security, massive inequality, and effective government will benefit from reading this book. David Riemer offers a timely and highly useful primer on the successes and shortcomings of the New Deal and its expansions up to now. He focuses on the ways that a reinvigorated (and recalibrated) New Deal—what he calls New Deal 3.0—can help the US become more democratic and better prepared to deal with the challenges of the 21st century."
— **John M. Bryson** and **Barbara C. Crosby**, professors at the Humphrey School
of Public Affairs at the University of Minnesota, co-authors of *Leadership for
the Common Good*, and co-editors of *Public Value and Public Administration*

"Part history, part economic theory, David Riemer's new book *Putting Government In Its Place: The Case for a New Deal 3.0*, clearly delineates the successes and failures of FDR's New Deal and the many follow-on policies that came after World War II. But, perhaps most importantly, he offers in his work thoughtful ideas and policy prescriptions for a New Deal 3.0 that he convincingly argues would 'create a comprehensive structure of economic security for all Americans.' Leaders in state capitals and Washington, DC, should take heed; Riemer's work warrants a close review."
— **Michael Morgan**, former Secretary of Revenue, State of Wisconsin

"The Social Security Act is the heart and soul of American social policy. But it's growing a little brittle around the edges. In this spectacular volume, Riemer proposes a facelift. If you need surgery, get someone who loves and respects you to do it. If the nation were to follow Riemer's recommendations, Social Security would be greatly improved and ready for anther three or four decades of serving children, adults, and the elderly."
— **Ron Haskins**, The Cabot Family Chair and a Senior Fellow in Economic Studies,
Co-Director of the Center on Children and Families, The Brookings Institution

"In his new book, David Riemer finds inspiration in Franklin D. Roosevelt's New Deal of the 1930s in drawing up a blueprint for prosperity of all Americans, particularly lower-income and working-class citizens. He looks at how the New Deal has changed through the years, has succeeded and failed, and calls for a New Deal 3.0 to meet 21st-century challenges. His arguments are drawn from a lifetime of experience in government, research, and advocating for the less fortunate. This book is a must for anyone who cares about the state of our union."

     — **Kenneth A. Germanson**, President Emeritus, Wisconsin Labor History Society

"David Riemer's new book is a must read for anyone interested in federal social programs' public policy in the 21st century. First, it provides an historical, comprehensive account and superb analysis of how we got to our current programs and their respective structure. His legal and public policy training and experience form the basis for his ideas and prescriptions for what our country needs to change — they would be considered 'disruptive' in today's parlance — to better serve our residents. Though not all will find David's perspective to fit their own, all will find his contribution a compelling discourse and one that we should seriously consider."

     — **Enrique E. Figueroa**, Ph.D., Emeritus, Associate Professor, Department of Urban Planning, University of Wisconsin-Milwaukee

"David Riemer has provided us with a sweeping and provocative analysis of what's wrong with America's domestic policy and where it should go from here. His diagnosis of the U.S. health system's many flaws is insightful. Of greatest importance, he recommends a new health insurance model — based on his experience with the Wisconsin state employee health plan in Dane County — that is both compelling and detailed. Above all, it would fundamentally reform the health system's now perverse cost-increasing incentives, and replace them with incentives for all to seek and to provide quality cost-effective care."

     — **Alain C. Enthoven**, Ph.D., Marriner S. Eccles Professor of Public and Private Management, Emeritus, Knight Management Center, Stanford University

"In this innovative book, David Riemer demonstrates his intimate familiarity and experience with both crafting and implementing public policy at the local, state, and federal levels. He argues persuasively that a New Deal 3.0 requires a fundamental change in the government's role in the economy. It needs to focus exclusively on two objectives: 1) economic security for all Americans and 2) market regulation to address external costs, such as pollution, and to ensure that consumers' interests are well served. In contrast, he calls for the elimination of existent New Deal means tested welfare policies, which he views as poverty traps, and market manipulation through subsidies of particular products and services, which reward the politically powerful at the expense of American households. In short, he argues that governments and markets both have critical roles in improving our economic well-being. Those interested in the recent history of national public policy, as well as those interested in reforming it, will benefit greatly from this book."

     — **Merton D. Finkler**, Ph.D., John R. Kimberly Distinguished Professor Emeritus in the American Economic System, Lawrence University

"This book is a must-read for anyone interested in social and economic justice in the US. In *Putting the Government in Its Place: The Case for a New Deal 3.0*, David Riemer offers a renewed concept of the role of government based on the bold actions Franklin Roosevelt's administration took from 1933 to 1938 in the depths of the Great Depression. This, he argues compellingly, is necessary if America is to thrive into the 21st century. He presents a pragmatic but visionary set of policies and programs that would very likely provide real economic security to American citizens and, at the same time, bring an end to unpopular and inefficient means-tested welfare programs and government manipulation of the market economy.

"Building on the innovative and successful elements of Roosevelt's New Deal, some of which withered in the post 1970 era, Riemer calls for a bold action plan consisting of gradually introducing transitional jobs for the unemployed or underemployed, free child care, higher minimum wages, paid leave, increased income supplements, sufficient retirement and disability payments, the guarantee of collective bargaining, improved environmental protection, protection for consumers, workers, and investors, and universal health care as a supplement to Medicare. These government-sponsored reforms, he convincingly argues, if introduced incrementally, will increase the income of families and individuals, substantially reduce poverty in the United States, and greatly enhance the standard of living for all Americans. This third iteration of the New Deal can bring about an expansion of and the fulfillment of the government's constitutional mandate to ensure the general welfare of its citizens.

"New Dealer Harry Hopkins, my grandfather and champion of the underdog, would wholeheartedly buy into this concept of a newly energized federal government providing transitional jobs to those who, because of the hazards and vicissitudes of a modern capitalist economy, find themselves unemployed, or underemployed. Hopkins fervently believed that the simple solution to poverty is a job paying a decent wage and a government leveling the playing field. Riemer's plan for New Deal 3.0 would go a long way in achieving this end."

—**Dr. June Hopkins**, Professor of History, Emerita,
Georgia Southern University, Armstrong Campus

"So much rhetoric today is about good vs. evil. Sadly, sometimes that's appropriate, but if you want to actually improve government policy outcomes read David Riemer's *Putting Government In Its Place*. Mayors, governors, legislators, policy analysts, and concerned citizens will be inspired when they're reminded that with thoughtfulness and determination public policy can significantly improve people's lives."

—**John Norquist**, Mayor of Milwaukee (1988 to 2004) and former
President and CEO of Congress for the New Urbanism

"It is important to give credit for massive sea policy changes in the basic 'social contract' of government with its citizenry. But government's duty is to continually evaluate whether what served best in the past serves best for the future. Riemer's book compels us to do just that. And he goes yet a step further by posing what a better government, a better future, could look like. That is why it ought to be a 'must read' for all of us citizens."

—**Kathleen Falk**, Dane County Executive (1997-2011) and former Regional
Director, U.S. Department of Health and Human Services

PUTTING GOVERNMENT IN ITS PLACE:
THE CASE FOR A NEW DEAL 3.0

November 2019

For Henry Wells —

Thank you for your
interest in improving
American government.

I hope you enjoy
reading this book.

David Riemer

Other books by David R. Riemer:

The Prisoners of Welfare: Liberating America's Poor from Unemployment and Low Wages (Praeger, 1988)

PUTTING GOVERNMENT IN ITS PLACE: THE CASE FOR A NEW DEAL 3.0

David R. Riemer

HenschelHAUS Publishing
Milwaukee, Wisconsin

Published by HenschelHAUS Publishing, Inc.
www.henschelHAUSbooks.com

Quantity discounts are available for non-profit, academic, and other institutions. Please contact the publisher directly for inquiries.

ISBN (paperback): 978159598-712-9
ISBN (hardcover): 978159598-741-9
E-ISBN: 978159598-713-6
Audio ISBN: 978159598-742-6
LCCN: 2019932724

Publisher's Cataloging-In-Publication Data
(Prepared by The Donohue Group, Inc.)

Names: Riemer, David R., author.
Title: Putting government in its place : the case for a New Deal 3.0 / David R. Riemer.
Other Titles: New Deal 3.0
Description: Milwaukee, Wisconsin : HenschelHAUS Publishing, [2019] | Includes bibliographical references and index.
Identifiers: ISBN 9781595987129 (paperback) | ISBN 9781595987419 (hardcover) | ISBN 9781595987136 (ebook)
Subjects: LCSH: United States--Economic policy--2009- | New Deal, 1933-1939. | United States--Politics and government--2017- | Public welfare--United States --History--21st century. | Trade regulation--United States--History--21st century.
Classification: LCC HC106.84 .R54 2019 (print) | LCC HC106.84 (ebook) | DDC 330.973--dc23

For Ellie Graan, with love,
and with great admiration for who you are and what you do.

CONTENTS

FOREWORD

by GWEN MOORE

I WAS DELIGHTED AND HONORED that my friend and colleague of thirty years, David Riemer, asked me to provide a foreword for his new book, *Putting Government In Its Place: The Case for a New Deal 3.0*. In thirty years, David and I have agreed on a lot; we've differed a lot too. But I have always been convinced of one thing.

There are few people who understand better than David what is right, wrong, and reformable when it comes to America's domestic public policy.

David and I first crossed paths in 1989 when David was the City of Milwaukee's Director of Administration and playing a lead role in creating Milwaukee's New Hope Project for the unemployed and working poor and I was serving in the Wisconsin Legislature. I laugh thinking back to those days because, later when David became the State Budget Director, I would kid him that he was now the gatekeeper to the $30 million annual state budget. However, the truth was that I immediately recognized that he had the heart of a public servant who also possessed the knowledge and drive to enact public policy that worked for the last, least, and lost.

I was right.

Between the years of 1989 and 2003, while I was serving in the Wisconsin Legislature and David held both city and state positions, David and I came to agreement on key policies, such as a more generous state Earned Income Tax Credit (EITC), enhanced childcare for low-income workers, and a major expansion of Medicaid known as BadgerCare.

In 2004, our lives took new political turns. David ran for Milwaukee County Executive, losing a hard-fought campaign. I ran for Congress and won a surprising victory as the first Black women elected to Congress from Wisconsin. Over the years, each of us spent countless hours going door to door in the chilly Wisconsin evenings, taking nothing for granted and talking to every city and suburban resident who would open their door. We heard their fears about jobs, rising cost of health care, and quality and accessibility of education. We listened to their hopes for a better future for themselves and their children.

Now, David Riemer has given us the gift of his lifetime of experience in public policy in his new book, *Putting Government In Its Place: The Case for a New Deal 3.0.* Do not be misled by the title. The essence of the book is that government has an essential place in our society. It necessarily occupies a large and uniquely important place in our lives. Finally, the book lays out how much of what government does today is actually highly successful.

But, as David explains in clear and convincing language, the current structure of government policy—especially the federal government—has significant gaps, flaws, and mistakes. His book lays out a compelling case for exactly how those policy gaps should be filled, flaws corrected, and mistakes ended so that

America can achieve full economic security, equal opportunity, and a truly safe and efficient market economy.

The book tells the story of what David calls the House that FDR Built (that is the formation of the original New Deal during the Great Depression), its expansion after World War II, its partial success, its major drawbacks, and how it should be rejuvenated. One of the great strengths of David's work is that he does not prescribe fuzzy solutions. He provides the reader with usable, detailed solutions. The book outlines an imaginative and often provocative vision for reforming the overall design of American government. It is a challenging narrative about our increasingly fraying covenant with government and how to rejuvenate voters' trust and belief in government as a positive force in their lives that meets the needs of the times.

I can tell you that the specifications in this book are concrete enough to draft a dozen pieces of new federal legislation. I'm glad you've begun the book. I encourage you to finish it. You will not agree 100%. Nobody will. I don't. But David's book is a "must read" for anyone interested in public policy and current events. It offers a thorough, gripping account of:

- How U.S. domestic policy underwent a sea change during the original New Deal of 1933-1938, creating for the first time a large, permanent federal structure for economic security and market regulation; and

- How the New Deal design continued to evolve and expand between World War II and Watergate, but began in the 1970s to lose its capacity to deliver increasing economic security and properly regulated markets in the face of a "new normal" of intense international trade and highly disruptive technological change.

Of greatest importance, the book makes a highly persuasive case for why a sweeping redesign of the New Deal model—a New Deal 3.0—is now necessary to undo the inequality and uncertainly that are tearing our country apart. It makes a compelling argument for how to get America back on a path of equitable and enduring economic security for unemployed, underemployed, working, disabled, and retired seniors (including health insurance, long-term care, and education reforms), and how to more effectively regulate markets to prevent damage to the environment, workers, consumers, and investors.

I believe you will agree that this timely and important book presents an overarching analysis, and spells out dozens of recommendations, that are right on target. I am grateful to David Riemer, as I hope you will be, for giving us such an insightful examination of government's achievements and shortfalls, and for making such a powerful case for a new direction for America's domestic policy.

Gwen Moore
Milwaukee, WI
August 2019

Preface:

Elevator Speech

I wrote this book to answer three questions that Americans are asking:

- Why has the economic progress that the majority of Americans made after World War II ground to a halt or shifted into reverse?

- Specifically, what shortcomings in government policy — what missing policies, messed-up policies, or mistaken policies — have caused or contributed to the drift or decline since the mid-1970s in economic security and the weakening of an effective market?

- Finally, what specific reforms in government policy would set things right, and get all Americans back on a rising economic and social path?

Focus on the New Deal

The focus of the book is the New Deal — its formation, its partial success, its major shortcomings, and its future. To avoid confusion, it will help to explain what I mean by the New Deal. I use the term in three different ways.

The Original New Deal

Sometimes it refers to the original New Deal. By this I mean the set of laws enacted during the first two terms of President Franklin Roosevelt, specifically from 1933 to 1938, in the four areas of:

(1) broad-based economic security guarantees,
(2) means-tested welfare programs,
(3) market regulation, and
(4) market manipulation.

The "jewel in the crown" of the original New Deal was of course the Social Security Act of 1935. But the category also includes the National Labor Relations Act, Fair Labor Standards Act, Banking Act, Securities and Exchange Act, and Agricultural Adjustment Act. Occasionally, I refer to the original New Deal as Version 1.0.

The New Deal Writ Large

Often I speak of the New Deal *writ large*. By this I mean the sum of the original New Deal plus its enlargement, over approximately the next 80 years (i.e., from 1938 to today), through new laws enacted in the same four areas of public policy.

Within the realm of broad-based economic security guarantees, the New Deal *writ large* combines the original provisions of the Social Security Act (e.g., Unemployment Insurance and old-age pensions) with subsequent Social Security Act programs (e.g., disability insurance and Medicare). Within the realm of means-tested welfare programs, the New Deal *writ large* combines the original New Deal welfare program (what we now call

Temporary Assistance to Needy Families, or TANF) with additions from the 1960s and 1970s such as Food Stamps and Medicaid.

The market regulation that the original New Deal launched from 1933 to 1938 has been similarly augmented over the following 80 years of the New Deal *writ large*. The same is true of federal manipulation of the market designed to subsidize specific types of consumption and investment, including entire industries and economic sectors.

Occasionally, I refer to the New Deal *writ large* as Version 2.0.

The New Deal Settlement

Finally, at times I refer to the sum of the original New Deal, plus its 80-year enlargement over the course of the New Deal *writ large*, as the New Deal "settlement." I have strived to use each term in an appropriate context.

WHY CONCENTRATE ON THE NEW DEAL?

The focus on the New Deal is not arbitrary. The questions that I asked at the beginning—(1) Why has economic progress for the majority of Americans ended or reversed? (2) What government policies are contributing to the drift and decline in economic security and the weakening of the market? (3) What reforms in government do we need to get America back on track—are ultimately questions about the New Deal's design, its defects, and its destiny. The greatest domestic challenge America faces in the 21st century is how to reform the New Deal so fundamentally that we end up with a New Deal Version 3.0.

The New Deal has come down to us as a label, a campaign pledge, a response to the Great Depression, and an alphabet soup of government agencies and programs. But its meaning goes deeper, its imprint is larger, and the challenge it presents is profound.

The federal government did not do much before the Great Depression. But the economic collapse of 1929-1932 so shattered the country that President Franklin Roosevelt and Congress felt compelled to pursue what FDR called "a complete change of concept" in government's role. The New Deal's two-part revolution was to put the federal government in charge of:

1) legally guaranteeing that Americans did not suffer the full brunt of unemployment and poverty caused by the shortcomings of the labor market, and

2) safeguarding both individuals and businesses from the damage and undue risks that can arise from the market's malfunctioning in general.

We now take for granted FDR's "complete change of concept" in government's functions. We accept as given the New Deal programs put in place from 1933 to 1938, and expanded over 80 years, within four clusters of domestic policy:

1) broad-based economic security guarantees,

2) means-tested welfare programs,

3) market regulation, and

4) market manipulation.

Most of us also recognize that the New Deal *writ large* did enormous good. It helped to lift millions of Americans out of poverty and into the middle class. It improved our health and education. It spurred the nation's economy during the "old normal" era of 1945-1970, when the U.S. totally dominated the world's markets and technology usually seemed a friend.

But since the 1970s, the New Deal settlement has steadily fallen short. The gaps, flaws, and mistakes in its design—interacting with a "new normal" of intense foreign competition and highly disruptive technology—have thwarted the New Deal settlement in solving our worsening domestic problems.

As a result, millions today face unemployment or underemployment, unstable jobs, volatile hours of work, static or slowly creeping earnings, faltering incomes (especially after health care costs are taken into account), imperiled retirements, and severe racial disparities. All suffer from a defective health insurance system. We have a flagging K12 education system, and a debt-crushing college education system. Means-tested welfare programs, aimed merely at preventing destitution, discourage work and marriage.

Persistent dumping on the environment, workers, consumers, and investors corrodes U.S. productivity and wealth. Overriding consumers' sovereignty over the market, massive subsidies for politically favored economic sectors further distort the economy's efficiency. In addition, some of the New Deal's most egregious mistakes—particularly housing and transportation policies that greatly worsened racial segregation and disparities during the post-war era—continue to inflict harm on minorities and society as a whole.

Within our tradition of pragmatic experimentalism, we now need another fundamental "change of concept" in government's role if the United States is to thrive. The heart of this book spells out what that next "change of concept" — a New Deal 3.0 — should be.

The approach should be pragmatic. Step-by-step reform is acceptable when large-scale advances are not viable. But the Bible reminds us of the need to tie specific steps to a broad vision. We need above all a new vision for reforming the New Deal.

ELEVATOR SPEECH

In telling this book's story, the toughest challenge I have faced is simplification. *Putting Government In Its Place* covers a lot of ground.

It goes back to the Declaration of Independence and the Constitution. It explores the formation of the New Deal's policy structure in 1933-1938. It analyzes the growth of the New Deal's four policy clusters from 1938 to today.

The book also deals with more than a dozen domestic policy topics: unemployment, underemployment, wages, earnings and their supplementation, disability income, retirement income, health insurance, K12 education, college education, means-tested welfare programs, market regulation, market manipulation, budgets, taxes, and more. In each area, I present specific recommendations for policy reform.

Because of the book's broad scope and multiple topics, I have sought to boil down the story to an "elevator speech."

Indeed, friends and colleagues have begged me to do so. It's not easy, but here goes. (Remember: it's a slow-moving elevator in a tall building.)

1st Floor: Government in the United States today is everywhere. It touches our lives in dozens of important ways. But while government today is ubiquitous, it typically is invisible, hiding in plain sight.

2nd Floor: The ubiquity of government in the U.S. is a 20th century phenomenon. Prior to the 1930s, government did a lot less, especially at the federal level.

3rd Floor: But starting in 1933 in the midst of the Great Depression, the New Deal responded to the collapse of the U.S. economy by completely changing the very concept of what government—particularly the federal government—does.

4th Floor: The nation's central problem, as President Franklin Roosevelt and his allies recognized, was the federal government's outdated and inadequate relationship with the markets—in particular the labor market and the financial market. Going forward, the federal government would fundamentally and permanently overhaul its relationship with these two broad swaths of the overall market.

5th Floor: The New Deal's two main goals were to ensure that Americans enjoyed much greater economic security by correcting for the labor market's deficiencies, and to protect individuals and businesses from damage caused by financial market abuse and malfunction.

6th Floor: To achieve these results, Roosevelt, his New Deal administrators, and supporters in Congress, between 1933 and 1938, created four large clusters of federal domestic policy:

broad-based economic security guarantees, means-tested welfare programs, market regulation, and market manipulation. The result: New Deal 1.0.

7th Floor: From 1938 to today, the U.S. greatly expanded the New Deal within these four policy clusters. The outcome: New Deal 2.0.

8th Floor: Unfortunately, starting roughly in the mid-1970s, the New Deal thus *writ large* has been steadily losing the battle to protect Americans from the "hazards and vicissitudes" of a new U.S. economy that has been radically reshaped by powerful foreign competition and breakneck technological innovation.

9th Floor: Huge gaps, major flaws, and big mistakes in the New Deal's structure have spread economic insecurity, tolerated serious market abuses, and undermined the economy's efficiency and the nation's wealth.

10th Floor: The solution—the way to jumpstart America's forward progress—is to stop tinkering and make fundamental changes in the New Deal's structure, thus creating a New Deal 3.0. Two New Deal policy clusters should be greatly strengthened. The other two policy clusters should be entirely eliminated.

11th Floor: Specifically, we should expand and improve the design of the New Deal's broad-based economic security guarantees and its market regulation safeguards.

12th Floor. At the same time, we should phase out the New Deal's means-tested welfare programs, as well as wind down its market manipulations that replace consumer sovereignty with subsidies for politically favored types of consumption and investment.

13th Floor. Unless we act thus to fundamentally restructure the New Deal settlement, the U.S. will continue to drift and falter, economically, socially, and politically.

14th Floor. Our tradition of pragmatic experimentalism requires that we redesign the New Deal settlement in pieces and in stages, bringing in specific reforms over time.

15th Floor. In taking this pragmatic approach, however, we must never lose sight of the ultimate shape of reform.

16th Floor: America's future success hinges in large part on whether we manage to move steadily—along what FDR called "lines of attack"—to put in place the fundamental restructuring proposed here in the New Deal's design.

The chapters of this book follow the elevator's journey. The start is the view from a typical American's front porch. Government is omnipresent but almost invisible. The journey's end is a set of detailed proposals for fundamental reform of the New Deal that add up to another "complete change of concept" in the functions of government: New Deal 3.0.

The proposals' aim is dramatic improvement in Americans' economic security and the efficiency of our market. But there is another overarching goal. To paraphrase Lincoln at Gettysburg, the ultimate goal is the nation's next birth of freedom.

Introduction:

Government's Hidden Ubiquity

"You see, but you do not observe."
— Sherlock Holmes to Dr. Watson

Imagine it is 4 PM on a Friday in early June. Imagine you live in Milwaukee, Wisconsin.

You worked hard all week. The boss let you leave early. You put a slice of pizza in the microwave, grab an ice-cold beer, and plop down on your front porch to enjoy an early dinner and check out what's happening in the neighborhood.

The last thing you are thinking about—the last thing you see—is government. The furthest thing from your mind is the New Deal.

You are certainly not thinking about the three big "D" questions. What should government *do*? How should government get the *dollars* it needs to operate? What's the best way to *deliver* government?

Yet government is everywhere. It is hiding from you in plain sight. It's so obvious you don't notice it. It's so visible you see right through it. It's omnipresent; it's a big deal in your life; and it escapes your observation.

Spy thrillers like to make us imagine that a hidden government is secretly dominating the world from a bunker under the Rocky Mountains or a fortress floating above the Arctic ice cap.

But the real hidden government lies just beyond your doorstep. It's right in front of you, unnoticed.

In front of you lies a city street—built by government, maintained by government, lit by government, regulated by government stoplights and yield signs and no-parking signs, cooled by government trees, cleaned by government sweepers in summer, plowed by government trucks in winter, and patrolled by government police and parking checkers.

A single street does not do much good. To get where you want to go—and to bring family, friends, and packages to your door—your street needs to be connected to hundreds of other local streets. The local street grid in turn must be connected to county roads, state highways, and the interstate system.

Government built it all, maintains it all, and controls it all. Every inch of this vast network of pavement was planned, engineered, and paid for by government. Every mile of concrete or asphalt is kept in shape by government, lit by government, dotted with signals and signs by government, shaded by government, swept and plowed by government, and monitored by government.

So far, we've only been talking about streets. As you munch on your pizza and take another swig of beer, you can observe a lot more of government's imprint. Your porch leads to a walkway that ends at a sidewalk—a government sidewalk. A few hundred feet down the sidewalk, there is a fire hydrant on the corner—a hydrant maintained by one government agency, the water department, so that another government agency, the fire department, can get high-pressure water into its hoses to stop your house from burning down.

That fire hydrant is just the most visible sign, a big red sentinel, that advertises the government's vast web of underground pipes that bring water to your home all the way from Lake Michigan. Before the water gets to you, the government has roughed it up pretty bad in the municipal water treatment plant: chlorinated it, sand-filtered it, and (just to be sure you don't get cryptosporidium) ozonized it.

Government's web of underground water pipes parallels government's underground web of sewer pipes. The government-owned laterals, connectors, and (if it really pours) deep tunnels convey your household sewage and that of your neighbors, sometimes mixed with storm-water runoff, to a giant government-owned treatment plant. The treatment plant mixes the nasty stuff with chemicals, and discharges the resulting effluent into Lake Michigan.

As you dig into your second slice of pepperoni-and-mushroom pizza and finish off that bottle of Miller High Life, many of the vehicles you glance at also belong to government. Their drivers are carrying out important governmental functions. A government owned- and-operated police car slowly cruises by, then flashes its lights and turns on its siren as the government-employed police officers take off after a speeder. You observe a government owned-and-operated fire engine returning to your neighborhood fire station after its government-employed firefighters put out a kitchen fire. A government owned-and-operated EMS vehicle whizzes by on an emergency run.

The heavy snowfalls that Milwaukee gets socked with have melted. No need to shovel your government-built, government-repaired sidewalk until the winter. Nor will you see any government owned-and-operated snowplows or salt-spreaders until the snow flies again. As you enjoy the spring weather, you remember how during last January's blizzard the city government's crews kept plowing and re-plowing the streets so you could go to your favorite niece's wedding.

You've also lived in Milwaukee long enough to know that, when the snow melts away in March (or April, or May), the Department of Public Works sets other government crews to work. They fix street lights, clean out drains, sweep streets to remove litter and dirt, trim the beautiful tall trees that the city's foresters planted decades ago, chop down dead trees, and plant new ones.

The weekend has begun, but your neighbors down the block failed once again to roll back their government-owned garbage cart before heading up north to their cottage. Damn! You'll have to look at that government-owned cart for a week as it sits on the government-owned sidewalk. For a moment you remember that when you left for work early this morning, the street was crawling with Bureau of Sanitation crews and equipment. Government owned-and-operated garbage trucks were picking up refuse. Government owned-and-operated recycling trucks were picking up old newspapers, aluminum cans, and glass bottles, plus #1, #2 (not #3), #4, and #5 plastic.

You look again. That government-owned garbage cart is still sitting on the government-owned sidewalk. Why don't your neighbors get the kids next door to roll it back where it belongs?

All those kids ever do is goof off at the government-built, government-maintained basketball court in the government-owned, government-operated park at the end of the street.

The kids will be off to a government-financed school on Monday. The neighborhood school is just four blocks away. In Milwaukee, approximately 75,000 children go to public schools that government owns and operates, while another 35,000 go to government-funded private charter schools or government-funded private "choice" schools. The single biggest part of the property tax bill you paid last December goes to government-financed K12 schools.

While you've been eating pizza and drinking beer, your senses of taste and smell have been hard at work. If you were so inclined, you might also use your sense of sight and (thanks to Sherlock Holmes) your powers of observation to draw distinctions between the different levels of government.

The level of government that is most visible from your porch is local government. The City of Milwaukee built and maintains the very visible street you live on, hired the police officers and firefighters who drove by your home, and assigned the sanitation crews to pick up your garbage and recyclables. The public school district—a specialized form of local government—hired your children's teachers and operates the beautiful old school four blocks away.

But the immediate visibility of a governmental service is hardly the sole measure of its importance. In our daily lives, some of the most essential services that government performs are distant and hard to observe

Close your eyes. Think. Your street, like most streets in America, is not on a bus line (or streetcar, light-rail, subway, or train line). You don't live across from a park. But at times in your life, you and your family have taken rides on government-financed public transportation and counted on government owned-and-operated parks for recreation. In your mind's eye, you can conjure up from your front porch a panoramic vision of the nearby presence of government-provided bus shelters, golf courses, tennis courts, basketball courts, baseball diamonds, football fields, soccer pitches, splash pads, and swimming pools. In Milwaukee, and in many other metropolitan areas, public transit and parks are the responsibility of some sort of regional government, such as a county, transit authority, or parks district.

Even with high-powered X-ray vision, however, you will have great difficulty seeing from your front porch the many ways in which your life is touched by state government and the federal government. The higher the level of government, the harder it is to observe.

It's true that, for a small fraction of Americans, observing state and federal government in action is easy. If you happen to be a state or federal employee; if you're a lobbyist or government contractor; if you live in a state capital or the Washington, DC, area; or if your home is near a state park, national park, or military base; then you have a personal connection with state or federal government.

But you yourself, sitting on your front porch in Milwaukee, are like most Americans. You take notice of the state and federal governments in only a limited number of situations, such as when you: (1) read, hear, or watch news accounts about those governments; (2) file a state or federal income tax return; (3) catch sight of a State Patrol vehicle on the interstate; (4) buy or renew a state vehicle registration, driver's license, hunting license, or fishing license; (5) go on a vacation that takes you to a state or national park; (6) see your letter carrier delivering the mail; or (7) start paying attention to Social Security and Medicare.

And yet the impact on your life of both state government and the U.S. government is enormous.

You live in Wisconsin. Your local property taxes are pretty high. But they would be dramatically higher if your state government did not pick up over 50% of the cost of local publicly financed schools. In this respect, you are not unique. In many states, over half of the cost of local K12 education is absorbed by state government. Paying for local K12 schools is in fact either the first or second biggest expenditure of state government.

You are fortunate to have good health insurance. Not everyone in your family has been so lucky. When your brother Bart lost his job during the Great Recession, he lost his employer-sponsored health coverage. Thank goodness he was able to enroll in Medicaid, along with his uninsured wife Beth, and their uninsured kids Bill and Bob. Your Aunt Harriet also signed up for Medicaid when she needed to go into a nursing home, but had no money left because Uncle Ozzie made a lot of bad investments and then ran off.

Medicaid, of course, is not an abstraction. State governments run Medicaid and pay for a big chunk of it. States do get reimbursed for 50% or more of their Medicaid costs with federal funds. Despite this, Medicaid costs are one of the states' biggest—and most rapidly growing—expenditures.

Far beyond what you can see from your front porch, your state government is busy providing you and your fellow citizens with dozens of valuable services. State governments operate prisons and courts. State governments fund technical schools. Each state government operates one or more state universities. State governments own and maintain tens of thousand of acres of forests and lakes, including dozens of state parks.

As you ponder whether to head inside for another slice of pizza and a second bottle of beer, your thoughts turn to the even more invisible federal government.

To begin with, you pay a lot in federal taxes. You earn a comfortable salary. You make a few thousand extra each year in interest, dividends, and capital gains. The federal government probably claims the biggest slice of your taxes, when you add up the two federal payroll taxes you pay (the FICA or Social Security Tax of 6.0% and the Medicare tax of 1.65%) plus your federal income taxes.

You can tell how important the federal government is by the sounds you do not hear. When you were growing up, the music of Simon and Garfunkel was popular. Their song "The Sounds of Silence" rose to the top of the charts. As the late afternoon shadows start to fall over Milwaukee, there are also a lot of sounds of silence, thanks to the U.S. government. You do not hear the gunfire of invading armies. You do not hear the explosion of missiles fired by attacking aircraft. Nor—with rare, tragic exceptions—are you ever likely to hear the detonation of suicide bombs or the gunfire of terrorists. For much of this, you owe thanks to the federal government: the Army, Navy, Air Force, Marines, and Coast Guard, as well as the Central Intelligence Agency (CIA) and Department of Homeland Security (DHS).

But protecting our safety and health is only the beginning of the important role of the federal government.

Let's take another look—literally—at the rest of the pizza that is waiting for you on the kitchen counter. You paid for the pizza with dollars printed by the federal government and whose value the United States Federal Reserve protects.

When you decided which pizza to order, you never thought about whether it would be safe to eat or whether the price would be fair. You assumed its safety and a competitive price. But in doing so, you were again relying heavily on the federal government.

Through multiple federal laws and agencies aimed at ensuring food safety and a competitive market, the federal government oversees the companies and transactions in the long chain of production and sale that escorted your pizza's ingredients to your mouth:

- The Environmental Protection Agency (EPA) oversees the Clean Water Act and the Clear Air Act with the twin goals of ensuring that safe water is used to make the pizza dough and that the air is not fouled by the companies that produce pepperoni, mushrooms, cheese, tomatoes, onions, and black olives.

- The federal agencies that administer the Fair Labor Standards Act (FLSA), the National Labor Relations Act (NLRA), and the Occupational Safety and Health Act (OSHA) aim to ensure that the workers who produce the pizza dough are paid at least the minimum wage, are free to organize unions and bargain collectively, and are not injured on the job.

- The Food and Drug Administration (FDA) seeks to guarantee that the pizza itself is safe to eat. Uncle Sam also regulates the safety of the microwave you used to "nuke" the pizza through the Consumer Product Safety Commission (CPSC). And the federal government also helps make sure your microwave has a steady supply of electricity.

- Finally, the Securities and Exchange Commission (SEC) tries to prevent potential investors from being fleeced as they consider whether to buy stock in Pizza Hut or Domino's. Indeed, several federal agencies seek to ensure the transparency and integrity of the string of businesses — manufacturers, banks, insurers, and more — that made money from your pizza's long trip to your taste buds.

In short, when you eat a pizza, you are consuming the federal government.

It is nearly 6 PM. Time to face up to today's mail. Now that you've had a bite to eat and some suds to drink, the bills won't look so bad. What's this? Not another invitation to join the AARP? You only just turned 60! OK, go ahead and recycle it. But in a few years, you will want to participate in the two giant programs of the federal government that the AARP cares most about: Social Security and Medicare.

The kids playing basketball at the local government park and other younger workers will, in a few years, be helping to pay a big part of your federal government pension (Social Security) and health insurance (Medicare). Feel free, though, to believe that you and others in your age group financed the entire cost, and that Washington is simply giving your own money back to you. It's a pleasant fiction, but you deserve it.

After all, you're hardly getting a free ride. You've been kicking in federal payroll taxes for decades. Those taxes help to ensure that your widowed mother, age 85, gets enough in her government Social Security checks to stay in your childhood home. And thank goodness she has the government Medicare program to pay for her visits to the doctor, cover the cost of her cataract operation, and defray the cost of the drugs she must take for her diabetes and high blood pressure.

As you turn to open the front door and go inside, you notice a soggy newspaper stuck in the bushes by your porch. Damn! Why can't the newspaper carrier throw straight?

You forgive her quickly. She gets up at 5 AM every day to deliver your copy of the *Milwaukee Journal Sentinel,* and then heads off to work for only a few bucks above the federal minimum wage at McDonald's. You've seen her there by 7 AM, scrambling eggs and frying bacon. You count yourself lucky.

But as you retrieve the newspaper, you can't help but glance at the dismal headlines:

"Many Still Stuck in Low-Wage Jobs"

"Poverty Rate in U.S. Barely Budges"

"Despite Obamacare, More Than 25 Million Uninsured"

"U.S. Students Lag Other Nations in Test Scores"

"Potholes Spread as American Roads Decay"

"Government Debt Rises to Record Level"

You mutter out loud, "Why can't government get *anything* right?"

You have to admit, though, that (except for the soggy paper and the depressing headlines) it's actually been a great start to the weekend. Warm weather. Blue sky. A slight breeze. Tasty pizza. Cold beer.

So before heading indoors, you toss the soggy paper into your government-owned recycling cart. Next week, government sanitation workers will dump its contents into a government-owned recycling truck and haul the truckload to a government-run recycling center.

On their way, the sanitation workers will drive along government-owned, government-operated streets. They may wave at the government police offers and government firefighters they see en route. They will pass two government-owned elementary schools, a government-financed high school, and a government-operated university.

Summer's here, so they may even discuss which government national park to visit on vacation. Grand Canyon? Yellowstone? Statue of Liberty?

As the sanitation workers take their lunch break, they may debate whether, once they turn 65 and switch to the government Medicare program, should they also claim their Social Security benefits or wait until age 70?

Now back to you—the Milwaukeean who just enjoyed several slices of pizza and a cold beer.

You are a fair-minded person. As you sit down to catch a little TV, you realize you let the soggy newspaper tick you off too much. You may not pay a lot of attention to government, but you know in your heart that the accusation you made— "Why can't government get anything right?"—is untrue and unfair.

The true and fair question is: "Why can't government do all the things it's meant to do…do them really well…and stop doing the stuff it has no business doing?"

You pay enough in taxes. You pay local property taxes, state sales and income taxes, and federal income and payroll taxes. So does almost everyone on your block, in your city and state, and across the country.

So with all that money and power in hand, why is government often missing, or broken, where we need it the most? And why does government so frequently intrude, and try to boss us around, when we don't want it or need it?

But then, what exactly is government supposed to do?

Out of the corner of your eye, you notice an old copy of *Reader's Digest*. Too bad someone ripped out the jokes. But what's this? A special feature—a quiz—on "What Should the Federal Government Do?" How fortuitous! (See Appendix A, "The Government Quiz.")

Half an hour and two broken pencils later, you admit that deciding exactly what government should do is not simple. Those were tough questions. Maybe you can get some help. Perhaps on a website. Maybe from a podcast. How about a book?

For a second, you think back to your high school class in U.S. history. The teacher was so-so, but the textbook was great: Henry Wilkinson Bragdon's and Samuel Proctor McCutchen's *History of a Free People*. It explained how, in response to the Great Depression, the New Deal dramatically changed what government did. That, at least, was an attempt to have government do the right thing.

Maybe, you say to yourself, we should go back to the New Deal to figure out how to fix today's problems. What did the New Deal do right? What did it leave out? Where did it go wrong?

Maybe, you wonder, the United States needs another New Deal.

CHAPTER 1

"A COMPLETE CHANGE OF CONCEPT"

Washington, DC. March 4, 1933

AT 12:00 NOON, FRANKLIN DELANO ROOSEVELT placed his right hand on his family Bible and swore to preserve the Constitution of the United States. Minutes later—in an Inaugural Address made famous by FDR's insistence that "the only thing we have to fear is . . . fear itself"—the new President promised "action, and action now."[1]

Action was clearly needed. Nearly 25% of U.S. workers were unemployed, as factory after factory shut down.[2] For those who kept their jobs, the average workweek fell by more than 10%.[3] From 1929 to 1933, national income dropped by roughly 50% and real GDP by more than 45%.[4, 5] Industrial production plummeted by over half, and the average index prices received by farmers also fell by half.[6, 7] Between 1929 and 1933, the number of banks in the U.S. fell by a third.[8] The Dow-Jones Industrial Average closed at an all-time high of 362.35 in September 1929, the month before the stock market crashed. The Dow dropped for the next three years, sinking to 57.75 for March 1933.[9]

On the Friday before FDR's inauguration, the New York Stock Exchange suspended trading and the Chicago Board of Trade shut down. In the days leading up to the Inauguration, bank after bank failed. Just hours before FDR took the oath of office, the governors of New York, Illinois, and Pennsylvania ordered their states' banks to close indefinitely. The U.S. had 48 states at the time, and 34 had shut down their banks.[10]

Not since the bleakest days of the Civil War, 70 years earlier, had the United States faced so terrible a crisis. Never in its history as a nation had the U.S. plunged into so deep an economic abyss. The collapse was not limited to America; it was worldwide. John Maynard Keynes, the eminent British economist, wryly told a reporter the previous summer that there was a precedent for what had happened to the world's economy. The precedent was the Dark Ages, and it lasted 400 years.[11]

Few could dispute that the United States of America needed "action, and action now."

THE NEW DEAL'S NON-PLAN

But *exactly* what action would President Roosevelt recommend to Congress to get America back on its feet?

Candidate Roosevelt had said little about specifics. "By the spring of 1932, almost every prominent Democratic progressive had become committed to the candidacy of New York's Governor Franklin Delano Roosevelt," New Deal historian William Leuchtenburg has written, but liberal Democrats were "disturbed by the vagueness of his formula for recovery."[12] FDR's vagueness no doubt unsettled conservative Democrats and Republicans as well.

In July, as the nation's economic crisis worsened, FDR secured his party's nomination and pledged a "New Deal" to the American people.[13] But what *precisely* would the New Deal be when translated into legislation, appropriations, and regulation?

In accepting the Democratic Party's nomination and in his campaign speeches throughout the summer and fall of 1932, Roosevelt shared tantalizing ideas about how he wanted to address the crisis. A scattering of ideas, however, is not a program for economic recovery. As the campaign marched closer and closer to Election Day on November 8, 1932 — the last possible day it could be held — the New Deal remained a collection of fuzzy notions.

Part of FDR's reticence was political shrewdness. In a campaign for high office, values plus vision can produce victory. Specifics — such as detailed policy papers, precise legislative language, or intricate budget calculations — are baffling, boring, and a turnoff for voters. It was hardly a surprise that, during the 1932 campaign, Roosevelt avoided making promises with a high level of programmatic, legal, or fiscal detail.

When FDR did venture into the realm of policy — even broad policy, shorn of specific detail — he often contradicted himself. According to Leuchtenburg's account of the 1932 campaign:

> Roosevelt's campaign did little to reassure critics who
> thought him a vacillating politician. His speeches
> sounded painfully discordant themes. He assailed the
> Hoover administration because it was "committed to
> the idea that we ought to center control of everything in
> Washington as rapidly as possible" but he advanced
> policies which would greatly extend the power of the
> national government. He struck out at the disastrous
> high-tariff policies of the Republicans but by the end of
> the campaign, taunted by Hoover, he had eaten so
> many of his words that no real difference separated the
> two candidates on the tariff issue. ... His Topeka speech

left farm leaders, as it was to leave historians, arguing over precisely what he intended. He would initiate a far-reaching plan to help the farmer; but he would do it in such a fashion that it would not "cost the Government any money." [14]

Ironically, one of the few specific pledges that candidate Roosevelt did make was his commitment to cut by 25% "the cost of current Federal Government operations" that had become "the most reckless and extravagant...that I have been able to discover in the statistical record of any peacetime Government anywhere, any time."[15] It was entirely the wrong prescription for the nation's illness. Had FDR kept his promise to cut federal spending by 25%, the Great Depression would have become the Humongous Depression.

But for the most part, Roosevelt avoided specifics. While part of his vagueness and vacillation was political shrewdness, there was a deeper reason. FDR did not have a carefully thought-out, spelled-out, or costed-out plan for economic recovery.

Leuchtenburg, disagreeing with writers who insisted that Roosevelt's campaign "foretold" virtually all of the New Deal, concluded that:

> [W]hat is striking...is what he did not mention in
> 1932—deficit spending, a gigantic federal works
> program, federal housing and slum clearance, the NRA,
> the TVA, sharply increased income taxes on the
> wealthy, massive and imaginative relief programs, a
> national labor relations board with federal sanctions to
> enforce collective bargaining—and this does not begin
> to exhaust the list.[16]

Roosevelt did not advocate such proposals because "his primary task was to get himself elected, and, as the front runner, he saw little point in jeopardizing his chances by engaging in controversies that might cost him more than they would win."[17]

But there was another, more fundamental, reason: "Roosevelt did not advocate such proposals in part because they had not yet crystallized...."[18] FDR simply did not know how he would convert his instincts and impulses about reform into concrete policies, much less detailed legislation to create new programs that would lift the U.S. out of the Great Depression.

Thus, up to the very moment that the nation's leadership passed from sour Herbert Hoover to upbeat Franklin Roosevelt, FDR was in doubt about exactly how he would attempt to get the unemployed back to work, save desperate farmers, jump-start idle factories, rescue the banks, revive the stock market, and in general save the nation's economy. The New Deal's lack of substance did not go unnoticed. "Both before and after Roosevelt took office," Leuchtenburg noted, "many deplored the absence of a coherent New Deal ideology."[19]

Not only did FDR not know precisely what he would do; his closest advisors were also perplexed. The leader of the New Deal's "Brain Trust," Professor Raymond Moley, who wrote many of FDR's speeches during the 1932 campaign and the stretch between election and inauguration, later admitted that no comprehensive plan guided the torrent of New Deal policies that would soon flow into law: "[T]o look upon these policies as the result of a unified plan," Moley wrote, "was to believe that the accumulation of stuffed snakes, baseball pictures, school flags, old tennis shoes, carpenter's tools, geometry books, and chemistry sets in a boy's bedroom could have been put there by an interior decorator."[20]

Frances Perkins, FDR's choice for Secretary of Labor, the first woman to hold a cabinet post, and later the chief architect of the Social Security Act, was blunter: "The notion that the New Deal had a preconceived theoretical position is ridiculous."[21] In her 1946 book *The Roosevelt I Knew*, Perkins wrote about the New Deal:

> It expressed a new attitude, not a fixed program. When he [Franklin Roosevelt] got to Washington he had no fixed program.
>
> The notion that the New Deal had a preconceived theoretical position is ridiculous. The pattern it was to assume was not clear or specific in Roosevelt's mind, in the mind of the Democratic Party, or in the mind of anyone else taking part in the 1932 campaign.[22]

Perkins, who worked closely with Roosevelt in enacting much of the New Deal's legislative program, was so convinced that the New Deal was unplanned that she repeated the assertion in her book:

> It is important to repeat the New Deal was not a plan, not even an agreement, and it was certainly not a plot, as was later charged. Most of the programs later called the New Deal arose out of the emergency which Roosevelt faced when he took office at the low point of the depression."[23]
>
> ....
>
> But there was no central unified plan. There wasn't time or organization for that. The New Deal grew out of these emerging and necessary rescue actions.[24]

It is unfair to say that Franklin Roosevelt was without a clue when he took the oath of office on March 4, 1933. But it is accurate to say that FDR and his inner circle had no overall plan, no ready-to-go proposals, no draft legislation in their back pockets, no projections for the cost of specific programs, and no wording for concrete regulations. As they themselves understood, they would need to invent the details of the New Deal on the run.

For better or worse, the Constitution provided little help. The U.S. Constitution defines the powers that the President and Congress may exercise. But it provides virtually no guidance in telling them exactly whether, when, or how to use those powers to combat a Great Depression or any other national problem. For a detailed discussion of the Constitution's limits, visit: www.govinplace.org/content/Constitution.pdf.

For many, the challenge was terrifying. As one of the President's advisors, his wife Eleanor Roosevelt, told a reporter: "One has a feeling of going it blindly, because we're in a tremendous stream, and none of us knows where we're going to land."[25]

THE HEART OF THE PROBLEM: FAILING MARKETS

Yet if Franklin Roosevelt lacked an overall plan and was short on specifics about exactly how to steer the American economy back to a safe shore, FDR was fairly clear where the heart of the problem lay. The American people themselves were not the problem. Neither fate, nor nature, nor the conduct of most Americans was at fault. Rather, the malfunctioning of the nation's markets had created the Great Depression. The market malfunction was driven by Wall Street, and mishandled by the federal government under the failed leadership of President Herbert Hoover.

Indeed, the U.S. faced two market malfunctions. First, the labor market had imploded. The labor market was massively failing to provide workers with an adequate supply of jobs, sufficient hours of work, and decent wages. The labor market's implosion had in turn spilled over into collapsing farm prices and skyrocketing mortgage foreclosure rates.

Second, the financial market—the banks and stock exchanges in particular—had exploded. Bankers, stockbrokers, and other key actors in the financial sector had failed to act honestly or prudently. As a result, millions of Americans had lost their savings and seen the value of their investments plummet or even vanish.

The nation's markets, however, had not "just" collapsed. Government, Roosevelt and his allies believed, had allowed the markets to disintegrate. The central problem of the United States, FDR maintained, was that the federal government under Hoover had perpetuated an outdated, out-of-touch, and wholly insufficient relationship with the markets—especially the labor market and financial market.

If Roosevelt's campaign advisors in 1932 had wished to coin a pithy slogan to sum up the essence of FDR's campaign message (as James Carville did for Bill Clinton in 1992), the slogan would have been: "It's the market and Hoover, stupid." Or, to be more precise but less pithy: "It's the failure of the federal government to correct now, and prevent in the future, the malfunctioning of the labor market and the financial market, for which President Herbert Hoover in particular is responsible."

Franklin Roosevelt believed, and for political reasons needed to make clear, that the markets' collapse was not inevitable. Government could have prevented the catastrophe. Government could avoid it in the future. FDR was equally convinced, and again for political reasons needed to emphasize, that the inattention and missteps of his opponent, President Herbert Hoover, had induced the market's collapse and prevented its recovery. FDR was likewise convinced that, if the American electorate put him in charge, he could clean up the mess and spare the U.S. from future disaster.

Roosevelt's belief that the Great Depression was caused by the preventable malfunction of the labor market and the financial market came out loud and clear in his March 1933 Inaugural Address.

Was fate, or nature, or the general conduct of the American people to blame for the Great Depression? Not a bit, said FDR:

> [O]ur distress comes from no failure of substance. We are stricken by no plague of locusts. Compared with the perils which our forefathers conquered because they believed and were not afraid, we have still much to be thankful for. Nature still offers her bounty and human efforts have multiplied it.[26]

As he concluded the address, Roosevelt drove home the point: "The people of the United States have not failed."[27]

What, then, had gone wrong? For starters, the labor market had been hollowed out:

[A] host of unemployed citizens face the grim problem
of existence, and an equally great number toil with little
return. Only a foolish optimist can deny the dark
realities of the moment.[28]

Linked to the collapse of the labor market, the financial market—
the nation's banks and stock exchanges—had failed. It was a
failure FDR attributed in large measure to the misdeeds and
ineptitude of bankers ("unscrupulous money changers") and
stock exchange managers ("rulers of the exchange of mankind's
goods"):[29]

> Plenty is at our doorstep, but a generous use of it
> languishes in the very sight of the supply. Primarily this
> is because rulers of the exchange of mankind's goods
> have failed through their own stubbornness and their
> own incompetence, have admitted their failure, and
> have abdicated. Practices of the unscrupulous money
> changers stand indicted in the court of public opinion,
> rejected by the hearts and minds of men.
>   True they have tried, but their efforts have been cast
> in the pattern of an outworn tradition. Faced by failure
> of credit they have proposed only the lending of more
> money. Stripped of the lure of profit by which to induce
> our people to follow their false leadership, they have
> resorted to exhortations, pleading tearfully for restored
> confidence. They know only the rules of a generation of
> self-seekers. They have no vision, and when there is no
> vision the people perish.
>   The money changers have fled from their high seats
> in the temple of our civilization.[30]

The dual failure of the labor market and financial market had
devastated the American people's jobs, earnings, income,
savings, homes, and hopes. "[T]he withered leaves of industrial

enterprise lie on every side; farmers find no markets for their produce; the savings of many years in thousands of families are gone," FDR declared. "Values have shrunken to fantastic levels; taxes have risen; our ability to pay has fallen."[31]

Roosevelt then proceeded to emphasize (without personally castigating poor Herbert Hoover, who sat a few feet away) his belief that it was the duty of the federal government—now his federal government—to take strong action to revive both the labor market and the financial market:

> Our greatest primary task is to put people to work. This is no unsolvable problem if we face it wisely and courageously. It can be accomplished in part by direct recruiting by the Government itself, treating the task as we would treat the emergency of a war, but at the same time, through this employment, accomplishing greatly needed projects to stimulate and reorganize the use of our natural resources.
>
> …
>
> Finally, in our progress toward a resumption of work we require two safeguards against a return of the evils of the old order: there must be a strict supervision of all banking and credits and investments, so that there will be an end to speculation with other people's money; and there must be provision for an adequate but sound currency.[32]

As Roosevelt approached his peroration, he made it clear that governmental action—"We must act, and act quickly"—would involve the prompt enactment by Congress of specific laws:

> These [i.e., restoring the labor market and fixing the financial market] are the lines of attack. I shall presently urge upon a new Congress, in special session, detailed

measures for their fulfillment, and I shall seek the immediate assistance of the several States.[33]

The target and task were clear. The federal government, under Roosevelt's leadership, would work with Congress to correct the terrible malfunctioning of both the labor market and the financial market. But as Inauguration Day moved from the ceremony on Capitol Hill to the celebration along Pennsylvania Avenue, the detailed measures FDR mentioned for carrying out his lines of attack did not exist.

What proposals did Roosevelt and his team intend to presently urge upon the new Congress? Nobody, FDR included, knew. There was no plan. There were no "detailed measures." Not yet.

Indeed, Franklin Roosevelt's call for the nation's government to act now to restore the labor market and financial market left wide open the nature, scope, and duration of what I call the "policy approach" that the federal government would take (much less the nitty-gritty of specific laws). Would the New Deal be small or big? Narrow or sweeping? Temporary or permanent?

Roosevelt and his allies probably were not pondering on March 4, 1933, whether one or another policy approach would fit the specific solutions they needed to fashion. But in reality they faced a stark choice between going small, narrow, and temporary vs. big, sweeping, and permanent across a broad front on the policy menu. Based on both the constitutional authority and past precedents for what the federal government *might* do, FDR's and Congress' choices *could* be drawn from either Column A or Column B on the policy approach menu:

Column A: Small Change	Column B: Big Change
Superficial	*Fundamental*
Narrow in scope	*Sweeping in scope*
Provide opportunities	*Create guarantees*
Voluntary	*Compulsory*
No risk sharing	*Extensive risk sharing*
Inexpensive	*Costly*
Temporary	*Permanent*
Based on status	*Based on activity*
Heavy reliance on states	*Dominant federal role*
Variation across the U.S.	*Uniform across the U.S.*

For further discussion of the two competing policy approaches that Roosevelt and his allies might pursue as they began in 1933 to shape the New Deal, visit: www.govinplace.org/content/ WhatKindNewDeal.pdf.

Every President and Congress faces the same choice of policy approaches—how much from Column A's menu of small, narrow, and temporary policies, and how much from Column B's menu of big, sweeping, and permanent policies—in pursuing any specific, new, domestic legislation. The difference was that Roosevelt and the 73rd Congress had little room for error. If they blundered in redefining the federal government's relationship with the labor market and financial market, the nation's economic meltdown would continue, an even greater catastrophe would ensue, and the U.S. might be unable to recover. The stakes were enormous.

So which choices would Roosevelt and his New Deal allies make in March 1933, the next 100 days, and the months that followed? How much of the "action now" that they wanted would be drawn from Column A or Column B? So far, FDR the candidate had not shown his hand (or, as some observers felt, he had revealed all his cards in vague terms but not said which cards he would play).

We now know the final outcome. As Roosevelt and the New Dealers assumed power in March 1933, however, the policy approach they would settle on for redefining the federal government's relationship with the labor market and financial market might have gone either way.

Yet if FDR had not settled on a policy approach for tackling the Great Depression, at a key moment in the campaign he had hinted at the direction he was likely to take.

"A COMPLETE CHANGE OF CONCEPT"

For Franklin Roosevelt had offered a glimpse — buried deep in a campaign speech — of how he would proceed.

By Inauguration Day, FDR had not yet formulated "detailed measures" that were potentially capable of correcting the market's double failure and rescuing the U.S. from the economic crisis. Nor had he formulated a coherent if broad recovery plan. But one of the statements that FDR let slip during the midst of the 1932 campaign was a stunning revelation of how he intended to move forward.

Roosevelt had strongly suggested that he believed it was necessary to fundamentally transform the role of the federal government — to reshape profoundly and permanently the functions that Washington performed — in order to overcome the economic crisis and lay the foundation for enduring national success.

In a speech in Pittsburgh on October 19, 1932, Roosevelt had urged the necessity of "a complete change of concept of what are the proper functions and limits of the Federal Government itself."[34] It was not enough, he argued, to use the federal government to tackle the Great Depression and then go back to the *status quo*. Rather, it was necessary to drastically alter the very idea of what the government should do. FDR aimed not merely to resuscitate the U.S. economy and then return to pre-emergency arrangements. He intended to radically and irrevocably revise the place of government in the nation's economy and, as an inevitable result, the nation's culture.

It is important to note that Roosevelt was talking about the pursuit of federal "economy" — that is: cutting federal spending by 25%, balancing the federal budget, and reducing federal debt — when he spoke in Pittsburgh of the need for "a complete change of concept of what are the proper functions and limits of the Federal Government itself." Here is the context of FDR's statement:

> The air is now surcharged with Republican death-bed repentance on the subject of economy, but it is too late. We must look deeper than these eleventh-hour pronouncements. You cannot go very far with any real Federal economy, without a complete change of concept of what are the proper functions and limits of the Federal Government itself.[35]

But it is equally important to emphasize that, a few minutes after Roosevelt pledged his troth to fiscal retrenchment, he also promised not to cut federal spending and not to balance the federal budget. He promised, rather, to go in the opposite direction, spend additional millions of federal dollars, and run a large deficit if required to save the American people from "starvation and dire need." FDR's statement about spending more and running a deficit, totally contradicting his prior commitment, also deserves quoting in full:

> At the same time, let me repeat from now to election day so that every man, woman and child in the United States will know what I mean: If starvation and dire need on the part of any of our citizens make necessary the appropriation of additional funds which would keep the budget out of balance, I shall not hesitate to tell the American people the full truth and ask them to authorize the expenditure of additional funds.[36]

It was certainly true in the United States in 1932-1933 that you could not "go very far" in cutting federal spending by 25% without undertaking "a complete change of concept" in government's functions. It was just as true, however, that Roosevelt and Congress could not "go very far" in preventing "starvation and dire need on the part of any of our citizens" without also pursuing "a complete change of concept" in government's functions. Whichever direction FDR faced, he was committing himself to a sweeping and lasting transformation in the role of government.

The importance of Franklin Roosevelt's speech in Pittsburgh, therefore, does not lie in understanding whether he believed that only fiscal retrenchment, or only fiscal expansion, or (somehow) both would require a "complete change of concept" about the federal government's future role. What mattered most in the speech was FDR's recognition of the need for—and, it appears, his commitment to—such a "complete change of concept."

It would be impossible to bring about a "complete change of concept" in the functions of government, however, if all the federal government did in 1933 was to draw upon Column A's menu of superficial, narrow, and temporary changes. If the New Deal were to usher in a true "change of concept" in the role of the federal government *vis-à-vis* the labor market and the financial market, it would be necessary to turn to Colum B's menu of fundamental, extensive, and permanent change.

The big takeaway from Roosevelt's speech is thus the light it shines on how he was thinking about the future of American government, particularly the federal government. To get out of the quicksand the U.S. was mired in, FDR was open to pushing for "a complete change of concept" in the government's functions. Roosevelt was more than open to the strategy. He called for it. Small change, partial change, temporary change would not suffice. Profound, across-the-board, and enduring changes in what government did—particularly *vis-à-vis* the labor market and the financial market—were required. FDR had unlocked the door to a revolution in government's role.

Roosevelt's statement that the United States required "a complete change of concept" in the functions and limits of the federal government may seem like a throwaway line in a campaign speech, but it was a logical step in the progression of his experience and thinking. FDR's 1932 campaign across the United States had driven home to him how miserably the federal government had failed to combat the dual market failures that had allowed the nation to sink into an economic abyss. Day after day, he had seen the desperation of thousands of Americans.

Speech after speech, he gradually came to recognize that the U.S. needed much more than a grab bag of random, unlinked policy changes in order to stem the nation's collapse and restore prosperity.

FDR had competed in many prior elections, but he had never competed in an election whose stakes were as high. Long before he arrived in Pittsburgh in mid-October, it must have become clear to him that the nation's decision in November 1932 went far beyond a power struggle between two individuals with strikingly different temperaments. It involved more than a contest between two parties with divergent histories and impulses. It was even bigger than a choice between different approaches to restoring America's economic health. It was (to use an expression FDR would later make famous) a "rendezvous with destiny" that spelled a profound historical choice for the United States.

It must steadily have dawned on Roosevelt, as the 1932 campaign wound to a close, that the heart of the profound national choice that American voters would be making in November involved the very future of American government itself, particularly at the federal level. It was thus entirely fitting for FDR to urge in Pittsburgh that the functions of American government had to dramatically alter—had to undergo a "complete change of concept"—in order to overcome the Great Depression and prevent the recurrence of a future catastrophe.

Few politicians have understood the country's mood as well as Franklin Roosevelt. Few have better grasped the nation's needs at pivotal moments in U.S. history. Roosevelt could not but recognize that he was running to become the 32nd President, at least in part, so as to lead a peaceful, sweeping, and permanent revolution in the federal government's role in correcting for the flaws and risks inherent in the labor market and the financial market. Nor could FDR fail to understand that success would permanently reshape the nation's economy and culture.

Conclusion: A Profound Admission

Roosevelt's short, veiled, but public pledge in Pittsburgh to pursue "a complete change of concept of what are the proper functions and limits of the Federal Government itself" was thus a profoundly important admission. Not surprisingly, FDR said nothing in Pittsburgh about exactly what he meant. He neither explained the current concept of government's functions he wanted to replace, nor outlined the sharply new concept of government's functions he wanted to establish. FDR also presented no vision of what the federal government should never do, i.e., the "limits of the Federal government itself."

It should likewise come as no surprise that Roosevelt did not repeat or amplify his Pittsburgh comment in the few weeks left before the election. Doing so might inflict political damage. But there was another, more important, reason. FDR did not know what his proposed "complete change of concept" would entail. It was a vague vision, not a concrete plan. It was an approach to policy, not a set of specific policies

Roosevelt's vagueness was entirely in keeping with the essential features of his personality. One of FDR's many insightful biographers, Joseph Lelyveld, speaks of "his customary slyness."[37] It was Roosevelt's engrained habit to keep his vision fixed on lofty goals, but pursue them with a deep-seated pragmatism that involved compromise, contradiction, and delay:

At key junctures, as the scholar Warren Kimball has
suggested, [FDR] showed himself to be 'a man with a
conception but without a plan.' His goals were clear, in
his own mind at least; his means of attaining them were
left to whatever improvisation and maneuvering
circumstances might favor. [38]

Yet despite the fuzziness of the big idea that Roosevelt floated in
Pittsburgh a few weeks before his election, the importance of that
big idea should not be overlooked. It provides a valuable clue to
the direction FDR wanted to take the United States—and in fact
steered the nation.

On the cusp of taking over the presidency, already smelling
a big victory, and fully grasping the severity of the crisis that he
would be obliged—indeed, that he wanted—to tackle, Franklin
Roosevelt recognized that the New Deal could not turn into a
small deal. It could not just be about tiny or temporary tinkering
with the labor market and the financial market. It had no chance
of success if it simply added, modified, and subtracted a handful
or even a large number of programs that created jobs, stabilized
banks, and propped up the stock exchanges.

Rather, FDR grasped that the New Deal necessarily would
require a dramatic and enduring alteration in the overall role—
the "functions and limits"—of government itself, particularly the
federal government's interaction with two of the nation's biggest
markets. The task of the New Deal was to rescue the United
States from the deepening crisis by means of putting the federal
government in a fundamentally different place, a place so
changed that the American people and economy would never
again descend into an abyss.

CHAPTER 2

THE NEW DEAL'S
FOUR POLICY CLUSTERS

AS THE GREAT DEPRESSION WORSENED month by month—as the economic catastrophe of 1928-1932 descended into the economic collapse of early 1933—most Americans were giving little attention to the notion of "a complete change of concept of...the proper functions and limits of the Federal Government itself." The immediate struggle of tens of millions of individuals to find work, keep a roof over their heads, stay clothed, and stave off hunger overshadowed for most any impulse to examine or dispute whether there ought to be a fundamental change in the functions of government. The imperative of survival trumped the temptation to indulge in such a high-level debate.

To the extent that a relatively small group of Americans in 1932-1933 did pay attention to what a radical change in government might look like, their focus was likely to be on the power of the President. The Dictator Question had entered the nation's discourse. Should the U.S. move away from the Constitution's model of separation of powers and adopt a dictatorial model that vested unchecked power in an elected President, at least until the President imposed solutions (whatever they might be) that rescued America from its economic crisis?

As Jonathan Alter has explained in *The Defining Moment*, "dictator" was not a dirty word in 1932-1933.

> That word — "dictator" — had been in the air for weeks, endorsed vaguely as a remedy for the Depression by establishment figures ranging from the owners of the New York Daily News, the nation's largest circulation newspaper, to Walter Lippmann, the eminent columnist who spoke for the American political elite. "The situation is critical, Franklin. You may have no alternative but to assume dictatorial powers," Lippmann had told FDR during a visit to Warm Springs on February 1, before the crisis escalated. ... Even Eleanor Roosevelt, more liberal than her husband, privately suggested that "a benevolent dictator" might be what the country needed. The vague idea was not a police state but deference to a strong leader unfettered by Congress or the other inconveniences of democracy.

"Roosevelt came to office," Alter continues, "just as the appetite for strong leadership seemed to be surging worldwide."[1] Some Americans shared the same appetite. Mussolini was popular in the U.S. in 1932-1933. Stalin had a following. So did Hitler, appointed chancellor in January of 1933 and given dictatorial powers over the following months.

The popularity of Europe's dictators' stemmed in part from the fact that they stood for replacing the two prime features of constitutional democracy — legislative debate (bickering and dithering) and judicial review (obstruction and delay) — with decisive and quick action by a single-minded leader. Il Duce, the General Secretary, and Der Führer appeared on the surface to be solving their nations' economic crises. Why should not America imitate their example by having a President who ignored

Congress and the courts and wielded dictatorial power to end the Great Depression?

Franklin Roosevelt flirted with the idea. In his 1933 Inaugural Address, he pledged to use constitutional methods to rescue the U.S. from economic collapse.[2] But FDR also strongly hinted that, if Congress and the courts failed to cooperate, he would consider dictatorship. Towards the end of the speech, FDR put it this way:

> It is to be hoped that the normal balance of executive
> and legislative authority may be wholly adequate to
> meet the unprecedented task before us. But it may be
> that an unprecedented demand and need for undelayed
> action may call for temporary departure from that
> normal balance of public procedure.[3]

Thus, to the extent that Americans were thinking at all about any kind of complete change of concept that involved the federal government, it is as likely as not that they were thinking about the power of the President vis-à-vis the countervailing powers of Congress and the courts. Far less attention, even at the highest levels, focused on the question of whether the overall functions of government—its place in American society *vis-à-vis* the labor market, financial market, economy, and culture—should fundamentally and permanently change.

That the New Deal's revolution in the functions of American government was largely unplanned, however, does not diminish its historical importance. Only a small chunk of history is about what leaders plan in advance of events. The core of history is about what actually happened, regardless of what leaders (or anyone else) wished or proposed. What counts most is what changed from year to year, and from era to era. What matters in the main is emergence. What emerged from the past? How and why did the emergence take place? What is the meaning of what emerged for the future?

The focus of this book is therefore on the story, the meaning, and the future of the New Deal revolution in the functions of American government that in fact emerged between 1933-1938 (New Deal Version 1.0) and evolved over the course of the next 80 years (New Deal Version 2.0). What FDR, his New Deal team, and their allies in Congress thought and sought—as well as fought—helps to illuminate what happened. My primary concern, however, is the "complete change of concept" in government's functions that actually took place.

A few hours after 12:00 noon on March 4, 1933, as Herbert Hoover headed to New York City and the Waldorf-Astoria Hotel, Franklin Roosevelt moved into the White House and launched the famous First 100 Days of rapid, intense, and—at last—very detailed efforts to jump-start the economy. During the five years from 1933 to 1938, FDR and the New Dealers pushed through Congress (or accepted from Congress) dozens of specific laws, spending provisions, tax changes, and other measures that were unprecedented in their scope and cost. Some were temporary, and meant to be so. Many were permanent, thus meant to make enduring changes in the role of the federal government. A "complete change of concept of … the proper functions and limits of the Federal Government" in fact began to unfold. It kept on unfolding for decades.

Beyond the dozens of new programs, and beyond the alphabet soup of new federal agencies, what did the New Deal's "complete change of concept" in government's role turn into? What, in hindsight, did the Roosevelt Revolution actually bring about in the functions of American government?

And, looking beyond what the New Deal amounted to, how has it fared? What are its successes and its failures? To the extent it has shortcomings, how should we fill its gaps, fix its flaws, and correct its mistakes? What should be the shape and details of a New Deal Version 3.0?

ECONOMIC GUARANTEES AND MARKET REGULATION

In the end, the New Deal's "complete change of concept" in the functions of government was at once huge and simple.

Going forward from Roosevelt's inauguration, the meaning of the New Deal—its inner logic, its central thrust—was that it would be the responsibility of the federal government to correct for the catastrophic failures that had already occurred in both the labor market and financial market. That responsibility included creating policies strong enough to prevent future devastation of both branches of the U.S. economy.

The New Deal's primary approach in correcting for the labor market's defects was to guarantee economic security. It could have been otherwise. The New Deal might have adopted policies that guaranteed nothing, but merely increased the odds that some people would be better off. But Roosevelt and his New Deal allies, to a high degree, put in place policies that provided permanent legal guarantees to different types of economic security, primarily for adults in their capacity as workers (unemployed, active, or retired) *vis-à-vis* employers. The new legal guarantees relied heavily on social insurance and labor market standards.

Of equal importance, the New Deal rested on the principle that the federal government needed to permanently correct for the inherent risks of abuse and failure that arise in the nation's financial market and the economy in general. Roosevelt and most New Dealers were not socialists. They believed in a market economy; they valued its great strengths.

But they had seen enough and learned enough to know that the possibility of abuse and failure—resulting in devastating damage to people, families, businesses, and the economy—is inevitable in a market economy. Declining income due to high unemployment, falling wages, insufficient pensions, and other labor market shortcomings was always a risk. Bank failures, stock exchange collapses, and other major breakdowns in the financial market were always risks. Thus, the collapse of a market economy was always a risk. FDR and his New Deal allies believed that the pronouncements of laissez-faire economists, some business leaders, and a large chunk of the Republican Party establishment that the market will self-correct its problems were as foolish as they were self-serving.

In brief, the central design of the original New Deal was that the federal government would permanently undertake two new enormous functions:

1) Guarantee economic security—primarily by means of offering unemployment insurance and employment itself, setting a minimum wage, enabling collective bargaining, and ensuring a basic retirement income—for the great majority of American adults in their

multiple relationships with the labor market as unemployed, employed, and retired workers; and

2) Regulate the market as a whole — not just bits and pieces of the market as before, but banks and exchanges and other major market sectors — so as to block the market from harming America's environment, workers, consumers, and investors, and so as to prevent future meltdowns.

Both of these mega-functions of government were brand new concepts in 1932, as far as mainstream U.S. politics and federal policy were concerned. The fact that the New Deal made both mega-functions permanent — that is: intended to outlast the Great Depression and thus prevent future episodes of mass unemployment, overwhelming poverty, and economic catastrophe — underscores the magnitude of the "complete change of concept" they represented in government's place in the national landscape.

Today, there is widespread agreement, evinced less in theory than in practice, that government — at least in a democratic society with a market economy — has three primary purposes:

1) Protecting and enhancing the public's safety, health, resources, and infrastructure;

2) Promoting individuals' economic security, including health care and education; and

3) Furthering an effective market.

Within each of these broad purposes, governments perform numerous functions.[4]

What many do not appreciate—because we are so familiar with history's outcome—is how much the New Deal radically altered the mission of government, especially at the federal level, by adding meat and bone to the latter two purposes of government. The New Deal converted the vague notion of "promoting" economic security into specific *guarantees* of economic security for millions of Americans. Simultaneously, the New Deal converted the abstract notion of "furthering" an effective market into a vast expansion of specific *regulations* of the market—not just here and there, but across the board.

In short, between FDR's taking office in 1933 and his signing the Fair Labor Standards Act in 1938, government's day job underwent a wholesale transformation. By 1938, it had become government's duty to broadly guarantee economic security and to systematically regulate the market. The original New Deal's fundamental revision of government's job description, especially at the federal level, continued to be refined for another 80 years.

THE NEW DEAL'S FOUR POLICY CLUSTERS

It can be argued—and for the purposes of this book, it is helpful to explain—that Franklin Roosevelt and his New Deal allies in fact launched not two, but four, fairly distinct, "complete change[s] of concept of what are the proper functions and limits of the Federal Government itself."

The effort to guarantee economic security involved two different policy clusters: (1) broad-based economic security guarantees, and (2) means-tested welfare programs.

1) **Broad-Based Economic Security Guarantees:** The first cluster of programs gave broad-based (often called "universal") legal rights to economic security to U.S. adults, whether poor or not, in their various relationships with the labor market, i.e., as unemployed, employed, disabled, or retired workers.

2) **Means-Tested Welfare Programs**: A second cluster of programs aimed to catch in a safety net the individuals who fell through the cracks of the broad-based economic security system, but required them to be and remain poor (or near-poor) to receive a mix of cash and non-cash assistance.

Likewise, the effort to regulate the markets also involved two different policy clusters: (3) market regulation, and (4) market manipulation.

3) **Market Regulation**: The third cluster of programs imposed restrictions on businesses that restrained them from inflicting damage on the environment, workers, consumers, and investors, and that helped to preserve the overall stability of the market.

4) **Market Manipulation**: The fourth cluster of programs intervened in the market by heavily subsidizing or otherwise conferring benefits on politically preferred types of consumption and investment.

Most of the original New Deal's domestic policy initiatives fell within one of these four policy clusters. The four categories emerged during the early days of the New Deal, continued to define American domestic policy for the remainder of the 20th century, and extended into the 21st century. Today, the same four policy clusters still form the template for most of our domestic policy debate and action.

Following is a description of the major New Deal laws and programs—encompassing both those created during the original New Deal of 1933-1938 and those added over the next 80 years of the New Deal *writ large*—as organized by policy cluster.[5]

1st Policy Cluster: Broad-Based Economic Security Guarantees

Prior to March of 1933, it was not common wisdom that government, and in particular the federal government, should play an active, large, and costly role in promoting economic security. Above all, it was inconceivable that the federal government would give Americans individual legal rights to economic security—to employment, wages, income, or health care—unless they happened to be veterans or government employees.

Within weeks of Franklin Roosevelt's taking office in March of 1933, however, the New Deal launched its initial program to directly provide wage-paying jobs to unemployed adults. On March 21, only 17 days after his inauguration, FDR asked Congress to create the Civilian Conservation Corps (CCC). Congress passed the necessary law, and FDR signed it, 10 days later. Within a month, the first CCC camp—Camp Roosevelt in the George Washington National Forest near Luray, Virginia— began operation.

By the end of 1935, there were over 2,650 camps, operating in all states and providing more than 500,000 unemployed men with wage-paying jobs. CCC workers planted more than three billion trees, erected 3,470 fire towers, built 97,000 miles of fire roads, devoted 4,235,000 man-days to fighting fires, and spent 7,153,000 man-days on other conservation activities. The CCC also provided disaster relief during floods and blizzards. The CCC remained in business until Congress phased it out in 1942.[6]

The CCC was the prelude to much larger jobs programs. In the fall of 1933, Roosevelt and Harry Hopkins (then Administrator of the Federal Emergency Relief Administration) moved millions of "relief" recipients into wage-paying jobs under the auspices of the quickly created Civil Works Administration (CWA). The CWA hired as many as 4.2 million workers. In 1934, the CWA wound down. But in 1935, the federal government put in place a longer lasting program to hire more millions of jobless adults, the Works Progress Administration (WPA). At its height, the WPA employed 3.0 million workers.[7] The WPA ended in 1943.

Unemployed adults had no legal right to a CCC, CWA, or WPA job. But most New Deal economic security programs did vest workers with legal guarantees. The Fair Labor Standards Act (1938) gave large categories of workers a federal individual right to a minimum wage. The National Labor Relations Act (1935), commonly called the Wagner Act, provided large groups of workers with the legal right to organize unions for the purpose of bargaining collectively to raise wages even higher, as well as to improve hours, benefits, and working conditions. Perhaps the single most popular piece of federal legislation in American history — the Social Security Act (1935) — vested tens of millions of American workers with legal rights to several categories of income: unemployment benefits if they lost work, a pension once they retired from work, and a survivor's income if a working spouse or parent died.

Over the next 80 years, the federal government would provide a large share of adults who had a serious disability with a federal individual right to disability benefits. The New Deal *writ large* would also grant virtually every American a federal individual right at age 65 to enroll in a national health insurance program, Medicare.

Thus the original New Deal, as it pushed into a near-wilderness of public attitudes and political habits, was both creating specific new programs and launching a dramatic new concept of what it meant for government to create economic security. The concept soon became precedent. The last act in the 80-year drama of expanding federal individual rights to economic security was the Affordable Care Act, Obamacare, which granted seniors on Medicare a more generous prescription drug benefit.

With rare exceptions, the economic security programs of the New Deal *writ large* were permanent. Most were also huge in scope and cost. And each additional program was more than a stand-alone reform. Each filled a gap in a series of related gaps. Each contributed to reshaping the very idea of what it meant for American government to create economic security.

Of central importance, the New Deal's cluster of economic security programs went beyond the traditional notion of providing merely the opportunity to be economically secure. With a few exceptions, they gave individual Americans who met carefully defined criteria the formal legal right to enjoy—to have—specific benefits that lay a foundation of economic security.

Further, by relying heavily on social insurance as the vehicle for financing many (and the biggest) of its economic security guarantees, the New Deal established many of the new individual legal rights as *de facto* vested rights. Not only are workers legally entitled to claim Unemployment Insurance (UI) and Social Security benefits. They also believe (whether the belief is legally true or not) that, since they or their employers paid for UI and Social Security, those benefits belong to them and thus lie beyond the reach of a future act of Congress. As Franklin Roosevelt appreciated more than most (for FDR had worked for an insurance company for many years[8]), the choice of social insurance as a vehicle for financing UI and Social Security meant that most Americans would become so fiercely attached to their new individual rights to economic security that those rights would never be stripped away by lawmakers of any party. After FDR's death, the choice of social insurance to pay for Social Security Disability Insurance (SSDI) and Medicare added individual rights to the economic security cluster that have also enjoyed an insurance shield against political threats.

The broad-based economic security guarantees of the New Deal *writ large* from 1933 to today also generally share several other key features that distinguish them from the New Deal's means-tested welfare programs. Each guarantee is explicitly designed to counteract one of the "hazards and vicissitudes" that arises from the perilous nature of the labor market. Accordingly, each broad-based economic security program is based on work—either loss of work (Unemployment Insurance), work itself (minimum wage, collective bargaining, and eligibility for Social Security and Medicare), inability to work (Disability Insurance), retirement from work (most recipients of Social Security and Medicare), or the death of a working spouse or parent (Social Security).

Most striking, the cluster of economic security programs is available to everyone regardless of income. You do not have to be poor to receive Unemployment Insurance benefits, get the minimum wage, form a union, qualify for Social Security Disability Insurance benefits (as opposed to Supplemental Security Income benefits), get a Social Security pension or Social Security survivor's pension, or enroll in Medicare (as opposed to Medicaid). You may be poor. But poverty is not required to exercise your individual right to these benefits. Nor does escaping poverty, via work or marriage, cause you to lose your right to any of these benefits. The New Deal's economic security guarantees are poverty-neutral. They extend to the working class, the middle class, and the rich.

Seen as a whole, the big cluster of New Deal broad-based economic security guarantees—not only because of their sheer scope and cost, but also because of the legal rights they create, their reliance on social insurance, their essential relationship to work, and their indifference to poverty—take center stage in FDR's "complete change of concept of ... the proper functions" of the federal government. When we think or talk about the New Deal, Social Security and its broad-based companions are most likely what we have in mind.

2nd Policy Cluster: Means-Tested Welfare Programs

The New Deal might have stopped at broad-based economic security guarantees in its efforts to lift Americans out of poverty. But the crisis of destitution that the U.S. faced in 1933, combined with an unwillingness and inability to push this policy cluster further, impelled the Roosevelt administration and its allies in Congress to launch a second "complete change of concept" in the federal government's functions: means-tested welfare programs.

Frances Perkins recalled how severe the crisis of destitution had grown prior to FDR's election in a speech she delivered 30 years after her tenure as Secretary of Labor had ended:

> People were so alarmed that all through the rest of 1929, 1930, and 1931, the specter of unemployment—of starvation, of hunger, of the wandering boys, of the broken homes, of the families separated while somebody went out to look for work—stalked everywhere. The unpaid rent, the eviction notices, the furniture and bedding on the sidewalk, the old lady weeping over it, the children crying, the father out looking for a truck to move their belongings himself to his sister's flat or some relative's already overcrowded tenement, or just sitting there bewilderedly waiting for some charity officer to come and move him somewhere. I saw goods stay on the sidewalk in front of the same house with the same children weeping on top of the blankets for 3 days before anybody came to relieve the situation![9]

Responding to this human catastrophe, the New Deal positioned the federal government to create a national safety net for millions of Americans who faced starvation and eviction. Or, if we think of the larger cluster of broad-based economic security guarantees as a primary safety net, we can think of the New Deal's cluster of means-tested welfare programs as a secondary safety net.

Prior to 1933, private individuals, religious organizations, and other charities played the biggest role in aiding the poor, particularly widows and orphans. As the U.S. developed, local and state government occasionally set up programs. The onset of the Great Depression brought the federal government into the picture for the first time. It was actually Herbert Hoover who established Washington's first program of "relief."[10]

Franklin Roosevelt hated the dole.[11] He twice replaced large chunks of what the era's policymakers called "relief" with jobs programs that instead paid workers wages: the CWA (1933-34) and the WPA (1935-1943). FDR also spoke repeatedly, most notably in his 1935 State of the Union Message to Congress, of his hope to "quit this business of relief."[12]

Nonetheless, Roosevelt and the New Deal did not abolish "relief" as a vehicle for helping a segment of poor Americans. The Social Security Act included a permanent means-tested welfare program for impoverished parents of dependent children, called Aid to Dependent Children (ADC). Overwhelmingly, they were destitute mothers who had been widowed or abandoned by husbands. The program continues to this day, renamed Aid to Families with Dependent Children (AFDC) and finally retitled Temporary Assistance to Needy Families (TANF). In addition, the original New Deal created non-cash programs to help the poor by "clearing" slums and providing their former inhabitants (or someone) with public housing.

After World War II, over the course of the New Deal *writ large*, the number of means-tested welfare programs grew in number, complexity, and cost. AFDC enrollment expanded substantially in the 1960s, 1970s, and 1980s, until TANF's adoption in 1996 both ended the federal legal entitlement and rolled back the growth.[13] The Food Stamps program, launched as an experiment by President Kennedy in 1961, became permanent in 1964 and expanded as part of President Johnson's War on Poverty.[14] Now called the Supplemental Nutrition Assistance Program (SNAP), it is one of the federal government's largest means-tested welfare programs. In 1965, Congress and LBJ amended the Social Security Act to create Medicaid, the means-tested companion to Medicare. Numerous other "categorical" programs joined the means-tested welfare cluster, providing the poor and near-poor with housing, nutrition, health, childcare, and other benefits via a mix of legal entitlements and first come/ first serve approaches.

The number of means-tested welfare programs is now so large, and the details so complex, that it is easy to allow the trees to obscure the forest. But in the end it is the forest that is most significant.

Prior to the Great Depression, alleviating poverty was a minor responsibility of local and state government. It was not at all a responsibility of the federal government. But since 1933, the remediation of poverty through multiple programs that only help the poor or near-poor has become a major, permanent facet of government, especially at the federal level.

All such programs require individuals to be poor and remain poor (or nearly so) to receive help. The programs typically phase out benefits as income rises. Sometimes, a recipient will lose an entire benefit, e.g., Medicaid, once income steps $1 beyond an arbitrary eligibility "cliff." The cluster of means-tested welfare programs provides the poor with cash in several forms (TANF and SSI). It provides non-cash benefits in an even larger number of varieties (Food Stamps, LIHEAP's pick-up of energy costs, public housing subsidies and housing vouchers, and Medicaid health care coverage). Means-tested welfare programs constitute the New Deal's second "complete change of concept" in the functions of the federal government.

3rd Policy Cluster: Market Regulation

It was far from common wisdom in March of 1933 that it was the job of government, especially the federal government, to regulate the market across the board in order to prevent damage — or what economists call "cost externalization" — to the environment, workers, consumers, and investors, and to avoid wholesale economic catastrophe.

Hitherto, government's regulation of the market was small and piecemeal. The prudence of individuals arising from their self-interest (*caveat emptor*), the right to sue for negligence and win damages in court, self-regulation by banks and stock exchanges, limited regulation at the state level of various market actors, and even more limited federal regulation were accepted as sufficient to control abuses. Washington played a narrow role, deploying only a few agencies — such as the Federal Reserve, the Food and Drug Administration (FDA), the Interstate Commerce Commission (ICC), and the Federal Trade Commission (FTC) — to prevent only a scattering of harmful practices.

The original New Deal of 1933-1938 quickly advanced along a broad front to enact an array of federal programs to regulate the financial market, and soon to regulate many other market sectors. The Emergency Banking Act (signed into law a mere five days after FDR's inauguration, on March 9, 1933) and the Glass-Steagall Banking Act (signed into law three months later, on June 16, 1933) created a new federal system of bank regulation. The Securities Act (which became law on May 27, 1933) and Securities Exchange Act (1934) introduced federal regulation of securities and their exchange. The Public Utility Holding Company Act (1935) regulated electric utilities, either limiting them to a single state and state regulation, or compelling multi-state utilities to divest and serve a limited geographic area, as well as preventing them from engaging in unregulated businesses.

The process of adding stronger regulations continued over the course of the New Deal *writ large*. The Clean Air Act (1970) and Clean Water Act (1972) eponymously helped protect the environment. The Occupational Safety and Health Act (1970) added workplace safeguards, while the Employee Retirement Income Security Act (ERISA, 1974) set minimum standards for most voluntarily established private pension and health plans. The Consumer Product Safety Act (1972) authorized a new Consumer Product Safety Commission (CPSC) to develop product safety standards, as well as pursue recalls of products that present unreasonable or substantial risks of injury or death to consumers. The Sarbanes-Oxley Act (2002) set new or expand-ed requirements for all U.S. public company boards, management, and public accounting firms. The Dodd-Frank Wall Street Reform and Consumer Protection Act (2010) further reformed the regulation of the U.S.'s financial institutions.

Altogether, across the decades stretching between the Emergency Banking Act of 1933 and the Dodd-Frank Act of 2010, the federal government enacted dozens of laws and amendments whose aim is to protect the environment and individuals from a wide range of harm and risks, pushing corporations to replace cost externalization with less damaging means of production.

The number and complexity of these laws and amendments tempt us to miss the big picture. As important as each individual enactment is the fact that the New Deal fundamentally altered the very concept of what government's role would be in making the market effective.

Up to 1933, government's primary role, especially at the federal level, was to "make the market" — to enable it to function — by protecting property rights, upholding valid contracts, creating a single currency and a single market, and freeing up interstate commerce while uniformly controlling foreign trade. Federal regulation was minimal.

From March 1933 onward, however, the very concept of government's role *vis-à-vis* the market dramatically changed. Government henceforward would have two primary roles. It would both "make the market" (as before) and systematically regulate the market, largely at the national level, to protect a wide range of potential victims from a widening spectrum of harm and risk, as well as trying to prevent the economy's meltdown.

4th Policy Cluster: Market Manipulation

Finally, the original New Deal greatly expanded—and the next eight decades of action by the New Deal *writ large* enormously expanded—the federal government's role in steering the U.S. economy in politically favored directions by subsidizing, or otherwise promoting, specific types of consumption and investment.

To rescue the U.S. from the Great Depression and prevent future economic crises, this surge of subsidies was unnecessary. Franklin Roosevelt and his New Deal allies did not need to manipulate the market as massively as they chose to do. The original New Deal in theory might have stuck to (A) creating an economic security structure that virtually eliminated unemployment and poverty, and (B) regulating the market to prevent damage to the environment, workers, consumers, and investors, as well as avoid national economic meltdowns. Had the New Deal taken this course, it could have avoided not only means-tested welfare programs but also massive interference in agriculture and other economic sectors.

The severity of the overall economic crisis and the collapse of the farm economy in particular, however, opened the door to direct interference. An unwillingness to push economic security further, uncertainty about the efficacy of the new system of market regulation, and good old-fashioned politics also helped lay the groundwork for market manipulation. In addition, central economic planning had a powerful appeal at a time when both Mussolini and Stalin were giving a good name (in different circles) to the wisdom of central governmental management of the economy. For these and other reasons, FDR and the New

Dealers embraced market manipulation in general and subsidies for farmers in particular.

There were precedents for their decision. Earlier in U.S. history, the 19th century had seen government efforts at all levels to promote particular economic sectors. State governments went gaga over canals and later railroads in the 1800s. Arkansas, Illinois, Indiana, Louisiana, Maryland, Michigan, Mississippi, and Pennsylvania went bankrupt in the 1840s due in many cases to lending support to private transportation "investments."[15] During and after the Civil War, the federal government launched a massive initiative (including land grants and government bonds) to support the building of the Transcontinental Railroad, with Abraham Lincoln signing a law that set the rail gauge at 4 feet and 8½ inches.[16,17]

The New Deal greatly upped the ante. The first Agricultural Adjustment Act (1933) paid subsidies to farmers not to plant crops (cotton, field corn, hogs, rice, wheat, and tobacco, and later barley, sugar beets, sugar cane, flax, peanuts, potatoes, rye, and grain sorghum) in order to reduce the agricultural sector's "surplus" of crops. The law also paid farmers to slaughter cattle and hogs, so as to reduce the nation's "excess" of beef, milk and its products, and pork. By reducing supply, the law aimed to raise the prices farmers could command in the resulting, manipulated, farm market. The Supreme Court struck down the law in 1938, but a second Agricultural Adjustment Act (1938) fixed the legal defect and continued the federal government's massive interference in the farm economy.[18]

It was only the beginning. Over the course of the New Deal *writ large*, the federal government enacted dozens of programs — many of them "tax expenditures" embedded in the tax code in the form of special exclusions of income from taxation, deductions from taxable income, credits against tax liability, and other tax-related devices—that subsidize consumption or investment in the energy, health, and housing sectors, as well the sale of bonds (especially government bonds) and stocks.[19]

Today, America's maze of subsidies is so vast and complex that it is difficult to pin down with precision how much they cost. A plausible conservative estimate for the subsidies that take the form of tax expenditures is $1.5 trillion—that is: $1,500 billion.[20] Subsidies that are doled out via direct expenditures no doubt raise the total to roughly $2.0 trillion—that is: $2,000 billion.[21]

In addition to these enormous subsidies, the federal government manipulates the market in other ways. For example, the federal Cranberry Marketing Committee established in 1963 to represent 100% of U.S. cranberry handlers requests "marketing orders" from the U.S. Department of Agriculture to legally limit the output of cranberries.[22] The cranberry growers' justification for their federally approved cartel is to "to safeguard the orderly supply of a quality product."[23] The major impact of this governmental mechanism for shrinking the supply of cranberries is, of course, to artificially jack up the prices consumers pay for cranberry juice for breakfast and cranberry relish for Thanksgiving.

The 19th century subsidies for canals and railroads were often limited to promoting the initial creation of infrastructure. Whether justified or not, at least they dealt with a traditional function of government, i.e., transportation. By contrast, the 20th century subsidies of the New Deal *writ large* crossed the Rubicon into a new realm of government interference in the economy.

The New Deal enacted continuing subsidies: payments or tax breaks that could (and do) go on and on for decades. New Deal subsidies also extended to multiple economic sectors. They directly infused—and continue to infuse—massive sums of taxpayers' money (either in the form of direct payments or cuts in tax liability) into economic activities that government previously never touched. And New Deal subsidies, rather than focusing on creating infrastructure, typically have aimed to increase consumption and investment in politically favored economic sectors.

Because so many of the subsidies that the New Deal *writ large* put in place now seem so ridiculous, e.g., paying farmers not to grow corn or giving homeowners a tax break that swells with their income, it is tempting to focus on the absurdity or grotesqueness of each subsidy's unique quirks. The larger issue, however, is whether the subsidization of particular types of consumption and investment is wise in the first place, on both moral and economic grounds.

The moral question is: Should consumers—or government—control the economy? It has historically been the view of both communists and fascists that government, in Lenin's words, should occupy "the commanding heights of the economy."[24] From those heights, opponents of free markets believe, government should decide how the economy moves and where it ends up. Congress has to some extent embraced Lenin's vision of central economic planning—or, at least, steering—of the U.S. economy. Should that continue? Or, rejecting Lenin's vision, should Congress allow American individuals and firms, through choices they make that are unfettered by government manipulation of preference, to freely decide the direction and shape of their economy?

The economic question is: Should the economy be more productive or less productive? Virtually all economists (who are not in the pay of a subsidized industry) agree that subsidies distort the market, reward less efficient firms, retard overall productivity, and shrink the nation's wealth. Do we want to continue to pay that steep price in order to help out certain politically favored sectors? Or (even if the subsidized firms and sectors complain) do we want to liberate our market from distortion, reward the most efficient firms, achieve maximum productivity, and enlarge as much as possible the nation's wealth?

CONCLUSION: THE HOUSE THAT FDR BUILT

Taken together, the policies enacted during the original New Deal of 1933-1938 dramatically reshaped the fundamental idea of what functions American government should perform. No single Roosevelt proposal, no single New Deal law, was revolutionary. But the sum of what New Deal Version 1.0 achieved—not just the lengthy list of laws, programs, and agencies, but their collective logic—added up to what can only be seen as a radical change in the notion of what American government should do. After 1933, it became the federal government's job to guarantee a measure of economic security for the majority of American adults in their multiple relationships with a perilous labor market, and to regulate the market as a whole to prevent it from inflicting harm and melting down.

But Roosevelt and the founders of the New Deal did far more than revolutionize what American government did. They also created the template—the agenda, the categories, and the vocabulary—that defined how government would organize its new responsibilities for decades to come. The original New Deal created, and the New Deal *writ large* cemented in place, four distinct and large clusters of domestic policy—(1) broad-based economic security guarantees, (2) means-tested welfare programs, (3) market regulation, and (4) market manipulation—that each rested on a unique set of assumptions, objectives, and mechanisms. Those four policy clusters lay the foundation for the House that FDR Built.

Today, we Americans still live in the House that FDR Built. Every now and then, we knock down a wall or add a window. More frequently, we repaint, re-carpet, or make other cosmetic changes. But the four big rooms created in 1933-1938 and enlarged over the next eight decades—the security room, the welfare room, the regulation room, and the manipulation room—all remain in place. From 1933 to today, we have honored the original conceptual blueprint and retained the core of the structure. Even some of the most intense critics of the New Deal legacy, from Ronald Reagan to Donald Trump, have operated inside the House that FDR Built, whether they know it (and admit it) or not.

Or, to shift metaphors, after retiring New Deal Version 1.0 and installing New Deal Version 2.0 in the 1950s, we have been updating that version ever since. Whenever pundits and politicians of any stripe propose a change in federal domestic policy, as likely as not their intent is to tweak New Deal Version 2.0.

A fundamental change, New Deal Version 3.0, still remains to be launched.

CHAPTER 3

SUCCESS AND FAILURE

DEFINING THE BROAD PURPOSES OF government is a good place to begin any detailed examination of the specific tasks we want government to perform. Identifying the broad purposes of government also helps us think more clearly about whether government has succeeded or failed, where the New Deal has done well or fallen short, and what a New Deal 3.0 might look like.

In the United States (as is true in any democratic society with a market economy), government has three broad purposes:

1) Protect and improve the public's overall safety, health, resources, and infrastructure.

   The focus is on society *as a whole*, in contrast to individuals' participation in programs that guarantee their economic security or the effective operation of the market. The primary aim is overall *preservation*: safeguarding and enhancing the entire population's lives and health; protecting private and public property; carefully managing the natural resources that all of us depend on; and maintaining the human-made grids that allow movement of people, vehicles, water, electricity, and electromagnetic waves.

2) Promote each individual's economic security, including equal access to health care and education.

The focus is on *individuals*, their status, and their development. The primary aim is *personal stability and advancement*: enrolling individuals in specific programs that shield, uplift, and empower them in specific ways that help them attain a stable and decent living standard, excellent health care, and a solid education.

3) Enable the market to work effectively.

The focus is on defining and overseeing *the market and the economy*. Economies are not always market economies. Sometimes dictators, "central committees," or thugs command their operation. But in a market economy, government limits itself — more or less — to setting the ground-rules and refereeing the competition. Individuals and firms make most of the resource allocation decisions, choosing among competing vendors (and regulated natural monopolies) as to which goods and services are purchased at what prices.

The primary aim is the *efficient allocation of resources* — labor and capital, primarily — towards the goods and services that individuals and firms most desire, based on low cost, high quality, and excellent reputation. The ultimate goal is to channel resources to the most efficient and creative organizations and individuals, thus strengthening the economy's productivity and spurring national wealth.

In carrying out these three broad purposes, government in the United States performs at least the following 28 major functions:

Protecting and Enhancing Public Safety,
Health, Resources, and Infrastructure

1. National defense
2. Law enforcement
3. Fire suppression
4. Public health
5. Drinkable water
6. Sewage treatment
7. Garbage disposal
8. Building inspection
9. Natural resource preservation
10. Infrastructure creation, maintenance and updating
11. Planning and zoning

Promoting Individual Economic Security,
Including Access to Health Care and Education

12. Help for unemployed and underemployed adults
13. Assistance to low-income workers
14. Benefits for adults with disabilities that prevent employment
15. Pensions for retired seniors
16. Health insurance, long-term care
17. K-12 education of children
18. College education of adults

Enabling the Market to Work Effectively

19. Guaranteeing property rights
20. Enforcement of valid contracts
21. Uniform standards
22. Full, accurate, and timely information
23. Trustworthy methods of exchange
24. A sound money supply
25. Basic scientific research
26. Single national market
27. Regulation of foreign trade
28. Prevention of damage to the environment, individuals, and firms

In carrying out these functions, government frequently succeeds. It also frequently fails. American government is neither "a" success nor "a" failure. It is both.

WHERE GOVERNMENT SUCCEEDS

We should not thank government alone, of course, for all of the great gains in safety, jobs, income, health, education, and more that have taken place in the U.S. over the last 80-plus years. The New Deal certainly cannot take full credit.

Much of the thanks goes to changes in values and culture, advances in science and technology, and the creativity of millions of individuals both obscure and famous. We owe much to the contributions of thousands of private organizations.

But government deserves a giant share of the credit. The New Deal especially — the House that FDR Built and subsequent policymakers enlarged — deserves a lot of thanks. Absent the specific policies that the original New Deal of 1933-1938 put in place and the New Deal *writ large* expanded over the next 80 years, the people of the United States would be poorer, sicker, and less educated. Our society would be shabbier. Our economy would not only be more panic-prone, but also far less dynamic and wealthy.

Following are five of our government's most spectacular successes:

1. Unemployment Insurance Benefits

Proposed by Franklin Roosevelt and enacted by Congress in 1935 as part of the Social Security Act, the federal Unemployment Insurance (UI) program invited states to participate in a joint federal-state effort to provide weekly benefits to qualifying unemployed workers. By the end of 1936, 35 states and the District of Columbia had enacted UI laws.[1] The first UI check in the amount of $15 went to Neils B. Ruud of Madison, Wisconsin, on August 17, 1936.[2] The number of UI beneficiaries and volume of UI payments fluctuate with the business cycle, but even in good times UI is a large program.

In 2017, an average of roughly 475,000 unemployed workers each month received first payments averaging $349 per week.[3] Altogether in 2017, UI recipients claimed nearly $30 billion in payments.[4] Implicitly financed by workers themselves in the form of reduced compensation (although their employers nominally pay the UI tax), the Unemployment Insurance program has enabled millions of laid-off American workers for over eight decades to keep up with the rent, pay off mortgages, put food on the table, and stay current with utility bills and car payments. Virtually all of the money gets recycled back into local economies.

2. Social Security Pensions

The most famous and biggest part of the 1935 Social Security Act is of course its pension program for retired workers.[5] Social Security delivered its first payment of $22.54 to Ida May Fuller of Vermont on January 31, 1940.[6] An estimated 175 million workers are covered under Social Security. It is the major source of income for most of America's elderly.[7] In 2017, Social Security provided over 41 million retired workers, whose average age was nearly 74, a monthly average payment of $1,202 for women and $1,519 for men.[8] The total cash benefits paid to retired workers in 2017 was $799 billion.[9] Without Social Security, over 40% of seniors would live below the "official" U.S. poverty line. Thanks to the program, fewer than 10% of America's seniors are "officially" poor.[10]

3. Bank Deposit Insurance and Banking Regulation

In 1930, over 1,300 banks failed. By 1933, the number of bank failures rose to 4,000. During the Great Depression as a whole, over 9,000 banks failed.[11] Virtually all of the Great Depression's bank failures occurred, however, prior to 1934. Soon after Franklin Roosevelt's inauguration, the 1933 Banking Act— sometimes called the Glass-Steagall Act—created the Federal Deposit Insurance Corporation (FDIC), which guarantees the safety of deposits in "member banks" up to a certain amount (now $250,000 per depositor per bank). The law also required banks to end high-risk activities and imposed criminal penalties for misconduct by bank officers and directors.[12]

The impact was immediate. The number of bank failures dropped precipitously to nine in 1934, 25 in 1935, and no more than 75 per year for the rest of FDR's life. From 1945 to 1975, the annual number of bank failures remained below ten. The numbers later rose to over 100 in two waves: 1982-1993 and 2009-2010. But since the 1933 launch of the Banking Act's system of insurance-plus-regulation, the highest annual number of bank failures, 534 in 1989, remained far below Great Depression levels. Since 2014, the number has again fallen below ten per year.[13] Of equal importance, since 1933 depositors in failing banks have generally enjoyed the protection of FDIC insurance.

4. Centers for Disease Prevention and Control

Founded a year after FDR's death in 1946, the CDC has success-fully contained many of the deadliest health threats, including: (A) closing in on the worldwide eradication of smallpox and polio; (B) control of malaria, typhus, and cholera epidemics; (C) combating malarial transmission in the United States; and (D) management of antibiotic-resistant infections, birth defects, and a number of chronic diseases.[14] Thanks to CDC's work with physicians such as the inventor of the polio vaccine, Dr. Jonas Salk, the U.S. has been polio-free since 1979.[15]

5. The City-to-City Segments of the Interstate Highway System

Starting in 1956, the U.S. government funded approximately 47,000 miles of roadway as part of the interstate ("I") system. The city-to-city portion of the network enabled vehicles to travel far more quickly across the vast distances of a continent-wide country.[16]

+ + +

These are just a few of government's many successes. In dozens of other areas where we have vested government with responsi-bility — national defense, law enforcement, fire suppression, public health, drinking water, sewage treatment, garbage disposal, building inspection, natural resource conservation, parks, roads, bridges, transit, airports, water ports, planning and zoning, Worker's Compensation, Unemployment Insurance, disability benefits, health care and health insurance, long-term care, day care, K12 schools, higher education, libraries, coinage and currency, money supply, environmental protection, worker protection, consumer protection, investor protection, scientific research, international commerce, and more—local, state, and the federal government (at times acting alone, often acting in concert) have provided Americans with genuine benefits.

We expect genuine benefits in exchange for the taxes we pay. As citizens and taxpayers, we should expect no less. But we should be candid in acknowledging that government frequently delivers the goods, in whole or in large part, in return for the payments and powers we give it.

WHERE GOVERNMENT FAILS

Yet just as it would be foolish to deny government's widespread success, it would be naive to ignore its extensive failures.

In a great many areas, government has entirely missed the boat; it has fallen short; it has done harm.

In large part because government has failed to act, or acted mistakenly, the United States today faces over a dozen serious problems, including:

- High levels of violence, with a murder rate higher than most developed nations;

- Daunting public health problems, including addiction to opioids and other drugs, addiction to tobacco, addiction to and abuse of alcohol, HIV/AIDS, and obesity;

- Inability or reluctance to join the labor market on the part of millions of adults who have the capacity to work, and often want a job, but are not counted as "officially" unemployed;

- Frequently high levels of "official" unemployment and, even when the unemployment rate dips below 4%, widespread underemployment;

- Extensive poverty, no matter how it is measured;

- Millions of workers who are unable to care for a newly born or adopted child, or assist an ailing parent, because they have no paid leave;

- Stark levels of inequality — and racial disparity — in income and wealth;

- Over 25 million Americans with no health insurance, and tens of millions more with inadequate health insurance due to exorbitant premiums and high deductibles;

- A large number of Americans with no dental insurance and poor dental care;

- No coherent system of long-term care insurance;

- Unaffordable childcare for millions of working parents of young children;

- Millions of children who drop out of K12 schools or graduate from high school without a real education;

- A large number of high school graduates who avoid college or drop out because of unaffordable tuition, or who graduate with a mountain of debt;

- Inadequate protection of the environment, workers, consumers, and investors;

- A sub-performing market, hamstrung by costly subsidies for politically-favored types of consumption and investment that subvert the market's productivity and capacity to maximize the nation's wealth;

- A deteriorating network of streets, roads, highways, bridges, and transit;

- A tax system that is unfair, complex, and onerous; and

- Massive federal deficits that have produced a troubling level of federal debt.

Why Things Looked So Good for So Long

Yet for most Americans in the quarter century after World War II, the overall model of American government appeared to serve the country well. As GI Joe married Rosie the Riveteer, the Baby Boom got underway, and Ed Sullivan hit the airwaves, it looked like the New Deal settlement and its four policy clusters were doing just fine. Franklin Roosevelt was gone, but happy days indeed seemed to be here again.

Two major reasons explain why, from roughly 1945 to the early 1970s, citizens and policymakers could not easily discern that anything was fundamentally amiss with the overall design of American government. First, the enormous economic advantages that the United States enjoyed, thanks to its utter domination of the world's economy, masked the New Deal's shortcomings. Second, several major but time-limited investments by the federal government also helped to hide the New Deal's gaps, flaws, and contradictions. Not until the U.S. economy in the 1970s began to undergo a wrenching transformation— especially in its labor market—did the underlying defects of the New Deal settlement slowly become visible.

We Owned The World

It can be said, with no trace of braggadocio, that the United States virtually owned the world's economy from 1945 until the early 1970s.

When World War II ended, Western Europe was in ruins, its biggest economies a wreck. Germany had been flattened by bombs and invasion, then divided in two and occupied by its conquerors. Victorious England had been badly bombed. It owed huge debts to the U.S. Its empire was vanishing, thanks in part to U.S. pressure. France and Italy suffered from intense political conflict. Spain and Portugal languished under dictators. Greece was torn apart by civil war. The notion of a single, powerful European market was just a dream in Jean Monnet's sleep.

To the east, the Soviet Union (while strong militarily) posed no economic challenge. The Soviet satellites in Eastern Europe likewise amounted to a blip in the world's economy. Further east, the economic powerhouses of Asia today—China, India, South Korea, and Taiwan—were still emerging as independent nations. Oppressed by colonial occupation, or ravaged by foreign invaders and civil war, their economies posed no threat to America's. If you had talked about products "Made in China" in the 1950s, 1960s, or 1970s, no one in the U.S. would have had a clue what you were talking about.

Bombs had also leveled Japan, culminating in the A-bombs' destruction of Hiroshima and Nagasaki. It would take decades for Japan to start competing with the U.S. Even into the 1960s, products "Made in Japan" were more likely to be mocked than feared. Japan then sold us junky radios that fell apart. High-tech

Toyotas and Hondas, with their superior maintenance and fuel efficiency, remained on the horizon.

Finally, neither Mexico, nor the nations of Central and South America, nor the new nations of Africa, provided any competition. When U.S. manufacturers moved their production to obtain cheaper labor, they moved from Massachusetts and Rhode Island to North Carolina and Georgia — not to Chihuahua or Monterrey.

In short, America's only serious economic competition came from Canada (which many Americans think of as an adjunct to the U.S. economy anyway). In addition, trade barriers impeded what international commerce there was. The world had not returned to the ruinous tariffs of Smoot-Hawley, but international trade was still a long way from GATT, WTO, and NAFTA.

The data make clear how fully the U.S. dominated the world economy.[17] In 1913, on the cusp of World War I, the Gross Domestic Product (GDP) of the three biggest European nations (Germany, the UK, and France) constituted 22.2% of the world's GDP. The combined GDP of the three biggest Asian nations (China, India, and Japan) stood at 18.9% of the world total. The U.S. tied with 18.9%.

Fast forward to 1950. The recovery of western Europe and Japan was underway. Still, the GDP of Europe's three biggest nations had slipped by nearly a third to 15.6% of the world's GDP, far behind the U.S. The GDP of Asia's three biggest nation's had plunged by an even greater degree to 11.8% of the world total. China's and India's shares had fallen by roughly half, offset by Japan's small gain. Meanwhile, the U.S. had increased its share of world GDP by nearly half, to 27.3% of the world total. Thus, in the wake of World War II, the combined

GDPs of the once and future economic giants of the planet—Germany, the UK, France, China, India, and Japan—was virtually the same as that of a single economic colossus: the United States.

Dominating the globe's economy tells only half the story of why America was in such good shape in the immediate post-war era. The other half of the story is the New Deal and its aftermath.

Federal Investments Made Us Even Stronger

The New Deal was not even a teenager in 1945, but it had already begun to strengthen the economic position of so many millions of Americans that it was bolstering the U.S. economy as a whole. For starters, New Deal economic security policies stabilized and raised incomes. Unemployment insurance cushioned laid-off workers when the U.S. economy faced occasional downturns. The federal minimum wage and collective bargaining increased workers' purchasing power. Social Security pension payments began to ensure that a growing share of retirees had a comfortable income.

Two other key federal policies that took hold in the post-war era also had a profound positive effect on the economy: interstate highways and the GI Bill.

Siphoning off the gas taxes paid by drivers of America's expanding fleet of vehicles, state and federal governments chose to divert much of the growing stream of revenue away from maintaining the existing local streets, county roads, and state highways that drivers overwhelmingly used. Instead, government redirected a huge slice of the revenue to finance construction of a vast new network of interstate highways. A big reason was the federal government's decision in 1956 to pick up 90-95% of states' costs for building interstate highways.[18]

The decision to run interstate highways through the heart of dozens of central cities ultimately did enormous damage to the environment, urban economies, and racial integration. In the short run, however, interstate highways achieved the one positive good that President Dwight Eisenhower envisioned. Ike was an admirer of Germany's autobahn system. He wanted an American version, and Congress agreed. The new "freeways" greatly shortened the time it took to transport goods between metropolitan areas. That piece of the investment accelerated the productivity of the nation's economy.

A second new federal policy, the GI Bill, probably did even more to stimulate the U.S. economy. For the first time in U.S. history, millions of low- to middle-income young men and women found it possible to afford a college education. Responding to the tuition that former GIs carried with them, the nation's colleges and universities expanded rapidly. Many were state universities, which also received growing subsidies from their state governments.

The program was far from perfect. Blacks faced severe discrimination, as they also did when trying to use the GI Bill's housing benefits. Overall, however, the GI Bill's investment in enabling millions of WWII veterans to acquire a higher education quickly began to pay off, as a more highly educated workforce entered the labor market in the 1950s.

A (MOSTLY) GOOD THING LASTS FOR THREE DECADES

Put the two halves of the puzzle together — (1) a recovering world economy that America totally dominated with its undamaged and robust domestic market, plus (2) America's new economic security policies, stronger market regulation, and massive public investments in infrastructure and education — and it is little wonder that the U.S. did so well from 1945 through the mid-1970s. Unemployment rarely rose above 4%. Incomes rose across the board. A growing share of the population acquired health insurance and earned college degrees. The middle class vastly expanded.

Yet ironically, the very success of the New Deal settlement helped to hide its shortcomings, flaws, and contradictions.

The post-war economy provided steady jobs for almost anyone who could set an alarm clock, get out of bed, and fog a mirror. Whenever the economy got a little tired, the still-new Unemployment Insurance program gave short-term cash to many who faced temporary layoffs. Why worry about the risk of unemployment, underemployment, or job volatility?

Since wages were rising steadily due to the triple-whammy of minimum wage laws, collective bargaining, and market forces, there was also little need to supplement them. Rising earnings and income would go on forever, right?

Collective bargaining also increasingly provided workers with good health insurance. And from 1965 onward Medicaid helped many of the poor while Medicare took care of seniors. The nation's 40+ million uninsured remained an embarrassment. The emergence of hyperinflation in health costs raised concerns.

But who could doubt that the downward trend in the uninsured rate would not continue until everyone had coverage? And surely the nation that had simultaneously defeated Nazi Germany, Fascist Italy, and Imperial Japan, and was holding its own in the new Cold War against the USSR, could whip inflation in its internal health care sector.

On the education front, many jobs required minimal education to begin with. Meanwhile, millions of young adults were flooding colleges and universities, thanks to the GI Bill and state expansion of public universities. Why express concern about the quality of K12 education or the cost of higher education?

Yes, blacks and Hispanics remained far behind whites on all fronts. But all groups were gaining ground compared to their Great Depression levels of unemployment, poverty, earnings, income, nutrition, housing, health, and education. Most of those in power saw little need (at least until the 1960s) to worry about racial, ethnic, or gender disparities.

Meanwhile, while recipients of means-tested welfare programs were often hassled and stigmatized, the size of those programs was fairly small until the late 1960s. Many of the welfare programs we know the best, like Food Stamps and Medicaid, did not even exist until the 1960s.

In short, for most of the two and a half decades following World War II, it would have been reasonable to conclude that the New Deal was correcting most of the shortcomings of the labor market and handling in a satisfactory way most of the problems stemming from the rest of the market. If there were major gaps, big flaws, and serious contradictions in the New Deal settlement, they were not apparent. Happy days were not just here again. Happy days were here to stay.

Until, as Don McLean wrote in 1971 in *American Pie*, the music died.

1960s: A Growing Critique, an Expanding New Deal

It can be argued, of course, that the New Deal settlement was never satisfactory.

Despite the progress that African-Americans and Hispanics made during the post-war era in obtaining jobs, earning higher incomes, gaining health insurance, and graduating from high school and college, both minority groups lagged behind whites on all fronts. The nation's minorities continued to experience higher rates of poverty, suffer more from a lack of health care, and receive less and worse education. Minority groups experienced brutal levels of discrimination in the labor market and in housing

Indeed, many white Americans experienced high levels of unemployment, poverty, lack of health care, and terrible housing. Michael Harrington's *The Other America* became a bestseller, in part because it exposed white poverty in Appalachia.[19]

The Other America's painful revelation of widespread poverty in the midst of abundance was published in 1962. The same year James Baldwin's deeply disturbing essay on race and religion appeared in print, subsequently published as part of *The Fire Next Time*.[20] In 1962, Rachel Carson's *Silent Spring* documented the environmental harm caused by the indiscriminate use of approved pesticides.[21] Ralph Nader's exposé of dangerous cars and carmakers' negligence, *Unsafe at any Speed*, appeared a few years later.[22] Less than 30 years after the original New Deal of 1933-1938 and less than 20 years after World War II ended, a growing number of critics had begun to shine more and brighter light on America's serious economic, environmental, and market problems. In essence, they were building a sweeping critique of the New Deal settlement, even as the New Deal *writ large* continued to expand.

Yet despite the Vietnam War, urban violence, racial strife, political assassinations, "burning" rivers, and unsafe cars that rocked the mid-to-late 1960s and early 1970s, one could still make the case that the New Deal settlement was working well and Americans' circumstances were improving. More of the same was a plausible argument. What ensued was more of the same. Not since 1933-1938 had the New Deal *writ large* expanded so quickly and widely as between 1964 and 1973.

In 1964-1965, Congress and President Johnson added a host of anti-poverty programs under the umbrella of the War on Poverty, as well as Medicaid and Medicare. Some pieces of the War on Poverty were later eliminated or downsized, but many survived. Some War on Poverty programs, such as Food Stamps and Head Start, greatly expanded. As a result, tens of millions of Americans got more to eat and had access to improved childcare. Then, in the early 1970s, Congress and President Nixon added a raft of environmental regulations. It took a few more years, but eventually the nation's dirty air and dirty water began to get cleaner.

Overall, compared to 1932, Americans were unquestionably much better off in 1975. Unemployed adults, lower-income workers, persons with serious disabilities, and retired seniors had far more economic security as they navigated the "hazards and vicissitudes" of work and life. The middle class was booming. Two big pillars of a comprehensive national health insurance system—Medicare and Medicaid—had been put in place. Since the Great Depression, there had been no collapse of the banking system or stock market. And if the environment was still being poisoned by pesticides and consumers were still buying dangerous cars, at least the federal government was implementing new laws and agencies to stop the damage.

1970s: Economic Security Gains Grind to a Halt

But the bigger story is that by the mid-1970s the New Deal *writ large* was reaching its limits, especially in achieving economic security. In key areas, the New Deal settlement hit a wall. Looking back with the help of historical data, we can clearly see how after 1973 many of the key indicators of economic security worsened, ground to a halt, or barely improved.

"Official" Poverty Stopped Falling

The Census Bureau began its systematic measurement of poverty in 1959. From then until 1973, the "official" U.S. poverty rate dropped dramatically. But after 1973, poverty stopped falling— in fact, it increased—for the U.S. population as a whole, for children, and for most adults.

During the 1959-1973 period, "official" U.S. poverty fell by half, from 22.4% to 11.1% of the population. But for the next 40+ years, the nation's poverty rate remained stuck. It was always higher than 11.1%. Most of the time, it hovered between 12%-15% of the population.[23]

For children under 18 the pattern was almost identical. From 1959 to 1973, the "official" child poverty rate declined by nearly half, from 27.3% to 14.4%. Then the steady decline hit a brick wall. After 1973, child poverty was always higher. It never again fell below 15.0%. For 40+ years, it floated between 15%-22% of the under-18 population.[24]

The story was the same for the majority of adults, those ages 18 to 64. Between 1959 and 1973, their "official" poverty rate fell by slightly more than half, from 17.0% to 8.3%. But for the next 40+ years, it never got any lower. Most of the time, the poverty rate for this largest segment of the U.S. population hovered between 9% and 13%.[25]

Only seniors—those ages 65 and older—set a somewhat different pattern. They experienced the sharpest drop in "official" poverty between 1959 and 1973. During that 14-year period, their rate plunged by more than half, from 35.2% to 16.3%. The difference is that the senior poverty rate kept falling, but its decline was slow and incremental. It took another 38 years, from 1973 to 2011, for the senior poverty rate to drop to its lowest point of 8.7%. It has since climbed back to a 2017 rate of 9.2%. For most of the last 20 years, senior poverty has jiggled back and forth in the very narrow range of 8.9% to 10.5%[26]

SPM Poverty Ended Its Steady Decline

The fact that the drop in "official" U.S. poverty came to a screeching halt in 1973 for the overall population, children, and most adults (and down-shifted to a crawl for seniors) is not a problem of methodology. Whether we use the much-questioned "official" poverty measure or the new and arguably more credible Supplemental Poverty Measure (SPM), the story is much the same.

The SPM makes two major changes in the measurement of poverty.

First, unlike the "official" approach of counting only cash income, the SPM counts both cash and non-cash resources (e.g., Food Stamps and tax credits).

Second, rather than use the "official" approach of setting poverty lines at the outdated multiple of three times the 1950s' cost of a nutritionally deficient "economy food plan" (adjusted for inflation and family size), the SPM sets its poverty thresholds at 120% of the 33rd percentile of Americans' expenditures for a basic set of goods—food clothing, shelter and utilities (FCSU)— as adjusted for family size.

Both ways of measuring poverty include a number of arbitrary decisions. Many experts believe, however, that the SPM is the better method.

Nonetheless, according to the Census Bureau, when "official" poverty rates are stacked up against SPM poverty rates, only a small difference emerges in the degree of overall poverty. Bigger differences occur for sub-populations, but they tend to offset each other. Generally, as Table 3.1 shows, SPM poverty is higher.[27]

The heart of this discussion is how the decline in American poverty stopped in the mid-1970s. As explained earlier, during the relatively brief 14-year period from 1959 to 1973, the "official" poverty rate for the overall U.S. population plummeted

Table 3-1: Poverty Rates Comparing the "Official" Measure vs. the SPM: 2017		
	"Official" Poverty Measure	Supplemental Poverty Measure
All people	12.3%	13.9%
Under 18 years	17.5%	15.6%
18-64 Years	11.2%	13.2%
64 and Older	9.2%	14.1%

from 22% to 11%, dropping by half. No further decline took place for 44 years, with the overall "official" poverty rate remaining stuck on a plateau between 12%-15% from 1974 to 2017. Does the Supplemental Poverty Measure (SPM) tell a fundamentally different story?

The answer is no. SPM data are not available prior to 1967. During the short 6-year period from 1967 to 1973, the SPM poverty rate for all Americans nonetheless fell sharply from 25% to 19%, an average of one percentage point per year.[28] For the next 44 years from 1973 to 2017—a period over seven times longer—the overall SPM poverty rate declined from 19% to only 14%, barely more than a scant average of one tenth of a percentage point per year.[29]

Moreover, for most of this 44-year period, the SPM poverty rate remained stuck on two long plateaus—the first of 20 years, the second of 18 years—separated by an interval over which the SPM poverty rate declined by four percentage points:

- On the first 20-year plateau, 1973 to 1993, the SPM poverty rate jumped a little, dipped a little, jumped a little, and dipped a little, starting at 19% and ending at 19%.

- Then, for a 6-year period, the SPM poverty rate fell. From 1993 to 1999, it dropped by four percentage points from 19% to 15%.

- But afterwards, atop a second 18-year plateau from 1999 to 2017, the SPM poverty rate remained almost constant in the 14%-16% range, rising slightly during the Great Recession before dipping slightly after the recovery.[30]

Table 3-2: "Official" Poverty Rate vs. SPM Poverty Rate: 1959 to 2017						
	1959	1967	1973			2017
"Official" Poverty	22%	14%	11%			12%
	>>> Big Drop >>>		>>> 44-Year Plateau >>>			
		1967	1973	1993	1999	2017
SPM Poverty		25%	19%	19%	15%	14%
		Big Drop	1st Plateau		2nd Plateau	

Thus, mimicking the "official" poverty rate's trajectory, the SPM poverty rate has essentially followed the same long-term path. After a big and rapid rate reduction that took place until the mid-1970s, both poverty rates underwent a long 44-year period of no-to-limited progress that lasted from 1973 to 2017. The only difference is that the "official" poverty rate hit a single brick wall in 1973 and has remained stuck on a single plateau ever since, while the SPM poverty rate got stuck on two long plateaus of no progress (1973-1993 and 1999-2017) broken by a short interval of rate reduction (1993-1999).

The data lead to three conclusions about government's role in reducing poverty.

1) As America's experience from 1950s through the mid-1970s shows, government policy has the power to dramatically and steadily reduce poverty when the policy is calibrated to address the specific "hazards and vicissitudes" of the economy.

2) Since the mid-1970s, U.S. public policy deserves credit for keeping poverty from worsening.

3) American government has nonetheless failed, beyond the mid-1970s, in continuing the earlier pattern of big and continuous drops in the poverty rate.

For over four decades, flaws in the design of U.S. economic security policy have thwarted it from making large and unceasing progress in shrinking poverty in the face of the labor market's transformation by intense foreign competition and highly disruptive technology.

To get back on the track of making steady reductions in poverty (until we reach a residual level of perhaps 2-3%), the U.S. has only one option: reform the design of its economic security policy.

Wages Fell, Earnings Flattened, and Income Barely Rose

It is perhaps no coincidence that, as the rapid decline in poverty that the U.S. experienced in the 1950s and 1960s ran into a brick wall in the mid-1970s, the federal minimum wage suffered one of its biggest drops. Between 1968 and 1974, the minimum wage fell from $10.86 per hour to $7.67 per hour, as expressed in 2015 dollars.[31] (All future references to the minimum wage through 2015 are shown in 2015 dollars.)

Table 3-3: Federal Minimum Wage Adjusted for Inflation (2015 Dollars): 1938-2015			
1938: $4.19	1958: $8.18	1978: $8.33	1998: $7.46
1939: $5.10	1959: $8.12	1979: $9.44	1999: $7.30
1940: $5.06	1960: $7.98	1980: $8.89	2000: $7.07
1941: $4.82	1961: $9.09	1981: $8.71	2001: $6.87
1942: $4.35	1962: $9.00	1982: $8.20	2002: $6.76
1943: $4.10	1963: $9.65	1983: $7.95	2003: $6.61
1944: $4.03	1964: $9.53	1984: $7.62	2004: $6.44
1945: $5.25	1965: $9.38	1985: $7.36	2005: $6.23
1946: $4.85	1966: $9.12	1986: $7.22	2006: $6.04
1947: $4.24	1967: $9.90	1987: $6.97	2007: $6.67
1948: $3.92	1968: $10.86	1988: $6.69	2008: $7.19
1949: $3.97	1969: $10.30	1989: $6.38	2009: $7.98
1950: $7.35	1970: $9.74	1990: $6.87	2010: $7.86
1951: $6.82	1971: $9.33	1991: $7.37	2011: $7.62
1952: $6.69	1972: $9.04	1992: $7.16	2012: $7.46
1953: $6.64	1973: $8.51	1993: $6.95	2013: $7.35
1954: $6.59	1974: $7.67	1994: $6.78	2014: $7.24
1955: $6.61	1975: $9.22	1995: $6.59	2015: $7.25
1956: $8.69	1976: $9.55	1996: $7.15	
1957: $8.41	1977: $8.97	1997: $7.58	

During the three decades between the federal minimum wage's launch in 1938 (the year the Fair Labor Standards Act became law) to its peak value in 1968, the minimum wage had steadily increased. It jumped in periodic increments, with occasional backsliding, from $4.19 per hour to $10.86 per hour.[32]

But starting in 1969, the minimum wage reversed direction, kicking off a slow (if herky-jerky) decline. By 1970 it fell below

$10 per hour. By 1980, it slid below $9.00 per hour. It reached its nadir in 2006, when it fell to $6.04 per hour. For most of the last 20 years, the federal minimum wage has oscillated within the $6.00 to $8.00 range.[33]

Today, the federal minimum wage is one-third below its $10.86 peak at $7.25 per hour.

The descent in the federal minimum wage hints at what happened to American workers' earnings and income, but hardly tells the story. It is possible for the minimum wage to fall, but workers' earnings to rise. Even if the minimum wage descends, it's possible that family income may ascend. Fortunately, we need not rely on the minimum wage's history as a surrogate for the earnings story or the income story. The Bureau of Labor Statistics surveys workers' earnings. The Census Bureau surveys families' incomes. Both of these data sets tell essentially the same story: no substantial progress since the mid-1970s.

Flat Average Wages: According to a 2018 analysis of BLS data by the Pew Research Center, "In real terms average hourly earnings [i.e., wages] peaked more than 45 years ago." Following "a long slide in the 1980s and early 1990s and bumpy, inconsistent growth since then," the average hourly wage in 1978 has "just about the same purchasing power" as "today's average hourly wage."[34]

Almost-Flat Median Weekly Earnings: The same pattern emerges when we shift from average hourly earnings to weekly median earnings. The BLS data analyzed by the Pew Research Center show that, before adjusting for inflation, "median usual weekly earnings rose from $232 in the first quarter of 1979 (when the data series began) to $879 in the second quarter of [2018]." But "in real, inflation-adjusted terms, the median has barely budged over that period: That $232 in 1979 had the same purchasing power as $840 in 2018 dollars." Thus, after the passage of four decades and with inflation factored in, the 1979 median usual weekly earnings level of $840 in 2018 dollars is a mere $39 less than the actual 2018 level of $879, despite the massive productivity growth in the American economy.[35]

After factoring in the increase in payroll taxes (FICA and Medicare) from 1979 (6.13%) to 2018 (7.65%), the net increase in median weekly earnings over the 39-year period shrinks to $23. For many, even that small gain has been eaten up by the rising cost of health care and housing.

Flattening of Median Annual Men's Earnings: We depend less on hourly wages and weekly earnings than we do on annual earnings. But since the mid-1970s, the annual earnings trend for men has also been bleak.

Men's earnings once rose sharply and quickly. Over the course of 13 years from 1960 to 1973, in inflation-adjusted dollars, the median annual earnings of men climbed from $32,686 to $42,934.

Then, for 24 straight years, men's median annual earnings were flat (with occasional small gains offset by bigger losses). It took 15 years, until 1998, before men once again experienced median earnings greater than $43,000. Once again, however, another long stretch of stagnant earnings kicked in. From 1999 to

2017, men's median earnings wandered within a narrow range between roughly $40,556 and $44,409.[36]

Here's the bottom line: in the relatively brief 13-year period from 1960 to 1973, men's median annual earnings rose by over $10,000. Over the much longer 44-year period that followed, men's median earnings rose by less than $1,500. The major increase in payroll taxes that occurred during this time (from 5.85% in 1973 to 7.65% in 2017) makes this weak growth in men's earnings even weaker. Just as the decline in poverty hit a brick wall in 1973, men's earnings hit a brick wall in 1973. It is reasonable to conclude that it was the same brick wall.

Sluggish Growth in Median Annual Women's Earnings: For women, the median annual earnings story is somewhat—but only somewhat—less bleak. Women constitute a smaller percentage of the workforce, but their numbers and share are increasing. The good news is that, for a substantially longer period than for men, women's median earnings kept rising. While gains for men stopped short in 1973, U.S. women's median earnings rose steadily from $13,285 in 1960 to $29,398 in 2003 in inflation-adjusted dollars.

But over the next 10 years, from 2003 to 2013, female median earnings (while falling and rising slightly) were essentially flat. Only after 2014 did they exceed $29,398, rising to $31,610 in 2017.[37]

Tepid Growth in Median Family Income: The downshift for men from rapidly rising earnings during the 1960-to-1973 period to nearly flat annual earnings over the following 44 years, combined with sluggish growth in annual earnings for women since 2003, suggest that total family income growth has cooled in recent decades. It has cooled a lot. With each passing decade, despite a strong upswing in women's participation in the labor market from the 1960s through the 1980s, U.S. family median income growth has gotten slower and slower.[38]

At the beginning of this era, paralleling the sharp decline in poverty that was taking place, median income grew strongly and rapidly. From 1967 to 1973, median family income in the U.S. (in 2017 dollars) rose from $45,965 to $51,984. It only took 6 years for U.S. households to have their median income grow by more than $6,000. The average annual growth in the median income was just over $1,000 per year.[39]

But it took another 25 years, four times as long from 1973 to 1998, for median family income to grow by the next increment of $6,000 to reach $58,612. The average annual growth in median income shrank by over three-quarters to $265 per year.[40]

And 19 years later, in 2017, median family income in the U.S. remained thousands of dollars below the next $6,000 increment of growth. It reached only $61,372. Over almost two decades, it rose by only $2,760. The average annual growth in median income during the 19-year period between 1998 and 2017 fell to a mere $145 per year.[41]

Thus, the trajectory that the American poverty rate followed (however poverty is measured) was not unique to poverty. From the 1960s through the mid-1970s, median earnings for men and women, as well as median family income, improved greatly and rapidly. Then, median earnings for men got stuck on a 44-year plateau. Even though more women worked, median family income rose much more slowly. Finally, as median earnings for women bogged down early in the 21st century on a 10-year plateau, median income growth for families nearly ground to a halt. Since 2000, U.S. median family income has risen by less than $85 each year.

The bottom line for public policy is simple. During the long stretch between the end of World War II and the Watergate era of the mid-1970s, government policies interacted with the economy to achieve large, continuous growth in earnings and incomes. But during the four decades that followed, the partnership fell apart. Just as the existing U.S. policy structure is no longer capable of reproducing the pre-1973 pattern of big and steady drops in poverty for those at the bottom, the current U.S. economic security policy machinery decades ago ran out of gas when it comes to producing sizeable annual gains in earnings and income for the American population as a whole.

In short, economic security for a vast and growing share of Americans has been overwhelmed by a radically different economy transformed by fierce international competition and intensely disruptive technology. For millions of lower-income and middle-class individuals and families, economic security has shifted into reverse. For millions more, progress has ground to a halt. To return to the kind of earnings and income gains that U.S. workers once enjoyed, government must put in place a new set of policies that are powerful enough to counter-balance the new risks arising from the rapidly morphing labor market.

Retirement Security Became More Perilous

It took a few years beyond 1973 for the crisis in retirement security to emerge. But since the end of the 1970s, the serious problem that many seniors face after retirement in maintaining a decent income has turned into a crisis that in time may descend into a catastrophe.

It is not only conventional wisdom—it is true—that seniors' income security in retirement depends on three sources of income:

1) Social Security;

2) Private pension plans that guarantee a "defined benefit" for the life of the retired worker and spouse; and

3) Individual savings.

Social Security faces challenges. Individual savings are often absent or scanty. But the most serious problem is the post-1970s' vanishing of "defined benefit" retirement plans for private-sector employees. If you work in the private sector, the middle leg of the three-legged stool of a secure retirement has been sawed off.

Early in the 1980s, the share of American workers in the private sector who relied on an employment-based "defined benefit" plan for their retirement started to plummet. As the name implies, "defined benefit" plans guarantee workers a specific retirement income for themselves, and often for their spouses, for as long as they live. But over the last several decades, an alternative approach, "defined contribution" plans, became the dominant mechanism for saving for retirement. "Defined benefit" plans, however, are generally more dependable and provide larger monthly pensions than "defined contribution" plans. There are several reasons why the latter are unreliable as a primary source of adequate retirement income.

To begin with, "defined contribution" plans require individual workers to set aside (to contribute) a portion of their current income to help them in a retirement that may lie decades in the future. Many workers, especially at younger ages, lack the income or discipline to do so. And even when workers do enroll in a "defined contribution" plan, it is impossible for them at any age to know how many years they, and perhaps a spouse, will survive in old age, or to predict health care and housing costs decades in the future. Thus, even the most prudent worker may easily fail to figure out and set aside the right amount.

In addition, "defined contribution" plans must be wisely invested in order to produce sufficient retirement income. Apart from the risk of choosing a fraudulent or foolhardy investment portfolio, workers' assets can be wiped out by economic disasters like the Great Recession of 2007-2009 or cut down by lesser downturns in the economy.

Finally, "defined contribution" plans do not necessarily include an insurance feature that guarantees a minimum — much less an adequate — pension. It is easy to outlive one's savings, particularly if one lives to be 85 or 95. It is particularly easy for retirees to outlive their savings if they need to pay out-of-pocket for nursing home care.

But despite the manifold advantages of "defined benefit" plans in contrast to the many shortcomings of "defined contribution" plans, the number of workers in the former has dropped precipitously since the 1970s, while workers' reliance on the latter has skyrocketed.

In 1979, 28% of private-sector workers with employment retirement plans had a "defined benefit" plan only. Another 10% had a combination of both types of retirement arrangement. But by 2014, the share of private-sector workers with a "defined benefit" plan only had nosedived to 2%. Those with a combination of plans stood at 11%. In other words, in 35 years, the proportion of private-sector employees with a "defined benefit" plan (alone or in combination) fell by two thirds, from 38% to 13%.[42]

By contrast, those who only had a "defined contribution" plan rose over the same 1979-2014 period from 7% to 34%, nearly a five-fold increase. After adding in private employees who had a combination of both types of retirement arrangement, the share with a "defined contribution" plan (alone or in combination) increased from 17% to 45%.[43]

Over 25 Million Still Uninsured

Finally, we come to health care. Today, more than 25 million Americans still have no health insurance (despite the Affordable Care Act). And health care costs continue to climb out of control.

Like the poverty rate, the "uninsurance" rate for the U.S. population under 65 also plunged from the 1950s until the mid-1970s. And then it too hit a wall.

In 1959, the percentage of under-65 Americans without hospital insurance was 31%. By 1968, it had dropped by one-third to 21%. (The under-65 population without surgical insurance likewise dropped from 36% to 22%.) After 1968, the National Center for Health Statistics began to measure overall health insurance and lack thereof. The steep downward trend rate continued. By 1972, only 17% of under-65 Americans were counted as uninsured. Two years later, in 1974, the uninsurance rate fell to 13%.[44]

Then, over the next 39 years before Obamacare kicked in, the uninsurance rate—like the poverty rate—got stuck on a long plateau. It fluctuated from 1974 to 2013 between 12% and 18%, rising and falling in small waves. Only twice did it go as low as 12%. For 20 years in a row (1989-2009), it never fell below 15.5% or rose about 17.8%.[45]

Table 3-4: Percentage of Americans Under 65 Without Health Insurance: 1959-2018 [46]			
Year Uninsured	Year Uninsured	Year Uninsured	Year Uninsured
1959: 30.9%	1986: 15.0%	1999: 16.1%	2010: 18.2%
1963: 27.7%	1989: 15.6%	2000: 16.8%	2011: 17.3%
1968: 20.7%	1990: 17.2%	2001: 16.1%	2012: 16.9%
1972: 16.7%	1991: 16.4%	2002: 16.5%	2013: 16.6%
1974: 13.1%	1992: 16.8%	2003: 16.5%	2014: 13.3%
1976: 14.1%	1993: 17.4%	2004: 16.4%	2015: 10.5%
1978: 12.0%	1994: 17.8%	2005: 16.4%	2016: 10.4%
1980: 12.0%	1995: 16.3%	2006: 17.0%	2017: 10.7%
1982: 13.9%	1996: 16.7%	2007: 16.6%	2018: 10.8%
1983: 14.6%	1997: 17.5%	2008: 16.8%	
1984: 14.5%	1998: 16.6%	2009: 17.5%	

Only after Congress passed and President Obama signed the Affordable Care Act did the pre-1973 pattern of improvement resume, and then for only a few years. The uninsurance rate finally fell substantially from 16.6% in 2013 to 10.4% in 2016. It was an historic drop. But it may have been a one-off. Since 2015, the share of uninsured Americans has varied little. In 2017, the uninsurance rate rose slightly to 10.7%. For the first nine months of 2018, it stood at 10.8%.[47]

As a result of the failure of U.S. economic security policy to guarantee health insurance for everyone, the Census Bureau reported that in 2017 a total of 28.5 million Americans had no insurance for the entire year.[48] Millions more went without health insurance for stretches of time. The 28.5 million Americans without any health insurance is larger than the entire population of Australia. It is more than the combined populations of Norway, Sweden, and Finland. It is over five times the population of Ireland.

As troubling as the inability of American government to provide health insurance for everyone is government's failure to create an effective mechanism to control the price of health care. Looking back to the beginning of the current century, a recent analysis of health care prices found: "On a broad level, since 2000, the Medical Care component of the Consumer Price Index (CPI) has been consistently increasing at a 1.5% to 2% higher annual rate than the CPI for all goods and services."[49]

According to another recent report by the Kaiser Family Foundation: "Since the end of 2007, healthcare prices have grown 21.6%, while prices in the general economy (measured by the GDP deflator) have grown 17.3%."[50]

The cumulative effect of 50 years of rising health care costs has been profound. When John F. Kennedy was elected President, Americans devoted 5% of GDP to health care. By the time Barack Obama neared the end of his second term as

President, America was spending nearly 18% of GDP on health care.

Just as the 1970s were an turning point in modern American history when it came poverty, earnings, and income — that is: no progress or very limited gains since then — the 1970s also provided an inflexion point when it comes to health care expenditure growth. During the two decades that encompassed the 1970s, i.e. 1960-1980, health care spending rose slowly by 3.9 percentage points (5.0% to 8.9%) as a share of GDP. But with the 1970s in the rear-view mirror, the pace of health care spending accelerated. Over the next two decades, from 1980 to 2000, health care spending jumped by 4.4 percentage points (from 8.9% to 13.3%) as a share of GDP. And over the shorter 15-year period that followed, from 2000 to 2015, health care spending rose by 5 full percentage points (from 13.3% to 17.8%).

Table 3-5: U.S. Health Care Expenditures as a Percent of U.S. GDP: 1960-2015 [51]	
Year	Percent of GDP
1960:	5.0%
1965:	5.6%
1970:	6.9%
1975:	7.9%
1980:	8.9%
1985:	10.2%
1990:	12.1%
1995:	13.3%
2000:	13.3%
2005:	15.5%
2010:	17.4%
2015:	17.8%

No other wealthy nation comes close to the United States in spending such a high share of its GDP on health care.

Looking at the problem another way, no other large and wealthy nation spends as much per capita as the United States on health care. Among OECD nations that are similarly large and wealthy (based on GDP and GDP per capita), in 2016 the average per capita expenditure on health care was $5,169. Germany had the third highest expense per capita: $5,550. Switzerland came in second: $7,919. The U.S. spent thousands more, and twice as much as the average: $10,348.[52]

If we continue to operate our health care system the same way, there is every reason to believe that U.S. health care spending will before long reach 20% of GDP, and keep on rising.[53] There is likewise no reason to doubt that, if we keep on keeping on with the same health care system, the yawning gap between what our economic competitors spend and we shell out per-capita for health care—a gap of thousands of dollars—will continue to gnaw away at the competitiveness of the U.S. economy.

Two explanations occasionally surface as Americans debate hyperinflation in our health care costs and the seemingly inexorable, out-of-line, growth in our overall level of health care spending as a percent of GDP or per capita. The first explanation: our aging population requires these excesses. The second explanation: the extra spending makes us healthier. The evidence contradicts both claims.

It is true that the U.S. population is aging. But one of the nation's foremost health care economists, the late Uwe Reinhardt of Princeton University, has debunked the notion that aging is a primary cause of America's rising and disproportionate health care spending. Writing in *Health Affairs* in 2003, Reinhardt concluded:

> The objective of this essay has been to deconstruct the popular myth that the aging of the population by itself is a major contributor to the annual increase in the demand for health care and, thus, to total national health spending. Although the projected increase in the fraction of elderly in the total population ... is not a trivial matter in health policy ... the bulk of the rapid annual growth in national spending in the past has been driven by other factors that increase per capita spending for all age groups. Key factors include rising per capita incomes, the availability of promising but costly new medical technology, workforce shortages that can drive up the unit cost of health care, and the asymmetric distribution of market power in health care that gives the supply side of the sector considerable sway over the demand side. These other factors will be the dominant drivers of health spending in the future as well.[54]

The relentless increase and excessive levels in U.S. spending on health care would perhaps be justified if those patterns resulted in making Americans healthier. But spending more and more on doctors, hospitals, drugs, and other inputs has not necessarily translated into gains in health outcomes. In recent years, in fact, more spending has been accompanied by worse outcomes. According to a 2016 report by Olga Khazan in *The Atlantic*:

> For the first time since the 1990s, Americans are dying at a faster rate, and they're dying younger. A pair of new studies suggests Americans are sicker than people in other rich countries, and in some states, progress on

stemming the tide of basic diseases like diabetes has stalled or even reversed. The studies suggest so-called "despair deaths" — alcoholism, drugs, and suicide — are a big part of the problem, but so is obesity, poverty, and social isolation.

American life expectancy fell by one-tenth of a year since 2014, from 78.9 to 78.8, according to a report ... by the National Center for Health Statistics. ... Meanwhile, the number of years people are expected to live at 65 remained unchanged, suggesting people are falling ill and dying young.[55]

The Structural Cause of Worsening Economic Insecurity

The economic security wall that America hit in the 1970s — that is: poverty no longer dropping, men's earnings turning flat, income growth downshifting to tepid, "defined benefit" pensions vanishing, and the percentage of uninsured stuck on a plateau interrupted only briefly by Obamacare — was no result of nature. Nor are the more recent outcroppings of economic insecurity — such as: more "temp" jobs, greater job instability, more volatile hours, and crushing college debt — mere acts of nature.[56]

Nor is it natural for over 25 million Americans today to still go without any health insurance, or for health care costs to consume such a rapidly accelerating and oversized share of the nation's GDP. None of these facets of rising economic insecurity is inevitable. As FDR might have put it, the United States after 1973 was not stricken by a plague of locusts.

Rather, the problem is that the overall policy structure that American government created in order to steadily expand economic security, the New Deal *writ large*, no longer works well in counteracting the powerful forces of economic insecurity unleashed by our "new normal" economy of intense international competition and highly disruptive technology. Since the mid-1970s, U.S. public policy has lost the dexterity and strength required to correct for the "hazards and vicissitudes" unleashed by the nation's morphing labor market. Tinkering with the status quo, New Deal Version 2.0, will be insufficient. The only choice that will succeed is to make fundamental changes in the New Deal settlement's overall policy structure: to design and implement a New Deal 3.0.

THE RISE AND TORPOR OF MARKET REGULATION

While the 1970s was the era when New Deal economic security policies began to lose their punch, the 1970s was also a period when the U.S. got serious about beefing up the regulatory apparatus that protects Americans from harm and improves the market's effectiveness. Congress enacted the Clean Air Act, the Clean Water Act, the Occupational Safety and Health Act, and the Consumer Product Safety Act. For a while, things got better in the marketplace.

But in recent years the nation's market regulation policy cluster has succumbed to lethargy or worse. Market regulation has four key tasks in addition to its overarching mission to prevent, halt, and reverse market meltdowns. All involve blocking cost externalization. They include:

1) Protecting the environment from pollution;

2) Shielding workers from injury and excessive risk;

3) Safeguarding consumers from harm and price-fixing; and

4) Protecting investors from fraud and deception.

But our laws for accomplishing these four tasks are insufficient and outdated. Enforcement mechanisms too often are weak. Under the Trump Administration, sound market regulation has shifted into reverse.

Compared to the "bad old days" of the late 19th century and early-to-mid 20th century, the U.S. has of course made enormous strides in pushing back on cost externalization. It once was the case that businesses could dump toxic pollutants in the nation's rivers and lakes with impunity. It once was normal for large numbers of miners and factory workers to lose their lives, limbs, and lungs in deadly, poisonous workplaces. Consumers commonly paid for products that malfunctioned or crumbled. Investors were often lured into buying bogus stocks, with no consequences for the scoundrels.

The New Deal—both the original New Deal, and the extension of the New Deal *writ large* over the following eight decades—made enormous gains in blocking and rolling back these forms of harm.

New Deal conservation projects, often carried out by the Civilian Conservation Corps (CCC), helped to protect the environment. (Other New Deal policies inflicted a great deal of harm, especially by mindlessly "taming" rivers.") The enactment of the National Labor Relations Act in 1935 and the Fair Labor Standards Act in 1938 began the process of improving workplace safety, through a dual approach of direct government regulation of the labor market and empowering unions to bargain for improved working conditions.

Building on the earlier work of the Federal Trade Commission (FTC) and the Food and Drug Administration (FDA), New Deal legislation strengthened consumer protections against unfair marketing practices and untested drugs. Most famously, the New Deal put in place a series of federal agencies—the Federal Deposit Insurance Corporation (FDIC, created by the Banking Act of 1933), the Federal Savings and Loan Insurance Corporation (FSLIC, created by the National Housing Act of 1934), and the Securities and Exchange Commission (SEC, created by the Securities Exchange Act of 1934)—to protect depositors from losing their savings and create an initial set of safeguards for investors in the stock market.

The original New Deal, however, only began the process. From the 1960s through 2010, the New Deal *writ large* expanded the entire range of regulatory protections. The 1970s was arguably the high point. The Clean Air Act (1970) and Clean Water Act (1972) further protected the environment. The Occupational Safety and Health Act (1970) added workplace safeguards. The Employee Retirement Income Security Act (aka ERISA, 1974) added protections for most voluntary private pension and health plans. The Consumer Product Safety Act (1972) created the Consumer Product Safety Commission (CPSC), which sets safety standards and recalls dangerous products. Later, the Sarbanes-Oxley Act (2002) and the Dodd-Frank Wall Street Reform and Consumer Protection Act (2010) strengthened the regulation of public companies, public accounting firms, and financial institutions.

And yet.

Despite the great gains that have flowed from the New Deal settlement, and despite the most recent waves and ripples of government regulation, America's environment, workers, consumers, and investors continue to suffer serious harm and face major risks. Following is a quick run-through of the major categories of cost externalization that continue to injure Americans and undermine the nation's market.

Environmental Pollution

The air we breathe continues to be fouled—in some cases, made toxic—by pollutants emitted by industry, agriculture, and transportation. The scientific evidence is now overwhelming that human activity has dramatically increased CO_2 and other greenhouse gas emissions. Human-driven climate change has caused global temperatures to rise, imperiling millions of people and thousands of communities in poor and rich nations alike.[57] According to a 2016 story in *The Guardian* on a report from the Organization for Economic Cooperation and Development (OECD), air pollution will cause as many as nine million premature deaths a year around the world—including thousands of deaths in the U.S.—in the next four decades. [58]

The Guardian account begins:

Air pollution is becoming a "terrifying" problem around the globe, one of the world's leading economic organisations has warned, and will get much worse in the coming decades if urgent steps are not taken to control the pollution.

> The Organisation for Economic Cooperation and
> Development (OECD) said ... that pollution of our air
> from industry, agriculture and transport was set to
> cause as many as 9 million premature deaths a year
> around the world in the next four decades, and the
> economic costs are likely to rise to about $2.6 [trillion] a
> year over the same period.[59]

"If current trends continue," *The Guardian* reported, "one person will die prematurely every four or five seconds from air pollution by 2060."[60] As the story makes clear, it is a worldwide problem. "India and China are likely to suffer the most, but the problem is increasing in many developing countries, where economic growth is lifting people out of poverty but where regulations on emissions have lagged behind. In developed countries, the problem is seen as likely to stabilize, though still with a high number of illnesses.[61]

Some of those whom air pollution prematurely kills and sickens are Americans. A recent story in Milwaukee's *Shepherd Express* illustrates how air pollution in the U.S. continues to poison people in this country:[62]

> Changing wind carries a suffocating air along the
> border of Racine County and Oak Creek. ... Black ash
> coats windowsills, TVs and cabinets. One of those
> cabinets is filled with more than a dozen medications to
> treat a young family's respiratory ailments, while their
> neighbors suffer from digestive issues, Crohn's disease
> and even cancer.
>
> "That's part of living near a coal-fired power plant,"
> said Frank Michna. He lives just south of the Oak Creek
> Power Plant on property homesteaded by his great-

grandfather. Michna, who has lived in the area his whole life, struggles with respiratory issues, while several other family members have developed heart conditions and severe forms of Crohn's disease. He said of the 12 families living on Michna Road, there's not one without some sort of respiratory ailment.

Bill Pringle also lived near the plant with his wife and three young children until 2014, when one too many trips to the emergency room forced them to move. In addition to the whole family being on medications for stomach issues, his wife's life-long breathing issues worsened, his daughter had to be put on an inhaler, and his oldest son was put in a breathing chamber. His youngest son, Jason, was born in the house and started having breathing problems a few months in. By age 3, he'd been in the hospital roughly five times.

One day, Pringle came home as his son was being taken away on a gurney. "He was blue; he couldn't breathe. His oxygen level was 82. They didn't find anything wrong with him," he said. A few months later, his son was admitted to the hospital for pneumonia with a 106.1-degree fever. "It almost killed Jason," Pringle said. "He looked at me while he was lying in the hospital bed and said, 'Daddy, am I going to die tonight?' That was the height of my patience. I was done."

The utility, WE Energy, maintains that "the Oak Creek plant is one of the cleanest and most efficient coal power plants in the country and operates in compliance with all environmental regulations." Nonetheless, the utility's own tests, as well as those conducted by the Wisconsin Department of Natural Resources and independent agencies, "revealed the presence of coal or coal ash in a number of homes surrounding the plant."

The tests also "showed elevated levels of molybdenum and boron in some residents' wells." Molybdenum and boron, two naturally occurring elements, can be found in higher concentrations in coal ash. According to the Centers for Disease Control and Prevention (CDC), "exposure to large amounts of boron over short periods of time can affect the stomach, intestines, liver, kidneys and brain and can eventually lead to death."[63]

From dirty air, we turn to filthy water.

The recent crisis of tainted water in Flint, Michigan, has reminded us that clean water is still far from guaranteed to every American. The Flint crisis began after residents complained that "the water started to look, smell, and taste funny." The Environmental Protection Agency and Virginia Tech then found "dangerous levels of lead in the water at residents' homes."[64]

According to CNN: "Lead consumption can affect the heart, kidneys and nerves. Health effects of lead exposure in children include impaired cognition, behavioral disorders, hearing problems and delayed puberty."[65]

Flint's tainted water is not unique. A report by Water Benefits Health found that, across the United States, water quality is in bad shape and water-related health risks are common:[66]

1) Over two-thirds of U.S. estuaries and bays are severely degraded because of nitrogen and phosphorous pollution.

2) Water quality reports indicate that 45% of U.S. streams, 47% of lakes, and 32% of bays are polluted.

3) Forty percent of America's rivers are too polluted for fishing, swimming or aquatic life. The lakes are even worse – over 46% are too polluted for fishing, swimming, or aquatic life.

4) Every year almost 25% of U.S. beaches are closed at least once because of water pollution.

5) Americans use over 2.2 billion pounds of pesticides every year, which eventually wash into our rivers and lakes.

6) Over 73 different kinds of pesticides have been found in U.S. groundwater that eventually ends up in our drinking water – unless it is adequately filtered.

7) The Mississippi River, which drains over 40% of the continental U.S., carries an estimated 1.5 million metric tons of nitrogen pollution into the Gulf of Mexico every year. This resulting pollution is the cause of a coastal dead zone the size of Massachusetts every summer.

8) Septic systems are failing all around the country, causing untreated waste materials to flow freely into streams, rivers, and lakes.

9) Over 1.2 trillion gallons of untreated sewage, groundwater, and industrial waste are discharged into U.S. waters annually.

10) The 5-minute daily shower most Americans take uses more water than a typical person in a developing country uses in a whole day.

Every month, the press runs stories about water pollution like this 2016 account in the *Milwaukee Journal Sentinel* of how manure runoff contaminates surface water in Ozaukee County, Wisconsin:

On Jan. 31, Ben Arnold watched a river of tainted, melting snow from a neighboring farm meander across his property and flow into one of his ponds.

The invading water — some of it dark as coffee — contained animal waste that the farmer had been spreading on a hillside.

"The manure runoff has started," Arnold wrote in the first of a flurry of emails he sent to state, county and local officials asking for help. "This will really get bad over the next few days."

Arnold's problem underscores the often contentious and protracted process of managing and regulating manure in Wisconsin. With the onset of spring, authorities say, the potential for such troubles can grow.[67]

Workplace Injuries and Worker Abuse

Pollution is often spread across a broad population and may take a long time to cause visible damage. But pollutants can also inflict intense and immediate damage to a specific set of workers in a specific workplace. A recent exposé in the *Milwaukee Journal Sentinel* documents how employees of Greif Inc., a $3.3 billion industrial packaging company that reconditions plastic containers and 55-gallon steel drums, suffered chemical and heat-related burns, plus injuries from explosions, due to chemicals left in barrels. According to the reporters, Grief "disregarded safe practices for handling hazardous materials."[68]

Mishandled chemicals are hardly the only cause of workplace injuries. The federal Occupational and Safety Health Administration (OSHA) reported that 5,147 workers (from all workplace sectors, public and private) were killed on the job in 2017.[69]

The majority of fatalities occur in private industry. According to OSHA's report:

> Out of 4,674 worker fatalities in private industry in calendar year 2017, 971 or 20.7% were in construction — that is, one in five worker deaths ... were in construction. The leading causes of private sector worker deaths (excluding highway collisions) in the construction industry were falls, followed by struck by object, electrocution, and caught-in/between. These "Fatal Four" were responsible for more than half (59.9%) the construction worker deaths in 2017, BLS reports. Eliminating the Fatal Four would save 582 workers' lives in America every year.[70]

OSHA correctly points out that, because of OSHA regulation, workplace injuries and fatalities have sharply declined. "In more than four decades, OSHA and our state partners, coupled with the efforts of employers, safety and health professionals, unions and advocates, have had a dramatic effect on workplace safety. Worker deaths in America are down, on average, from about 38 worker deaths a day in 1970 to 14 a day in 2017. Worker injuries and illnesses are also down, from 10.9 incidents per 100 workers in 1972 to 2.8 per 100 in 2017."[71]

Still, in 2017, the nation's workers suffered 5,147 on-the-job deaths that might have been prevented. That's an average of 99 deaths per week and 14 deaths per day. Over a five-year period (2012 to 2017), the number of workplace deaths rose by 11%.[72]

The vast majority of Americans, thankfully, work in safe workplaces. Safe work, however, does not necessarily mean safe wages.

According to the Economic Policy Institute (EPI), an "epidemic of wage theft" costs workers billions of dollars each year.[73] EPI's conclusion rests in part on a 2008 survey of over 4,000 workers in low-age industries in the three largest U.S. cities (Chicago, Los Angeles, and New York City) that found that "workplace violations are severe and widespread in the low-wage labor market."[74] Violations included failure to pay the minimum wage, failure to pay overtime wage rates, and theft of tips:

- Fully 26% of workers in our sample were paid less than the legally required minimum wage in the previous work week.

- These minimum wage violations were not trivial in magnitude: 60% of workers were underpaid by more than $1 per hour.

- Over a quarter worked more than 40 hours during the previous week, but of those 76% were not paid the legally required overtime rate by their employers.

- Like minimum wage violations, overtime violations were of substantial magnitude. The average worker with a violation had put in 11 hours of overtime — hours that were either underpaid or not paid at all.

- Of the tipped workers in our sample, 30% were not paid the tipped worker minimum wage (which in Illinois and New York is lower than the regular state minimum wage).

- In addition, 12 percent of tipped workers experienced tip stealing by their employer or supervisor, which is illegal.[75]

The aggregate impact is staggering. Looking at the three big cities studied, the researchers concluded that the average loss per worker over the course of a year was $2,634 out of total earnings of $17,616.[76] Their estimate of the total annual wage theft from front-line workers in low-wage industries in the three cities approached $3 billion.[77]

The preceding research focused on low-wage workers. As EPI points out, low-wage workers are particularly hard hit when employers fail to pay as required by law:

> Millions of Americans struggle to get by on low wages, often without any benefits such as paid sick leave, a pension, or even health insurance. Their difficult lives are made immeasurably harder when they do the work they have been hired to do, but their employers refuse to pay, pay for some hours but not others, or fail to pay overtime premiums when employees' hours exceed 40 in a week.[78]

But low-wage workers are not the only victims. Wage theft hurts some higher-wage workers. Its victims include the entire workforce and U.S. economy. The EPI report estimated that: "If these findings in New York, Chicago, and Los Angeles are generalizable to the rest of the U.S. low-wage workforce of 30 million, wage theft is costing workers more than $50 billion a year" in the U.S. as a whole.[79] To put in perspective its estimate of $50 billion in annual wage theft, EPI noted that in 2012 the FBI's Uniform Crime reports estimated that all of the nation's robberies, burglaries, larcenies, and motor vehicle thefts cost their victims less than $14 billion.[80]

Decades ago, Woody Guthrie contrasted different kinds of robbery in one of his most famous songs.[81] Some thieves use a gun, others prefer a pen. The only difference today is that wage thieves now use computers.

Consumer Harm

Compared to the era before the U.S. Consumer Product Safety Commission (CPSC) arrived, consumer products have become safer. But to make an extra buck, some businesses continue to sell products that put consumers at risk of death or injury.

The CPSC has found the incidence of consumer death and injury to be so widespread that it divides the data on dangerous products and harm into categories like:

1) Amusements (inflatable);

2) ATVs (All-Terrain Vehicles);

3) Carbon monoxide (via non-fire poisoning);

4) Fire (unintentionally occurring in residences);

5) Fuel, lighters, and fireworks;

6) Nursery products;

7) Toys; and

8) TV and furniture tipovers.[82]

In some areas, the level of harm is worsening. According to the CPSC, the number of persons who suffered injuries while using "inflatable amusements" — primarily "moon bounces" — rose from approximately 5,000 in 2003 to over 17,000 in 2013.[83] Following is a summary of how many Americans in 2013 (except as noted) were killed, or injured badly enough to go to the emergency room, as a result of accidents that were caused by or "associated with" the eight categories of products or harm listed below:

Table 3-6: Selected CPSC Data on Consumer Deaths and Injuries: 2013		
Type of Product or Harm	Deaths	ER-Treated Injuries
Amusement (inflatable)	0	17,377
All-Terrain Vehicles (ATVs)	426	99,600
Carbon monoxide (non-fire poisoning)	146	——
Fire (unintentional residential)	2,290	11,420
Fuel, lighters, fireworks	8	11,400
Nursery products	100*	74,900
Toys (under age 15)	9	256,700
TV and furniture tip-overs	22	33,100
* Approximate annual average		

Safety comes first. When consumers buy products or pay for services, above all else they deserve not to be killed, maimed, or sickened by their purchases.

But consumers deserve more than safety. They also deserve a market whose actors—primarily businesses—do not conspire to limit competition or collude to fix prices.

Illegal price-fixing and other cartel behavior are so widespread, however, that Purdue University Professor Emeritus John Connor, the "King of Cartels," has published three editions of his work on *Price-Fixing Overcharges*. According to the abstract that introduces Connor's work, the 700+ published economic studies and judicial decisions that contain 2,000+ quantitative estimates of "hard" cartels found that consumers have been heavily overcharged by cartels over the nation's post-industrial history. Among Connor's findings:

- The median average long-run overcharge for all types of cartels over all time periods is 23.0%;
- Historical penalty guidelines aimed at optimally deterring cartels are likely to be too low.[84]

Federal legislation like the Sherman Act and Clayton Act, and the enforcement activity by the Federal Trade Commission (FTC) and Anti-Trust Division of the U.S. Department of Justice, have helped to prevent the price-gouging of American consumers from being worse. But Connor's work makes clear that the United States needs to do more to protect consumers from price-fixing and other types of collusion.

Investor Deception

Finally, although Congress' and business' response to the Great Recession improved oversight of the financial system, investors still face perils. In 2015, the North American Securities Administrators Association (NASAA) announced its five top investor threats.[85] On the surface, they do not sound much different than the major perils that threatened American investors before the Great Recession. The weary cliché — *Plus ça change, plus c'est la même chose* — *the more things change, the more they stay the same* — seems to be particularly apt when it comes to investor fleecing.

NASAA's top five investor threats, based on input from state-level securities regulators, included:[86]

1) *Unregistered Products/Unlicensed Salesmen*: The offer of securities by an individual without a valid securities license should be a red alert for investors. Con artists also try to bypass stringent state registration requirements to pitch unregistered investments with a promise of "limited or no risk" and high returns.

2) *Promissory Notes*: In an environment of low interest rates, the promise of high-interest-bearing promissory notes may be tempting to investors, especially seniors and others living on a fixed income. Promissory notes generally are used by companies to raise capital. Legitimate promissory notes are marketed almost exclusively to sophisticated or corporate investors with the resources to research thoroughly the companies issuing the notes and to determine whether the issuers have the capacity to pay the promised interest and principal.

   Most promissory notes must be registered as securities with the SEC and the states in which they are sold. Average investors should be cautious about offers of promissory notes with a duration of nine months or less, which in some circumstances do not require registration. Short-term notes that appear to be exempt from securities registration have been the source of most—but not all—of the fraudulent activity involving promissory notes identified by regulators.

3) *Oil/Gas Investments*: Many oil and gas investment opportunities, while involving varying degrees of risks to the investor, are legitimate in their marketing and responsible in their operations. However, as in many other investment opportunities, it is not unusual for unscrupulous promoters to attempt to take advantage of investors by engaging in fraudulent

practices.

Fraudulent oil and gas deals frequently are structured with the limited partnership (or other legal entity) in one state, the operation and physical presence of the field in a second state, and the offerings made to prospective investors in states other than the initial two states. As a result, there is less chance of an investor dropping by a well site or a nonexistent company headquarters. Such a structure also makes it difficult for authorities and victims to identify and expose the fraud.

4) *Real Estate-Related Investments*: Troublesome real estate-related investments identified by securities regulators included non-traded real estate investment trusts (REITs), timeshare resales, and brokered mortgage notes. These types of products often carry higher risk. For example, non-traded REITs are sold directly to investors and are not traded on exchanges (as are conventional REITs). Non-traded REITS can be risky and have limited liquidity, which may make them unsuitable for certain investors.

5) *Ponzi Schemes*: The premise is simple: pay early investors with money raised from later investors. The only people certain to make money are the promoters who set the Ponzi in motion.

Judith Shaw, NASAA President, advises: "Investors should always be wary of unsolicited financial advice or investment opportunities."[87]

Caveat emptor is good advice. Buyers should beware. But investors — especially small investors — often lack the skills, tools, or time to fully protect themselves against shysters and liars. It is government's responsibility to help protect investors from fraudulent and deceptive schemes, and make sure that investors receive accurate, complete, and current information. Today's system of government protection is good, but it could be made better.

CONCLUSION: WHY SUCCESS AND FAILURE MATTER

This chapter has sought to make three key points about American government's successes and failures.

First, it is a foolish to speak of government as "a" success or "a" failure. It is both. Government frequently succeeds *and* frequently fails.

Second, for the roughly 30-year period between the end of World War II and the Watergate scandal (1945-1972), American government's achievements far outweighed its shortcomings. The four-cluster pattern of domestic policies that New Deal 1.0 launched from 1933 to 1938, and that subsequent federal leadership augmented over several decades to build New Deal 2.0, interacted with the U.S.'s world-dominating economy and generally benign technology to dramatically improve the wellbeing of most Americans. Poverty fell steeply. Earnings rose sharply for men and women. Family incomes grew steadily. Retirement became more secure. The number with health insurance climbed. Educational opportunities rapidly expanded. Urgently needed policies to protect the environment, workers, consumers, and investors became law.

These rapid improvements eventually ground to a halt or shifted into reverse. The mid-1970s was the tipping point. After the mid-1970s, the design of American domestic policy hit a wall in its ability to protect — much less advance — economic security for most Americans. Poverty stopped falling. Men's earnings flattened. Women's earnings leveled off. Median income crawled. Retirement began to grow more perilous. The share of uninsured individuals stopped dropping. Health care costs started rising at a hyperinflationary rate. College costs climbed, and college debt soared. Before long, regulation of the market to prevent cost externalization began to falter.

Occasionally, after the 1970s, a higher plateau ratcheted down to a lower plateau. Obamacare, for instance, has knocked down the rate of uninsured individuals from a 40-year mesa to a lower mesa, still leaving over 25 million without health insurance.

For most of the 45+ years from the mid-1970s to today, however, Americans as a whole have been stuck on a long plateau of no-to-little progress. And as the 20th century wound down and the 21st century kicked in, a large and growing number of adults (both young and old) have been compelled to grapple with a new set of economic difficulties: more temp employment, growing job instability, unpredictable and volatile hours of work, vanishing "defined benefit" pension plans, increased health insurance deductibles, and crushing college debt. For tens of millions of Americans, economic security has not merely failed to advance. It has retreated.

Yet despite the general lack of progress since the mid-1970s, an essential takeaway is that government, if properly designed, can make life better and better for almost everyone. *If* and *can* are the important words.

The third key point is that *if* the core structure of American government's domestic policy again gets a major upgrade—one that is powerful enough to counteract the new "hazards and vicissitudes" caused by a radical makeover of the labor market and the economy in general—government *can* again succeed in making life better and better for almost everyone.

Today, U.S. domestic policy is inherently incapable of helping us escape the plateau of economic insecurity on which tens of millions of Americans are stuck. But *if* the correct reforms occur, we *can* again resume our progress towards strong and enduring economic security for almost every American.

Along the wide front of market regulation, meanwhile, the expanded array of governmental safeguards created over the course of the New Deal *writ large* (much of it during the early 1970s) has run out of steam. The nation's environmental protection policies have failed to curb CO_2 and other greenhouse gas emissions, thus making the U.S. a major contributor to devastating climate change. Since the Great Depression, workplaces, consumer products, and investment activity are safer. But Americans continue to die, sicken, get hurt, and get fleeced because of inadequate rules, missing price signals, and weak enforcement. In short, sound market regulation is stuck, with dumping and dumpers at times gaining ground.

Yet here, too, fundamental change is possible. *If* government regulation of the market is enhanced in the right way, we *can* resume our progress in blocking cost externalization, thus safeguarding Americans from harm and making the market more effective.

The bottom line is this: Whether the focus is economic security or market regulation, the design of U.S. domestic policy—the heart of which is the New Deal 2.0—has become inherently incapable of getting America moving again toward greater, lasting economic security and a non-damaging, sound market. Further tinkering with New Deal 2.0 will not solve the problem. Big reform is necessary. Another "complete change of concept" in the domestic functions of government is needed. A New Deal 3.0 is required.

Understanding American government's past success *and* failure is the first essential step in moving forward with the fundamental overhaul needed in U.S. domestic policy. Coming to grips with both the New Deal settlement's great achievements *and* its manifold shortcomings is the necessary launching pad for designing a New Deal 3.0.

To spur us on, we should recognize that more is at stake than fixing government's policy defects. The public's confidence in America's future is at stake. The success of democracy is at stake.

During the last several decades the public's confidence in America's status and direction has badly eroded. Going back almost 40 years, more than 50% of those responding to Gallup's surveys have said on more than half the surveys that they were "dissatisfied with the way things are going in the United States at this time." For 13 of the most recent years (October 2005- October 2018), 60% or more of those polled by Gallup have stated each month that they were dissatisfied. [88]

Displeasure with the federal government is particularly intense. Like the public's general dissatisfaction "with the way things are going in the United States," distrust of "the government in Washington" is neither new nor ephemeral.

Prior to the inflexion point of the mid-1970s, according to decades of public opinion polling summarized by the Pew Research Center, public confidence in the federal government was strong. Usually, it far exceeded 50%.[89] But since the mid-1970s, Pew reports, fewer than 50% of Americans in virtually every poll have expressed trust in the federal government "to do what is right just about always/most of the time."[90] The most recent summary of surveys by Pew indicates that, for roughly a decade (2008 to 2017), an even smaller share of Americans—fewer than 30%, and at times below 20%—expressed confidence in the federal government to do what is right.[91]

A powerful reason for fashioning another "complete change of concept ... of the proper functions and limits" of the federal government, therefore, is the fact that most Americans are profoundly unhappy with the direction of their country and doubt that the national government will act correctly. A reasonable inference is that most Americans hold the federal government responsible for failing to solve the nation's problems, and want the federal government to change in major ways.

Part of the public's displeasure with government, particularly at the federal level, may just be typical grouchy American discontent with politicians. The public's level of discontent has no doubt been worsened by the proclivity of liars on social media or in elective office to spread fake news (that is: *truly* fake news) and the never-ending vapid carping of talk show hosts on radio and TV.

Yet Americans have a lot of real reasons to be dissatisfied with the performance of their government. Local and state government bear some of the responsibility. The heart of the problem, however, lies in Washington, DC. It is primarily the federal government's domestic policy shortcomings—a blend of inaction, deficient action, and mistaken action—that explain the inability to solve the U.S.'s serious economic and market problems.

And when we talk about the federal government's domestic policy shortcomings, what we mean above all is the shortcomings of the New Deal *writ large*.

CHAPTER 4

THE NEW DEAL'S SHORTCOMINGS

WHAT EXACTLY ARE THE NEW DEAL'S shortcomings?

It is one thing to summarize (as the prior chapter does) the two primary domestic failings of American government: (1) its inability since the mid-1970s to halt the spread of economic insecurity and resume the momentum towards greater and lasting economic security for almost everyone; and (2) its failure to referee the market so as to fully protect the environment, individuals, and business from cost externalization by corporations, as well as ensure the market's overall effectiveness. It is equally easy to generalize that these domestic policy failings are primarily the shortcomings of the New Deal *writ large*.

But in what *specific* ways has the New Deal settlement fallen short?

Only if we can identify and express with precision New Deal 2.0's gaps, flaws, and mistakes can we fix them. Like the ghostly images in a photographic negative, the detailed features of those gaps, flaws, and mistakes outline in reverse the spaces where the U.S. needs to fashion the concrete reforms that add up to a New Deal 3.0. Understanding with specificity the ongoing deficiencies of the New Deal settlement is the necessary prologue to forging the new policy design the U.S. needs.

Following is a summary of the New Deal's major gaps and flaws. I begin by listing the shortcomings that involve economic security. I then list those that involve the market in general. I conclude by explaining the fundamental contradictions that afflict the New Deal's policy clusters.

The primary shortcoming of the New Deal *writ large* is its failure to provide full economic security to American workers, persons with work disabilities, and seniors who have retired from work. There can be no question that the original New Deal of 1933-1938, as well as its 80-year expansion via the New Deal *writ large*, made great strides in advancing economic security. Yet the New Deal settlement, as it stands today, still does not:

- Offer jobs to unemployed and underemployed workers who cannot find work;

- Require an adequate minimum wage that automatically rises with inflation;

- Supplement earnings so that full-time work always yields an adequate income;

- Enable workers to easily form and sustain unions;

- Ensure workers paid leave;

- Provide all workers with free or affordable childcare;

- Guarantee adults with serious disabilities an adequate income;

- Guarantee retired seniors an adequate income;

- Guarantee all Americans excellent health insurance in a way that restrains costs;

- Provide seniors the resources to afford decent long-term care; or

- Educate children equally, effectively, and for free from K through college.

A second major shortcoming of the New Deal is its failure to adequately regulate the market. The New Deal settlement's policies that aim to protect the environment, workers, consumers, and investors are a good start. But major reforms of policy (including greater use of price signals), together with improved administration, are needed to:

- Stop environmental pollution, including climate change;
- Protect workers from avoidable death, injury, and illness, as well as prevent wage theft;
- Make products safer when used as intended; and
- Make sure that investors are neither fleeced, nor misled, nor punished by cartels.

In addition to safeguarding the environment and individuals, the preventing of cost externalization is necessary to make the market more efficient and add to the nation's wealth.

Finally, the New Deal *writ large* remains riven by two major contradictions in its overall design.

Its cluster of broad-based economic security guarantees rests on an entirely different foundation than its cluster of means-tested welfare programs. The broad-based guarantees depend heavily on adults' connection to the labor market. They prevent poverty, encourage work, and do not punish marriage. In stark contrast, the means-tested welfare programs are largely disconnected from work. They require poverty (or near-poverty), often discourage work, and frequently punish marriage. There is also a big political gulf. The New Deal's economic security guarantees are popular with the American public and politicians, and do nothing to stir up racial animus. The New Deal's means-tested welfare programs—especially the ones that hand out cash—are unpopular, and fuel racial bigotry.

The second of the New Deal settlement's major contradictions involves the market. One cluster of policies regulates the market to prohibit harm to the environment, workers, consumers, and investors. A key aim is to enable sovereign consumers and investors to allocate resources as they prefer, based on price and value and other factors, regardless of what politicians or corporations might want. In stark contrast, a separate cluster of market-manipulating policies deprives consumers and investors of market sovereignty by using tax dollars, tax breaks, and other schemes to maneuver resources towards politically favored types of consumption and investment.

This chapter spells out the New Deal's shortcomings in more detail. All of the gaps and flaws must be fixed (as spelled out in Chapter Five) to forge a New Deal 3.0.

The Failure to Guarantee Full Economic Security

The New Deal's single greatest shortcoming is that its economic security policies do not guarantee full economic security.

Lack of Fallback Paid Work

The New Deal's economic security apparatus tolerates high levels of unemployment and underemployment because of its greatest act of omission: the absence of a guarantee of fallback paid work for adults who want, but cannot find, 40 hours of paid employment in the regular labor market.

The original New Deal offered fallback wage-paying jobs to millions of unemployed individuals, from 1933 until the early 1940s, through the CCC, CWA, and WPA. Those jobs were never provided as a matter of right, however, and Franklin Roosevelt and Congress dropped the policy altogether soon after U.S. entry into World War II. Since the war's end, the New Deal *writ large* has never come close to offering—much less guaranteeing—fallback wage-paying jobs on the scale required to plug the job shortage that typically characterizes the U.S. labor market.[1]

As Tables 4-1 and 4-2 show, for the last 20 years, the U.S. job shortage has been real, continuous, and typically large. Ever since the Bureau of Labor Statistics (BLS) began collecting data that allow a comparison between jobseekers and job vacancies, the number of unemployed and underemployed American adults has persistently exceeded—typically by a large number—the supply of job openings that employers have available. We thus have an enduring aggregate job shortage. (See Appendix B, "The U.S. Job Shortage," for a fuller explanation of the nature and size of the job shortage.)

Especially when the economy is hot, some employers complain that they have trouble finding qualified workers to fill certain of their job vacancies. Their complaints are often true. Potential workers at times have trouble filling job openings because they lack the necessary skills, cannot get transportation to the jobsite, cannot obtain childcare, or cannot overcome unjustifiable barriers raised by the potential employers (e.g.,

Table 4-1: Jobseekers vs. Job Openings: 2000-2018
Using different counts of the unemployed / In thousands

Year	A	B	C	D
	Officially Unemployed	*Add :* Want Job Now Available to Work Searched for Work in the Last 12 months	*Also Add:* Working Part-time for Economic Reasons (Want more work)	Job Openings
Dec. 2000	5,634	6,820	10,063	4,736
Dec. 2001	8,258	9,589	13,982	3,385
Dec. 2002	8,640	10,080	14,401	2,943
Dec. 2003	8,317	9,823	14,573	3,214
Dec. 2004	7,934	9,424	13,851	3,650
Dec. 2005	7,279	8,883	12,998	4,064
Dec. 2006	6,762	8,190	12,377	4,278
Dec. 2007	7,645	9,006	13,624	4,123
Dec. 2008	11,286	13,180	21,209	2,830
Dec. 2009	15,098	17,612	26,710	2,407
Dec. 2010	14,348	17,045	25,980	2,857
Dec. 2011	13,093	15,688	23,859	3,369
Dec. 2012	12,298	15,004	22,947	3,570
Dec. 2013	10,404	12,923	20,750	3,783
Dec. 2014	8,704	11,038	17,855	4,820
Dec. 2015	7,907	9,782	15,809	5,395
Dec. 2016	7,502	9,200	14,754	5,486
Dec. 2017	6,576	8,176	13,091	5,667
Jun. 2018	6,564	7,977	12,720	6,662

Table 4-2: U.S. Job Shortage: 2000-2018
Number of unemployed remaining after filling all job openings
Using different counts of the unemployed / In thousands

Year	A Officially Unemployed *Minus job openings*	B *Add:* Want Job Now Available to Work Searched for Work In the Last 12 months *Minus job openings*	C *Also Add:* Working Part-time for Economic Reasons (Want more work) *Minus job openings*
Dec. 2000	898	2,084	5,327
Dec. 2001	4,873	6,204	10,597
Dec. 2002	5,697	7,137	11,458
Dec. 2003	5,103	6,609	11,359
Dec. 2004	4,284	5,774	10,201
Dec. 2005	3,215	4,819	8,934
Dec. 2006	2,484	3,912	8,099
Dec. 2007	3,522	4,883	9,501
Dec. 2008	8,456	10,350	18,379
Dec. 2009	12,691	15,205	24,303
Dec. 2010	11,491	14,188	23,123
Dec. 2011	9,724	12,319	20,490
Dec. 2012	8,728	11,434	19,377
Dec. 2013	6,621	9,140	16,967
Dec. 2014	3,884	6,218	13,035
Dec. 2015	2,512	4,387	10,414
Dec. 2016	2,016	3,714	9,268
Dec. 2017	909	2,509	7,424
Jun. 2018	(98)	1,315	6,058

irrational criminal background restrictions, inappropriate prior drug use rules, or racial or gender prejudice). Moreover, when the economy is super-hot, businesses in certain locales simply cannot find workers for certain positions, no matter how much they loosen their hiring requirements or raise their pay, benefits, and other conditions of employment.

The persistence of an overall job shortage, however, remains true. As the BLS data show, the overall job shortage is an ongoing reality that operates alongside the less frequent worker shortages that some employers, some of the time, complain of and that in fact exist for some employers, in certain locales, at various times. Typically, since the data have allowed us to measure the job shortage, it has been large. But large or small, the job shortage is always there.

In most years since the BLS has illuminated the question with data, the job shortage has indeed been very large. No matter which definition and count of the unemployed we use (see Table 4-1, Columns A, B, or C), the number of unemployed almost always exceeds the number of job openings (see Table 4-1, Column D) by a large margin.

Even using the conservative definition of the "officially" unemployed, since 2000 in 10 out of 19 years there have over four million more jobseekers than job openings. (See Table 4-2, Column A.) When we apply a broader definition of unemployment, the BLS data confirm that since 2000 in 14 out of 19 years, there have been over four million more jobseekers than job vacancies. (See Table 4-2, Column B.)

If the number of job seekers is further expanded to include a portion of the part-time workforce that is working part-time for economic reasons—that is the subset of this group that would like more work and is seeking extra work—the typical excess of job seekers over job openings grows even larger. (See Table 4-2, Column C.)

Yet despite the wake-up call of the Great Recession, and notwithstanding the post-recession inability to equalize the greater demand for paid work with the smaller supply of wage-paying jobs, the New Deal settlement's economic security policy structure fails to provide an adequate solution. It provides no fallback job mechanism that would allow the millions of unemployed and underemployed adults, whom the job market cannot absorb, to obtain the full-time, wage-paying employment they need and desire as they seek to transition into the regular labor market. The job shortage is likely to grow worse—and, thus, the need for a fallback job mechanism will grow more urgent—as the relentless pressures of trade and technology continue to squeeze out opportunities for steady employment in the regular labor market's bottom and middle ranks.

Inadequate Minimum Wage

The original New Deal gave many workers the legal right to a minimum wage (Fair Labor Standards Act, 1938). Subsequent laws expanded the scope of this right to additional categories of employees.

Nonetheless, as Chapter Three documents, the New Deal settlement's current economic security policies have failed to prevent low wages, low earnings, and the flattening of earnings growth for millions of Americans. Part of the problem is the inadequacy of the federal minimum wage. The federal minimum wage has dropped sharply (in inflation-adjusted dollars) from between $9-11 per hour during the late 1960s to $7.25 per hour today. Not since 2009 has Congress raised it. Nor has Congress added a requirement that adjusts the minimum wage for inflation.

Insufficient Earnings Supplement

For most adults, work is the precondition for escaping poverty and attaining an adequate income. One of the important vehicles for enabling workers to achieve an adequate income has already been mentioned: the federal minimum wage. Two more recent federal policy tools that supplement earnings — the Earned Income Tax Credit (EITC) and Child Tax Credit (CTC) — also play an important role.

Nonetheless, the New Deal's economic security policy cluster fails to raise the incomes of tens of millions of American workers to an adequate level. In 2017, nearly 40 million Americans, 12.3% of the population, subsisted on incomes below the "official" poverty line ($24,858 per year for a family of two adults and two children).[2] Many were workers, their spouses, and their children.

Moreover, the poverty line was designed to mark the boundary between penury and want, not to define the threshold to an adequate income.[3] On top of the nearly 40 million "officially" poor, tens of millions of additional Americans have incomes that fall short of the level that the public defines as an adequate income. An annual income of $43,600 was the target that lower-income Americans told the Gallup poll in 2013 was "the smallest amount of money a family of four needs to make each year to get by." A very large share of U.S. workers, their spouses, and their children have work-based incomes—that is: earnings + the EITC + the CTC—that fall short of what their fellow citizens define as an adequate income. (See Appendix C, "Defining an Adequate Income," for a fuller discussion of what an adequate income should be.)

A big part of the problem is that the New Deal settlement's current system of earnings supplementation is insufficient. The EITC and CTC are good, but not good enough. They fail to provide a large enough boost to the earnings of so-called "childless adults." They fail to provide a big enough supplement to the earnings of parents of dependent children. Further, the rapid phase-out of the EITC means that many workers face a very high combined effective marginal tax rate. The EITC's phase-out also subjects a significant slice of workers to a punishing marriage penalty.

A New Deal 3.0 can and should do better.

Weakness of Collective Bargaining

The original New Deal gave workers the legal right to form unions and bargain collectively (National Labor Relations Act, 1935). For several decades, union membership grew rapidly, and unions frequently succeeded in bargaining for gains in wages, benefits, and working conditions. Those gains improved the unionized workers' economic security, and also put pressure on employers to enhance economic security across the workforce.

During the last several years, however, union membership in the private sector has fallen sharply. Fewer and fewer private employees are covered by collective bargaining agreements. It is not a coincidence that this decline parallels the era since the mid-1970s during which poverty, men's earnings, and family median income leveled off and economic security become more tenuous across the labor market.

The sharp drop in the number of U.S. manufacturing employees, and the generally evolving nature of the U.S. labor market, explain some of this. But the diminished role of unions and collective bargaining has been greater in the U.S. than in other nations whose manufacturing workforces have also fallen and whose labor markets have morphed in similar ways.

Part of the problem, therefore, is that federal labor law and its implementation have grown weaker. It has become tougher for majorities of workers to form unions,. It is difficult to sustain collective bargaining. One of the New Deal 1.0's greatest achievements, the Wagner Act, has lost its punch.

Lack of Paid Leave and Free Childcare

The New Deal settlement has failed to follow the example of other developed nations in guaranteeing workers paid leave when they need to stay home to care for a newly born or adopted child, assist an ailing parent, or meet other essential personal obligations.

In addition, the U.S. lags behind other developed nations in guaranteeing job-seeking and working parents easy access to free childcare.

Insufficient Disability Income

There are several problems with the New Deal settlement's system of providing disabled adults with disability benefits. But one defect stands out.

The payments that Social Security Disability Insurance (SSDI) and Supplemental Security Income (SSI) pay are so low that a significant share of disabled adults end up below the poverty line. Their income falls even further below an adequate income as defined by the American public.

For more detail on how small are the monthly benefits that SSDI and SSI pay, visit: www.govinplace.org/content/ Disability_Policy_Reform.pdf.

Insufficient Retirement Income

The "jewel in the crown" of the New Deal, the Social Security pension program for retired seniors, has relatively few real problems (despite the perpetual complaints of critics that it is "in crisis").

But Social Security does have one serious deficiency. Its minimum payment is not enough to enable all recipients to rise out of poverty. As Chapter Three lays out in Table 3-1, in 2017 roughly 9% of seniors—nearly one in ten—were "officially" poor. A higher share, 14%, was poor in 2017 according to the more realistic Supplemental Poverty Measure (SPM).

The New Deal's "jewel in the crown" is chipped. A significant number of American seniors get so little income from Social Security that they are in poverty. An even larger number receive payments so low that they do not reach an adequate income as defined by the American public.

Lack of Health Insurance

The original New Deal was not able, despite Franklin Roosevelt's and Frances Perkins' hopes, to create a system of national health insurance that covered all Americans.

The New Deal *writ large* nonetheless deserves enormous credit for enacting policies that cover a huge swath of the population. The crowning achievement of the New Deal 2.0 was unquestionably the 1965 enactment of the Medicare program for seniors 65 and older. Other major health insurance accomplishments of the New Deal 2.0 include the passage of Medicaid (1965), the Children's Health Insurance Program (known as SCHIP or CHIP, 1997), and the Affordable Care Act (2010). The legal guarantees to coverage that these programs provide, together with countless voluntary private arrangements by individuals and firms, combine to provide health insurance to the vast majority of Americans.

It would be a mistake, however, to overlook the New Deal settlement's shortcomings in the area of health insurance. This essential branch of economic security policy—which also helps provide equal opportunity to health care—remains a long way from achieving its goal. Today, over 25 million Americans are still uninsured. Without further policy change, that number is unlikely to shrink.

Millions more who do have insurance must pay large premiums or struggle with insufficient coverage, characterized by high and rising deductibles that deter them from obtaining needed health care.[4] A major reason for big premiums and deductibles is persistent "hyper-inflation" in health care costs at rates in excess of the general growth in prices.

Absence of Long-Term Care Insurance

New Deal economic security policy also has failed to provide a comprehensive insurance mechanism for paying for long-term care, even as the number grows of seniors who need assisted living and nursing home care during their final years.

Inadequate Systems of K12 and Higher Education

Finally, the branch of economic security policy that involves equalizing opportunity for students to learn has fallen far short at both the K12 level and college level.

Two programs added as part of the New Deal *writ large*, the Elementary and Secondary Education Act (signed into law in 1965 as part of President Lyndon Johnson's "War on Poverty") and the G.I. Bill (signed into law by FDR in 1944, less than a year before his death) sought, respectively, to equalize educational opportunity for poor children and World War II veterans. The federal government also sought to help college students through Pell Grants and other loan programs.

But despite these add-ons to the New Deal settlement, K12 education remains unequal in funding and outcomes. American higher education policy meanwhile obliges millions of college students to bear high tuition and other costs that deter them from pursuing a college education or crush them with debt after they leave college.

Summing Up

These major gaps and flaws in the New Deal's economic security policy cluster are directly responsible for American government's failure to solve the multiple problems that block and hamper vast numbers of Americans as they try to live in comfort, maintain their health, and educate their children. The collateral damage is also great. The shortcomings in New Deal economic security policy contribute to crime and social disorder, insufficient nutrition, inadequate housing, premature death, higher rates of physical and mental illness, major problems in childhood education, and other social ills.

To make matters worse, the New Deal's shortcomings fall more heavily on blacks and Hispanics than other Americans, creating racial disparity. The holes and defects in the New Deal's economic security structure also feed the growing trend towards inequality in American society. Another probable side-effect is the willingness to embrace magical solutions, none of which involve fixing the New Deal's structural deficiencies but which instead scapegoat domestic minorities or foreign countries.

A MISTAKEN RELIANCE ON MEANS-TESTED WELFARE

The second major shortcoming of the New Deal is its reliance, which grew heavier over the course of the New Deal *writ large*, on means-tested welfare programs.

In attacking the poverty that inevitably arose from the gaps and flaws in the New Deal's policy cluster of economic security guarantees, the original New Deal began to put in place—and the New Deal *writ large* steadily expanded—a set of means-tested welfare programs. These programs by definition fail to eliminate poverty. They require the poor to be poor and remain poor (or nearly so) to get help. As poor individuals' income rises due to employment (i.e., finding work or earning more) or marriage (i.e., counting the spouse's income), means-tested welfare programs either rapidly withdraw their assistance due to "phase-out rates" or cut off benefits entirely at arbitrary "cliffs."

It is true that, thanks to ADC/AFDC/TANF, Food Stamps, and other means-tested programs, many of the poor have been spared the catastrophe of utter destitution. And in some states, even after poor individuals have technically crossed the "official" poverty line's boundary between penury and want, some means-tested programs will continue to provide meager but declining levels of cash benefits (e.g., TANF grants) or non-cash benefits (e.g., Food Stamps), or continue to offer Medicaid coverage.

In less generous states, however, the New Deal settlement's TANF program ceases to help well before its recipients cross the "official" poverty line's boundary between penury and want. Even in the more generous states that allow low-income individuals with multiple benefits (TANF + Food Stamps + LIHEAP + etc.) to cross the "official" poverty line and still receive help, benefits drop quickly. With the rarest exceptions, means-tested programs wind down or stop short many thousands of dollars before an individual or family attains the kind of cash flow that Americans say is needed to get out of real poverty, achieve an adequate income, and maintain a decent standard of living.[5]

To make matters worse, the New Deal's means-tested welfare programs almost invariably inflict the poor and near-poor with economic punishment if they try to improve their plight by making what they feel are good decisions (and most of the rest of us would say are good decisions), such as accepting a job, working for higher wages, or getting married to people they love. Their benefits are likely to be driven down, or entirely removed, as their earnings rise or marriage causes the spouse's income to be factored in.

On occasion, net disposable income may actually fall, should a gain in gross earnings be more than cancelled by the sum of (A) a reduction in welfare benefits, (B) an increase in payroll and possibly income taxes, and (C) extra childcare and transportation costs. More typically, net disposable income may creep up only a little, due to the rise in income being largely (but not entirely) offset by the decline in benefits, jump in taxes, and higher childcare and transport costs. In these circumstances, poor individuals' additional income, due either to improved employment or marriage, is subjected to the equivalent of a high marginal tax rate. At times, this "effective" marginal tax rate on the next dollar earned will exceed the highest marginal tax rate that Warren Buffett or Bill Gates must pay.

The New Deal settlement's means-tested welfare programs thus create a perverse incentive for the poor to hide their earnings from the government. There is also a perverse incentive to forego employment altogether, reject more hours of work, shy away from pay increases, and avoid marriage (where the spouse's income is counted). While these perverse incentives are real, the legends about the behavior of the poor in response to them may exaggerate the extent to which the welfare system actually causes low-income Americans to hide income, avoid work, and spurn marriage.

Nonetheless, there is evidence that some recipients of means-tested welfare benefits do in fact hide their earnings in order to avoid a benefit cut that wipes out part of their income, shortchanges their ability to house and feed their families, and undermines the logic of work. According to an analysis by Christopher Jencks and Kathryn Edin that appeared in 1990 in *The American Prospect*, most AFDC recipients at the time felt compelled to flout the system's rules—mostly by working, but not reporting their earnings—in order to take care of their families:[6]

> [T]he nation's 3.7 million welfare families confront an urgent problem: they do not get enough money from welfare to pay their bills. Nor can most single mothers earn enough to cover their expenses. The only way most welfare recipients can keep their families together is to combine work and welfare. Yet if they report that they are working, the welfare department will soon reduce their checks by almost the full amount of their earnings, leaving them as desperate as before. The only way most recipients can make ends meet, therefore, is to supplement their welfare checks without telling the welfare department.
>
> Welfare benefits have always been low . . . . [T]hey force most welfare recipients to lie and cheat in order to survive.

Jencks's and Edin's analysis highlights the moral commitment of most welfare recipients to care for their children by providing the basic necessities of food, shelter, and clothing. It is precisely that commitment that impels many of them to break the rules, primarily by working but not reporting their earnings, in order to survive. One result is the disdain that welfare recipients frequently feel towards government programs whose rules induce them to uphold their moral values only by telling lies and violating the law. Recipients' disdain is matched by the public's. One of the welfare system's most grievous outcomes has been the disparagement of the poor that it fosters, and the racial prejudice it reinforces among the U.S. population at large.

Perhaps worst of all, the New Deal settlement's means-tested welfare programs undermine the public's willingness to believe in government's capacity to enact effective measures to lift the poor out of poverty. According to a Rasmussen poll, 49% of Americans believe government programs increase the level of poverty in the U.S. as opposed to decrease it."[7]

It is not true. The data prove overwhelming, as laid out in the previous chapter, that the New Deal's economic security policies as a whole interacted with the labor market and national economy to dramatically reduce poverty from the end of World War II until the mid-1970s. The New Deal settlement has helped to keep poverty from rising ever since, despite the erosion of employment stability and earnings growth in the bottom half of the labor market. That experience strongly suggests that, if properly designed, a New Deal 3.0 can resume the rapid decline of the poverty rate towards a residual 2% to 3%.

But a big segment of Americans is not buying it. Underpinning their disbelief is their contempt for the smallest segment of New Deal economic security policy—its means- tested welfare programs—whose perverse incentives and morality-defying outcomes vex recipients, ex-recipients, and never-recipients alike.

In conclusion, the New Deal's policy cluster of means-tested welfare programs, however well meaning, has operated to trap many of the nation's poor in a welfare prison.[8] The programs typically fail to end poverty. They almost never lift the poor to an adequate level of income. They create perverse incentives to hide income, think twice about employment and raises, and avoid marriage. Not surprisingly, many Americans hold the welfare system in contempt. It has contributed to the public's doubting the capacity of government to solve big problems like poverty. The New Deal settlement's means-tested welfare programs have given the very concept of welfare—a concept enshrined in the Constitution's preamble—a dirty name.

THE FAILURE TO ADEQUATELY REGULATE THE MARKET

The gaps and flaws in the New Deal's system of market regulation are equally serious. The toleration of harmful levels of dumping on the environment, workers, consumers, and investors—that is: cost externalization by businesses—arises from a variety of sources.

In some cases, the problem is one of policy omission. For example, the U.S. still does not have in place adequate laws and rules for reducing agricultural runoff. Yet the Environmental Protection Agency (EPA) has determined that "[a]nimal manure, excess fertilizer applied to crops and fields, and soil erosion make agriculture one of the largest sources of nitrogen and phosphorus pollution in the country."[9] "Nutrient pollution" caused by excess nitrogen and phosphorus in the water and air, EPA states, is "one of America's most widespread, costly and challenging environmental problems."[10]

In other cases, the problem is one of method. For example, the U.S. has been slow to follow the recommendation of economists—and the example of other nations—in attacking climate change by using carbon pricing (through mechanisms like a carbon tax or cap-and-trade) as a way to give strong incentives to polluters to reduce harmful emissions.

To a high degree, the problem is one of enforcement and management. For example, workers continue to experience wage theft because the enforcement mechanism operated by government is inadequate.

What is needed above all is widespread recognition that there are major gaps and serious flaws that permeate the entire cluster of market regulation policies aimed at safeguarding the environment, workers, consumers, and investors. The policy cluster as a whole needs to be scrutinized and improved across the board, matching specific reforms to both the severity and the type of cost externalization.

A HARMFUL PATTERN OF MARKET MANIPULATION

Finally, the New Deal settlement's market manipulation policies have undermined both the U.S. budget and the nation's overall economy.

To begin with, the vast array of subsidies, which powerfully intervene in the market to favor politically preferred types of consumption and investment, carry a huge price tag. A conservative estimate of the cost is $2.0 trillion per year. The money comes from somewhere. Its primary source: the much higher taxes Americans will be compelled to pay (whether now, or when the massive debt being piled up comes due) in order to offset the hundreds of billions in direct spending and the giant portion of the $1.5 trillion in tax expenditures handed out to subsidized individuals and corporations.[11]

This higher taxation (which massive debt repayment will only make higher) acts as a drag on the American economy, reducing by substantial sums the amounts that average consumers and investors have available to spend or invest. The greater drag on the economy, however, flows from propping up the subsidized corporations and economic sectors. The subsidies give them far more money than their products and services would command in a truly free economy. Such artificial support provides unjustified shelter to less efficient producers, while malnourishing the revenue and profits of more efficient producers. Government's manipulation of the market thus diminishes the overall productivity of the U.S. economy. Our less productive economy in turn curtails the growth of the nation's wealth.

In short, the New Deal's market manipulation policy cluster imposes higher taxes on average American individuals and firms. It undermines the fairness of governmental budgets. It also makes the economy less efficient, less productive, and less wealthy. We all suffer—in the form of lost jobs, diminished earnings, and lower incomes—because government's manipulation of the economy makes it less competitive at the very time that greater competitiveness is demanded by the "new normal" of intense international trade and rapidly evolving technology.

INTERNAL CONTRADICTIONS: CLUSTER *VERSUS* CLUSTER

In addition to the major gaps and flaws *within* the New Deal's policy clusters, there are major contradictions *between* entire policy clusters.

The logic of the New Deal's cluster of broad-based economic security guarantees clashes with the logic of its cluster of means-tested welfare programs. The two sets of policy — both aiming to promote economic security — differ fundamentally in purpose, structure, and public approval.

At the same time, the New Deal's cluster of market regulation policies works entirely at cross-purposes with its cluster of market manipulation policies. The two sets of policies both intend to boost the nation's markets, but their rationales, architecture, and consequences could not be more different.

The New Deal may not be at war with itself, but it is certainly at odds with itself. A central argument of this book is that the New Deal will never achieve its underlying purpose until it is re-formed to eliminate its two big internal contradictions.

Broad-Based Economic Security Guarantees
vs. Means-Tested Welfare Programs

The first policy cluster, centering on broadly guaranteeing economic security for almost all Americans without regard to their level of income, helps workers absorb what Franklin Roosevelt called the "hazards and vicissitudes" of the labor market. During the Great Depression, that primarily meant the risk — for many, the reality — of unemployment and underemployment, low wage rates, meager earnings, and inadequate disability and old-age income. Today, we must add the impermanency of jobs and the volatility of hours, as well as racial disparity and economic inequality. Another key thrust of this policy cluster is to guarantee equal opportunity in health care and education.

The primary aim of this policy cluster is to prevent Americans from falling into poverty in the first place by stabilizing them economically, preserving their health and lengthening their lifespan, and helping them and their children attain the skills needed to prosper in the economy and life in general.

All of the cluster's programs legally guarantee some form of security. The vast majority of workers has a legal right to a minimum wage, and to strike, join a union, and bargain collectively. Qualifying individuals have a legal right to Unemployment Insurance, the EITC and CTC, Social Security Disability Insurance, Social Security pensions, and Medicare.

The cluster's guarantees are based on work. A sufficient degree of prior work, measured by a minimum number of dollars earned for a defined number of calendar year quarters, frequently determines eligibility. Current work effort—whether seeking work in the case of Unemployment Insurance, or doing work in the case of the minimum wage, collective bargaining rights, and eligibility for tax credits like the EITC and CTC— often shapes the guarantees' specific features.

The cluster's guarantees also typically provide universal benefits. By "universal benefits," I mean benefits for poor, middle-class, and rich alike. You do not have to be poor—it's OK to be middle-class or even rich—to get Unemployment Insurance, Social Security Disability Insurance, Social Security pensions, or Medicare.

The New Deal's list of policies that provide universal benefits is long. Technically, the federal minimum wage applies both to the person who cleans Jeff Bezos' swimming pool and to Jeff Bezos. The parking valets, nurses, and doctors at the Mayo Clinic can all decide to elect a union to bargain for their wages, hours, and working conditions. Although only lower-income workers now qualify for the EITC, virtually all wage or salary earners with young children can claim the Child Tax Credit.

On the health insurance side, Medicare covers almost all U.S. residents 65 and older. Access to public K-12 schools is likewise available to all school-age children.

The intent of these programs is of course to boost the economic security of the vast majority of Americans at the bottom and in the middle of the economic pyramid. None of these programs was enacted to help the rich. But the New Deal's economic security policy cluster seldom cuts off those near or at the top of the pyramid. The wealthy, too, qualify for eligibility and benefits under almost all of the programs mentioned.

Payments and other benefits vary, but the variation is almost always based on non-income factors, such as disability, age, family size, or whether children are officially "dependent." The two major tax credits—the EITC and CTC—do eventually phase out based on income. But the EITC provides help well beyond the poverty line, and the CTC does not even begin to phase out until well above the nation's median income.

Finally, an important feature of broad-based economic security guarantees that pay money is the typical stability of their payment amounts. Individuals who qualify for UI, SSDI, or Social Security benefits will receive different amounts. Their past work effort, their prior earnings, and inflation will determine how much, based on complex formulas. But these recipients' benefits will not vary from month to month as a result of changes in their overall income. Only the EITC and CTC provide payments whose amounts fluctuate yearly based on changes in earnings and income.

In short, the programs in the New Deal settlement's policy cluster of broad-based economic security guarantees are not limited to the poor or near-poor. They are either entirely universal (as far as recipients' income is concerned) or very broad in the income groups they reach. If they pay out money, the amount does not fluctuate due to recipients' income, except for the EITC and CTC.

Nonetheless, as already discussed, the New Deal's cluster of broad-based economic security guarantees has major gaps and serious flaws in the face of today's labor market. It allows high levels of unemployment and underemployment. It fails to drive down poverty to a residual level for unemployed, active, disabled, and retired workers. It leaves over 25 million uninsured despite Obamacare, and it allows health care costs to soar. It fails to equalize K-12 funding, fails to educate tens of millions of K12 students, and burdens millions of college students with crushing debt.

In addition, the cluster of broad-based economic security guarantees created over the course of the New Deal *writ large* has left major groups behind, particularly blacks and Hispanics. They are less likely to find work, earn a decent income, qualify for Unemployment Insurance, have access to doctors and hospitals, enroll their children in well-funded K12 schools, and send their kids to college. All of these shortcomings of the New Deal settlement in turn feed into the U.S.'s widening pattern of income and wealth inequality.

But instead of directly tackling the gaps and flaws in the New Deal's policy cluster of broad-based economic security guarantees, the federal government chose to plug some of the holes with narrowly "targeted" means-tested welfare programs for the poor. Begun under President Herbert Hoover; expanded under FDR; and greatly enlarged after World War II; successive waves of the New Deal *writ large* created a separate cluster of means-tested welfare programs that by the 1950s came to be lumped under the general heading of "welfare."

This second policy cluster—also intended to deal in its own way with economic security—operates on entirely contrary principles.

To begin with, unlike the first policy cluster, means-tested welfare programs by design do not prevent poverty. On the contrary, they require the poor to be in poverty (or nearly so) as a condition for getting help. Welfare programs certainly help shelter many of the poor from some of the most devastating effects of poverty such as homelessness, freezing, overheating, and starvation. But avoiding destitution should never be confused with either preventing poverty or escaping from poverty. Indeed, the enrollees in means-tested welfare programs must not only be poor (or nearly so) to get help. They must remain poor (or nearly so) to continue to get help.

Another departure from the New Deal's broad-based economic security guarantees is that means-tested welfare programs may—but may not—provide a legal guarantee. AFDC, the predecessor to TANF, once provided those who qualified with a guarantee of benefits. One of the main objectives of welfare reform in the 1990s, however, was to end the federal requirement of a guarantee. TANF lets states decide. Some states have opted not to guarantee benefits. Meanwhile, other means-tested welfare programs take different directions. SSI (Supplemental Security Income) and SNAP (Food Stamps) are federal legal entitlements. LIHEAP (the Low-Income Home Energy Assistance Program) and Head Start are not entitlements: they provide help on something akin to a first-come/first-serve basis until the money runs out.

An additional big difference from the New Deal's cluster of broad-based economic security guarantees is that means-tested welfare programs are not linked to work. Eligibility and initial benefits depend on overall income, regardless of whether the income has any connection to work. Only after eligibility has been confirmed, and initial benefits set, might work play a minor role, e.g., a "disregard" of a small amount of earnings in calculating benefit reductions, or an obligation to undergo training or pursue a job.

Another big structural difference is that means-tested welfare programs provide non-universal or "categorical" benefits. Narrow subsets of the poor (or near-poor) qualify for TANF, SSI, LIHEAP, and WIC. Only the poor (or near poor) get SNAP and Medicaid.

Finally, the benefits are often not stable. Where assistance comes in the form of cash or cash-like benefits, the amount fluctuates (both down and up) depending on the recipient's total income, family size, and whether children are "dependent." The poorer the recipient, and the bigger the family size, then the larger the benefit under most TANF programs or SNAP. As income rises and family size declines, benefits are likely to shrink until they vanish altogether.

Why this two-pronged approach to economic security? The reasons are complex. A thorough explanation lies beyond the scope of this book.

The point I want to make is that the New Deal's overall approach to achieving economic security has, from the era of Franklin Roosevelt to the days of Barack Obama, proceeded in two contradictory directions. The contradiction has exacted a high price. Both the public and the experts, unclear and often confused about the competing and inconsistent lines of attack, have generally defaulted to debating and enacting incremental changes on both policy fronts. Obamacare is a classic and the most recent example. It improved a work-based, universal guarantee: Medicare. It also improved a means-tested welfare program: Medicaid.

The tension—I consider it a contradiction—between the New Deal's primary thrust of broad-based economic security guarantees *versus* its backup approach of operating categorical, means-tested welfare programs raises a fundamental question about the future of the New Deal. Should we stick with this two-pronged approach? Or should the U.S. so thoroughly improve the New Deal's structure of broad-based economic security guarantees that, by virtually eliminating unemployment, poverty, insufficient incomes, lack of health insurance, etc., we can justify phasing out entirely the New Deal's means-tested welfare programs?

Market Regulation vs. Market Manipulation

The third policy cluster of New Deal programs, market regulation, aims to create an effective market that does not despoil the environment, damage or mistreat workers, harm or trick consumers, or swindle or mislead investors. In addition, of course, market regulation aspires to prevent, stop, and reverse financial meltdowns.

The policy cluster has four ultimate goals. Most obviously, market regulation seeks to protect individual Americans and businesses from getting hurt—"dumped on"—by corporations willing to inflict harm or shift excessive risk in order to shed production costs, lower prices, and increase sales, revenue, and profits.

A second goal of market regulation is to promote productivity by preventing corporations from gaining a competitive advantage by "dumping" instead of improving their productivity as the way to lower costs. To flip this goal around, its aim is to give firms a competitive advantage if, in lieu of "dumping," they achieve their advantage on a level playing field due their greater creativity or efficiency. No matter which way the goal is stated, a central purpose of sound regulation is to reward productivity throughout the U.S. economy and, thus, make the economy more productive as a whole and enlarge the nation's wealth.

A third goal of much of the New Deal's regulatory apparatus is to avoid market crashes. The crucible of the Great Depression of 1929 to 1939 was the origin of the original New Deal's regulation of banks, stock exchanges, and other major segments of the economy. The Great Recession of 2007- 2009 was the impetus for one of the final acts of the New Deal *writ large,* the Dodd-Frank law. A big part of the regulatory apparatus is aimed at ensuring that market downturns do not degenerate into wholesale meltdowns.

A final goal of the New Deal's cluster of market regulation policies is to put consumers (whether individuals or firms) in charge of the market itself. Sound regulation—precisely because it protects consumers from corporate "dumping" and levels the playing field so as to reward the most productive firms—is essential to making consumers the sovereigns of the market. Sound regulation helps to ensure that buyers' free interplay with sellers, rather than producer cartels and government manipulation, drives prices, demand, supply, and the market's shape and direction.

Consumer sovereignty is an end in itself. It embodies the overarching democratic value that what people freely choose, as individual and corporate buyers and investors, should rule the movement and destiny of the economy. Consumer sovereignty is the market's companion to voting in a free and fair election to choose the legislators and executives who will enact laws and oversee the machinery of government.

But consumer sovereignty is also a means to an end. It is the driving force in enhancing the nation's overall economic productivity and wealth. It is no coincidence that the link between consumer sovereignty, business productivity, and national wealth is a central theme in Adam Smith's treatise on *The Wealth of Nations*.

Unfortunately, despite the enactment of important regulatory programs during both the original New Deal of 1933-1938 and the post-WWII extension of the New Deal *writ large*, America's current regulatory policies and their enforcement have proven inadequate in practice. Air, water, and land pollution continue to endanger lives and health, as well as distort the market. Workers, consumers, and investors continue to be harmed, defrauded, and misled, hurting both them and the market. Consumers are far from sovereign.

All of these shortfalls in regulation can be remedied. But even if the regulatory system that has evolved during the New Deal *writ large* were to be perfected, the final goal of the New Deal's cluster of market regulation—the triumph of consumer sovereignty, and its capacity to promote the nation's economic productivity and wealth—would still be frustrated.

The reason is that the New Deal's fourth policy cluster, market manipulation, subverts consumer sovereignty by interposing massive government interference aimed at steering the market in centrally planned directions. The major tool for thus manipulating the market is the United States' vast array of subsidies (many embedded in the tax code) for politically favored types of consumption and investment.

Contradicting one of the key aims of the New Deal's cluster of market regulation policies, i.e., putting America's consumers and investors in charge of the market's direction and shape, the New Deal's cluster of market manipulation policies overrides free consumer and investor choice. By vesting government with the power to bend the economy's direction and twist its shape, market manipulation undermines economic productivity and diminishes the nation's wealth.

Like the New Deal's two-pronged approach to economic security, the New Deal's dual approach to the market has a complex history that lies beyond the scope of this book.

The essential point I want to make is that New Deal policy towards the market is riven with conflict. On the one hand, New Deal regulation tries to make the market work better so that individual and business consumers and investors — undamaged by harm, and shopping among firms that are competing on a level playing field — decide freely where the economy's resources go. On the other hand, New Deal manipulation strips dollars and control from consumers and investors. The New Deal settlement's massive subsidies for politically favored types of consumption and investment, both overtly (through direct spending) and covertly (through the tax code), play a heavy hand in deciding which economic sectors and even individual firms get Americans' money.

This tension between the two policy clusters — again, I consider it a contradiction — raises yet another fundamental question about the New Deal's future. Should we stick with this two-handed approach? Or should the U.S. fundamentally reform the New Deal's contradictory approach to the market by (A) strengthening its system of market regulation and (B) phasing out government manipulation of the market caused by the massive subsidies that channel hundreds of billions of our tax dollars to politically preferred types of consumption and investment?

Should Adam Smith or V.I. Lenin be the patron saint of the American economy?

CONCLUSION: AMERICA'S CAPACITY TO REPAIR ITS FAULTS

We should be cautious about the role that government can and should play in fixing the crises, problems, and stresses that all individuals and families experience. As Samuel Johnson said over 250 years ago: "How small, of all that human hearts endure/That part which laws or kings can cause or cure!"[12]

At the same time, government can do a lot to create an economic security structure that cushions and corrects the impact of the major "hazards and vicissitudes" of a labor market that is insufficiently large, stable, or well-paying. The cushioning and correcting capacity of government is particularly true of highly developed societies like the United States. Our democratic institutions incline us to help our beleaguered fellow-citizens. Our economy generates the economic resources to do so.

Government also can do a lot to safeguard the environment, workers, consumers, and investors from cost externalization by corporations, and to make consumers the true sovereigns of the market. The latter was precisely what Samuel Johnson's acquaintance, Adam Smith, was writing about in *The Wealth of Nations*. No "Laws of Nature and of Nature's God," to quote yet another 18th-century text, our Declaration of Independence, prohibits Congress from making the American market safe and free. Rather, it has been Congress's failure to use its powers to fully prevent dumping, combined with Congress's proclivity to use subsidies to manipulate the market, that have undermined the effectiveness of the market and weakened the U.S. economy. What Congress has messed up, Congress can set right.

It often takes a long time before Americans compel their government to admit error and change course. The resulting corrections are also often imperfect, as illustrated by the New Deal itself. But the impulse of many Americans to face up to national shortcomings and implement nationwide solutions is also strong. As Alexis de Tocqueville observed nearly 200 years ago, "The faults of the American democracy are for the most part reparable. ... The great privilege of the Americans [consists in] their being able to repair the faults they may commit."[13]

CHAPTER 5

THE NEXT CHANGE OF CONCEPT: A NEW DEAL 3.0

"As our case is new, so we must think anew, and act anew."
— Abraham Lincoln

WE WILL SOLVE THE U.S.'S MOST SERIOUS domestic problems only if we pursue another "complete change of concept" in the functions of American government.

The needed redesign should return to the original New Deal's underlying logic and embrace its core policies. Rather than roll back the New Deal settlement, we need to reaffirm its original aims: government's responsibility to guarantee economic security and properly regulate the market. We should also rejoice in the fact that many specific New Deal programs are sound in pattern and particulars.

At the same time, we need to be honest about the many fundamental defects in the New Deal settlement's structure. Leaving those defects in place, by fiddling with the status quo, will get us nowhere. Tinkering with the House that FDR Built will merely prolong the nation's many domestic crises, add fuel to public discontent and anger, and push America further down the path of scapegoating, avoidance, and drift.

A fundamental overhaul of the New Deal is needed. The overhaul needs to fill its gaps, fix its flaws, and drop its mistakes.

Based on Chapter Four's analysis of the existing New Deal settlement's major shortcomings, a New Deal 3.0 — that is: the next "complete change of concept" in the functions of American government — should aim to bring about four big changes in U.S. domestic policy.

First Big Change: Greatly Strengthen Economic Security Guarantees

The most pressing need is to widen the scope, and improve the power, of the nation's structure of broad-based economic security guarantees.

This means guaranteeing full-time employment; raising wages in the bottom of the labor market; increasing the incomes of the lowest-paid workers, impoverished persons with disabilities, and poor retired seniors; guaranteeing everyone excellent health insurance; creating a system of long-term care insurance; guaranteeing K12 students with identical needs the same resources; and making college education free.

Second Big Change: End Means-Tested Welfare Programs

The first big change justifies a second big change. With economic security guaranteed for virtually everyone, there will no longer be a need to perpetuate means-tested welfare programs. They should all be ended.

We should not "reform" welfare." Nor should we "end welfare as we know it." Rather, a New Deal 3.0 should fulfill at last Franklin Roosevelt's 1935 pledge "to quit this business of relief" by winding down all welfare programs that require poverty or near-poverty as a condition of eligibility.

Third Big Change: Enhance Market Regulation

The American market is imperiled by weak regulation. To protect individuals and businesses from damage—and to make the market work properly—it is essential to bolster the laws, rules, and enforcement that aim to safeguard the environment, workers, consumers, and investors from harm and undue risk. Where appropriate, price signals should be used to achieve the rollback of such cost externalization.

Fourth Big Change: End Market Manipulation

Finally, the nation's market is imperiled by another defect: massive government manipulation. To restore consumers to the seat of sovereignty that Adam Smith argued they must occupy in order to make the market optimally effective and enhance the nation's wealth, it is essential to eliminate rapidly all governmental subsidies for specific types of consumption and investment.

Instead, let individual Americans (with adequate incomes, health insurance, and education) and individual businesses (operating within a soundly regulated market) decide the direction and shape of the U.S. economy.

The following diagram illustrates what the New Deal settlement's four policy clusters look like today:

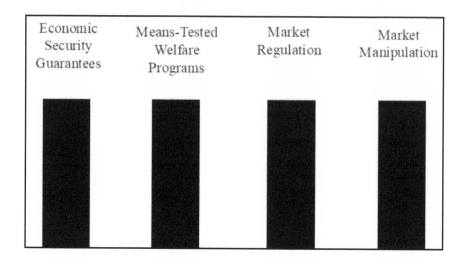

The next diagram shows what would happen to these four policy clusters under the New Deal 3.0's "complete change of concept" in the functions of government.

The existing four policy clusters would be downsized to two. The two remaining clusters would get bigger. The others

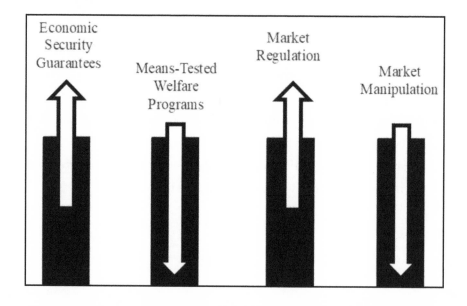

would quickly vanish. The following diagram presents the simpler, improved outline of a New Deal 3.0.

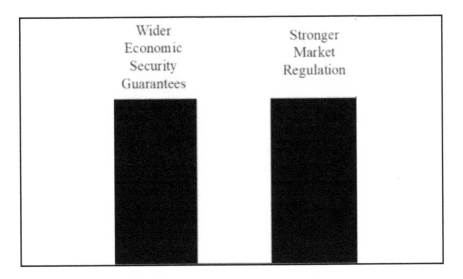

This chapter's account of the major policy reforms needed to create a New Deal 3.0 details the reasons for and shape of each policy improvement.

Additional detail can be found on the website with the same name as this book (*Putting Government In Its Place*, www.govinplace.org), Chapter Six ("Running the Numbers"), and Appendix D ("How a New Deal 3.0 Changes Budgets").

STRENGTHENING ECONOMIC SECURITY

The most essential task is to fill the major gaps and fix the most glaring flaws in the New Deal *writ large*. Most involve economic security. For an explanation of what I mean by economic security, and an overview of the principles I argue should govern economic security reform, visit: www.govinplace.org/content/ Economic_Security.pdf.

As Franklin Roosevelt and the original New Dealers undertook to create a comprehensive structure of economic security, they left a number of big holes. They typically did so for understandable reasons. FDR dropped national health insurance from the Social Security Act to avoid sinking the entire law in the face of intense opposition from the American Medical Association (AMA). There was no provision for long-term care because in 1935 far fewer Americans lived into old age.

The inheritors of the original New Deal of 1933-1938, the authors of New Deal 2.0 with its numerous updates, filled some of the gaps in economic security between 1945 and 2010. But they did not fill all the holes. New fissures in economic security also emerged, and old ones widened, as the nation's demographics changed and the labor market deteriorated under pressure from intense foreign competition and increasingly disruptive technology. As a result, today, America's economic security structure is riddled with cavities.

It is difficult to draw a bright line between the New Deal's gaps and its flaws. The policies that are totally absent from the New Deal settlement tend to blend into existing New Deal policies that are largely sound, but have serious defects. (The latter category in turn tends to blend into New Deal policies that are in good shape but need minor patching.)

Following are the 14 major repairs needed in U.S. economic security policy that a New Deal 3.0 would put in place. Some of the proposed policies fill gaps. Others correct flaws. Several add new legal guarantees. More than a few would best be implemented — if not immediately, then in time — through the creation of new programs of social insurance.

1. Transitional Job Guarantee

Whether the economy is tanking or flourishing, millions of unemployed and underemployed American adults who can work, want to work, and are expected to work by others, have difficulty finding wage-paying jobs that provide full-time work. To ensure that unemployed and underemployed adults always have easy access to 40 weekly hours of wage-paying employment whenever (despite a reasonable job search) they are unable to find a job at all or obtain 40 hours in the regular economy, the U.S. should guarantee such workers the right to a Transitional Job (TJ) at the minimum wage. The TJ should ensure that the worker is able to have 40 hours of paid work, when the TJ's hours are combined with any existing part-time employment in the regular labor market. (Raising the minimum wage will be discussed shortly.)

The work should be useful. The jobs could be in public service, like CCC and WPA jobs offered during the Great Depression. Or they could be in the private sector, either helping non-profit organizations to meet essential community needs or enabling small for-profit firms to decide if they can justify expanding their workforce on their own dime. It is essential to design the TJ program to avoid displacement of existing workers, interference with strikes or collective bargaining, and misuse of funds. It is also important that workers in Transitional Jobs have clear and strong incentives to leave TJs in order to take employment in the regular economy.

Unemployment and underemployment are risks that every worker faces. For that reason, it is reasonable for the TJ program eventually to be operated—and financed at least in part—as a new, payroll-based, social insurance program. Unemployment Insurance would then have a partner: Employment Insurance. In the short run, this may not be possible; but it should be the long-term goal.

For further detail about the design of a successful Transitional Job program, visit: www.govinplace.org/content/Successful_TJ_Program.pdf.

2. Unemployment Insurance Reform

The Unemployment Insurance (UI) program might be called the patron saint of federal social insurance policy. Worker's Compensation laws at the state level came first and paved the way. The Social Security Act became the first comprehensive, federal, social insurance law. UI was considered in 1935 to be the law's central feature because it directly addressed the Great Depression's most pressing problem. UI began delivering benefits to unemployed Americans as early as 1936, over three years before the Social Security retirement program made its first payment.[1]

In its 75-plus year history, UI has been seldom and only lightly changed. Its mechanism for providing unemployed workers with cash payments works well. Its major flaw is that it does not offer its beneficiaries what many really want: paid work. UI delivers the fruit of work, money, but not work itself.

UI should always be counted on to deliver the cash benefits that, on workers' behalf (and diminishing their compensation), their employers have paid in taxes. Workers in essence pre-pay for their UI benefits; they should have an absolute right to receive them. But UI would be a better program if it allowed UI recipients who want to work, but who have found it hard to find a regular job, to voluntarily convert their UI benefits into wages in exchange for doing useful work in a Transitional Job.[2]

In addition to the emotional benefits this might provide, it would produce specific economic benefits. While the receipt of UI benefits as TJ wages would subject them to FICA, Medicare, and income taxation, it would also enable many workers to claim thousands of dollars in earnings supplements via the EITC and CTC or the redesigned earnings supplement program discussed shortly. The worker's net annual income, therefore, would often be significantly higher. In addition, the TJ wages would count towards Medicare and Social Security eligibility, and might increase Social Security payments.

The primary economic benefit, however, is likely to be UI recipients' more rapid return to regular employment and a permanently higher net income. Compared to an unemployed adult who sits at home and periodically seeks out work, an active worker — interacting with colleagues, building up positive references, possibly learning new skills, perhaps hearing about a wider array of job opportunities — will typically be more likely to land, and sooner, a regular job.

3. Minimum Wage Increase

Work should pay a decent wage. But many minimum wage workers, including some who are employed full-time, do not earn enough to raise themselves and their families above the poverty line's boundary between penury and want (whether the "official" poverty line or a more realistic Supplemental Poverty Measure is applied). The minimum wage, even if paid for 40 hours per week and 52 weeks per year, falls far short of generating an adequate income—"the smallest amount of money… needed to get by" —as defined by the American public.[3]

As the first step in a two-step process (i.e., earnings plus an earnings supplement) for guaranteeing that all full-time work yields an earnings-based income that meets the test of an adequate income, the federal minimum wage should be increased to between $10 and $12 per hour. It should also be automatically indexed to rise with changes in the Consumer Price Index (or some other measure of inflation).

For further detail about why a minimum wage of this size would do significantly more good than harm, visit: www.govinplace.org/content/Raising_Minimum_Wage.pdf.

A second step must then be taken to ensure that full-time work consistently produces an income that crosses the threshold of an adequate income. The nation's system of earnings supplements requires major change, as I discuss in the next section.

4. Earnings Supplement Redesign and Enlargement

Raising and indexing the minimum wage is an essential step towards ensuring that full-time work yields an adequate income, but that policy reform alone is insufficient. Recognizing this, for nearly 40 years Congress has enabled many workers to supplement their earnings via the Earned Income Tax Credit (EITC) and Child Tax Credit (CTC).

The EITC and CTC are a good start. But their eligibility rules and structures are complex. Of equal importance, they do not guarantee that all full-time workers will end up with an earnings-based income — that is: earnings *plus* EITC *plus* CTC — that lifts them and their families far enough out of poverty to reach the threshold of an adequate income as defined by the American public.

To simplify the U.S. system of supplementing earnings, and to guarantee that all workers who are employed at least 40 hours per week end up with a truly adequate income, the EITC and CTC should be consolidated into a new, single, easy-to-use earnings supplement. Compared to the status quo, the new supplement for so-called "childless adults" (i.e., adults without dependent children) should be greatly increased. The supplement for working parents of dependent children should also be substantially enlarged. The specific formula proposed for the new earnings supplement is shown in Table 5-1. Its impact on achieving an adequate income is illustrated in Table 5-2.

As Table 5-2 illustrates, the proposed new earnings supplement ensures that full-time work at or above a minimum wage of $12 per hour would yield an adequate income as defined by the American public.[4] The new formula also solves two structural problems with the current EITC, i.e., the way its phase-out rates can create both a marriage penalty and a work disincentive. Finally, the new formula is compatible with solving the current EITC's third structural problem, i.e., its lack of a periodic payment mechanism because it is delivered only as a lump sum.

Table 5-1: Proposed Earning Supplement Formula

Each Worker

Phase-In Rate	20.00%
Minimum Income for Maximum Credit	$15,000
Maximum Credit	$3,000
Phase-Out Start	N/A
Phase Out Rate	N/A
Phase-Out End	N/A

Additional Amounts for Each Dependent Child

1st Child

Phase-In Rate	43.33%
Minimum Income for Maximum Credit	$15,000
Maximum Credit	$6,500
Phase-Out Start	N/A
Phase Out Rate	N/A
Phase-Out End	N/A

2nd Child

Phase-In Rate	36.67%
Minimum Income for Maximum Credit	$15,000
Maximum Credit	$5,500
Phase-Out Start	N/A
Phase Out Rate	N/A
Phase-Out End	N/A

3rd Child

Phase-In Rate	30.00%
Minimum Income for Maximum Credit	$15,000
Maximum Credit	$4,500
Phase-Out Start	N/A
Phase Out Rate	N/A
Phase-Out End	N/A

4th Child

Phase-In Rate	12.0%
Minimum Income for Maximum Credit	$15,000
Maximum Credit	$1,800
Phase-Out Start	N/A
Phase Out Rate	N/A
Phase-Out End	N/A

For the 5th, 6th and 7th child, the phase-in rates would be 11.5%, 11.0%, and 10.5%, respectively, of earnings up to $15,000. The maximum credits for these additional children would be $1,725, $1,650, and $1,575, respectively.

Table 5-2: Earnings + Supplement Compared to Adequate Income					
Family Size	Annual Earnings	Earnings Supplement	Annual Income	Adequate Income	Annual Income/ Adequate Income
1 Adult *plus* Following Number of Children	Full-time Year-Round at $12/ Hour	Per Year	Earnings *plus* Supplement	Based on 2013 Gallup Poll and Appendix C's Assumptions and Methodology	Ratio
0	$24,960	$3,000	$27,960	$27,500	102%
1	$24,960	$9,500	$34,460	$33,500	103%
2	$24,960	$15,000	$39,960	$39,000	102%
3	$24,960	$19,500	$44,460	$44,000	101%
4	$24,960	$21,300	$46,260	$45,750	101%
5	$24,960	$23,025	$47,985	$47,500	101%
6	$24,960	$24,675	$49,635	$49,250	101%
7	$24,960	$26,250	$51,210	$51,000	100%

The shortcomings of the current EITC do not simply involve its dollar amounts. There are at least three structural problems with the EITC as well.

First, the current EITC penalizes marriage. (So does the CTC, but to a much lesser extent.) When two adults who live together and both work in low-wage jobs decide to wed, they are likely to shift their tax status from "single" to "married filing jointly." They will then no longer fill out separate IRS 1040 forms, but will instead submit a single IRS 1040 that combines their earnings. As a result of reporting combined earnings, they could easily see a big drop in their EITC and thus their disposable income, even though their cost of living remains the same. In some cases, getting married can mean losing thousands of dollars.[5]

The new supplement should be structured so that it never—or at least seldom—penalizes marriage. The source of the problem is that the EITC is calculated based on a couple's combined earnings if they pay their federal income taxes as "married and filing jointly." The only ultimate solution is to "uncombine" the married couple's earnings so that the calculation of the new earnings supplement is driven by each worker's individual earnings. Marriage, then, will rarely impose a penalty.

Second, the current EITC utilizes phase-out rates that impose a high "effective" marginal tax rate on low-to-moderate income workers. Once the EITC begins to phase out, a worker with one child loses 15.98% of every EITC dollar for every extra dollar of earnings. Workers with two or more children lose 21.06% of each EITC dollar for every additional dollar of earnings.[6] When these "effective" marginal tax rates on EITC payments are combined with the official marginal tax rates imposed on wages by FICA and Medicare taxes, the total "effective" marginal tax rates that such typical workers pay for every extra dollar earned are 23.63% and 28.71%.

Such *de facto* tax rates on low-income workers may only be the beginning. The final "effective" marginal tax rate that results from earning an extra dollar gets larger if the worker (A) starts losing a means-tested welfare benefit like Food Stamps, or (B) starts paying income taxes.

There is only one solution to this problem. The new supplement should not be phased out. The next-best approach (used by the CTC) is to defer the phase-out until the worker's earnings reach a very high level. Even then, the phase-out rate should be low. The better approach to avoiding excessive "effective" marginal tax rates for lower-income and middle-class families would be to have no phase-out at all, but instead, reduce the supplement by the filer's existing top marginal tax rate.[7]

The third structural problem with both the EITC and CTC is that, although many workers need an earnings supplement to help meet their monthly costs of living (rent, heat, car payments, etc.) or to offset disruptive spikes in expenses (e.g., fixing a broken furnace, replacing a punctured tire, etc.), the EITC and CTC are now only available in the following year as one-time lump sum. The new earnings supplement should be structured to allow workers to claim a portion of the estimated supplement, e.g., 50%, on a periodic, as-you-earn, basis. It may also make sense to let workers draw down small "mini-lumps" every quarter that add up to perhaps 25% of the total. Any amounts not claimed, plus the remaining 25% balance, would be delivered as a final lump-sum payment.

5. Stronger Collective Bargaining

There can be no dispute that the increase in the percentage of unionized employees during the 1950s and 1960s was associated with—and, many would conclude, contributed to—Americans' rising level of earnings, income, health insurance coverage, health itself, retirement security, and home ownership during those decades. In recent decades, however, the share of unionized workers has declined, paralleling—and, many again would assert, contributing to—the worsening economic status of the middle class, as well as rising inequality.

We should reverse course, strengthen workers' right to unionize, and give collective bargaining a more important role in increasing wages, stabilizing hours, and setting working conditions. The following specific reforms to the National Labor Relations Act and its administration should be put in place:

First: When a majority of employees requests an election to decide if they will have a union, the election should be held immediately and without intimidation by the employer.

Second: It should also be legal in all circumstances for unions to negotiate a contract that requires all covered employees to contribute to the contract's negotiation and enforcement. In other words, Congress should remove the power of states, under the misleading label of "right to work," to impede unions and employers from agreeing to include such a requirement in their final contract.

6. Paid Leave Guarantee

Another big gap that the New Deal *writ large* has tolerated in the U.S. system of economic security involves paid leave. The U.S. lacks, on a nationwide basis, a simple and consistent mechanism for enabling workers to receive periodic payments when they leave work to take care of an urgent family need, such as caring for a newborn or newly adopted child, or helping an aging parent move into long-term care. Various local communities and states have experimented with solutions. A growing body of employers has voluntarily embraced paid leave.

But (as was true during the early development of Unemployment Insurance, Social Security pensions, and other social insurance programs), there are several serious problems with a local, state, or private approach. First, by definition, local or state action does not help people who live in the jurisdictions whose governments have been unwilling to act. Second, a region-by-region approach distorts the domestic labor market by creating an incentive for businesses to avoid location or expansion in the places that require paid leave, thus reducing the actual number of Americans who benefit from the policy.

A strong case can thus be made for a uniform, national paid-leave guarantee. In the long run, the best mechanism may be a payroll-based social insurance program.

Paid leave is by definition linked to work. It provides payments in lieu of wages. It includes a legal right to return to the job once the exigency has passed.

Paid leave is also linked to risk. It is impossible to tell in advance which workers face the risk of needing replacement income when they necessarily take a short-term break from work. Nor can we predict when that risk may materialize. Who can predict which worker next year may be adding a child to the household, or which employee two years later will need to care for an ailing parent? The risk factors are even more complex. The baby may be twins, or ill, or have special needs. There may be time-consuming complexities in completing an adoption. The ailing parent may be terribly sick.

Because work-related risk underpins the need for paid leave, structuring a national paid leave policy as a social insurance program is an appropriate solution.

For additional background on the need for a national paid leave program, visit: www.govinplace.org/content/PaidLeave.pdf.

7. Childcare Guarantee

From the 1930s through the 1950s, culture and demographics kept childcare for pre-school children off the radar screen. "Stay-at-home moms" (often the Rosie the Riveters and Army nurses of World War II who had relinquished their work tools) were frequently available to provide free care for babies, infants, toddlers, and other young children. The greater incidence of large and multi-generational families meant that, if mom took a job, a trusted (or not so trusted) family member was often available to care for the kids before they started school. The family "breadwinner" — typically a man — did not need to worry too much about children's safety or care as he headed off to work in a factory, mine, shipyard, or office. Or at least, that's how it seemed in the 1950s' and 1960s' world of *Leave It To Beaver*.

The reality was different. Even back in the immediate post-WWII era, many parents struggled to find good, affordable childcare. In recent decades, the evolution of American culture and demographics has increased the need. A national guarantee of affordable childcare for pre-school children is long overdue.

Such a program should offer free childcare for young kids whose parents work the day, evening, or night shift. It should be flexible enough to accommodate the fluctuating work schedules that a growing number of parents face. Free childcare should also be available to parents of young children while the parents are attending school. Since the need for childcare is a risk that arises primarily from parents' need to leave home for work, the childcare program could reasonably be operated and financed — at least in part — as a social insurance program.

For additional background on the logic and cost of a national program of free childcare, visit: www.govinplace.org/content/Childcare.pdf.

8. Disability Insurance Improvement

The major disability benefit program, Social Security Disability Insurance (SSDI), does not help all adults whose disabilities prevent them from working. Nor does SSDI guarantee its recipients a minimum income that is well above the poverty line. Like Unemployment Insurance, SSDI also does not make it easy for recipients who want to work — even a few hours — to convert their benefits into wages paid in exchange for useful employment.

SSDI should be revised to cover all adults who truly cannot work because of a severe disability. The means-tested Supplemental Security Income (SSI) program would thus be eliminated. The individuals with disabilities whom SSI covers would be folded into SSDI. The expanded SSDI program should then be restructured to guarantee all disability income recipients a minimum monthly payment that is well above the poverty line. The minimum payment should be 90% of the amount, adjusted for family size, that Americans say is the least needed to "get by."[8] The 90% target creates a modest incentive to prefer employment, which would often yield a higher total income. The current SSDI policy would continue under which recipients who contribute more into the SSDI system would receive proportionately higher payments.

SSDI should also become a more work-friendly program. Its recipients should gain the right to voluntarily convert part or all of their disability payments from cash into wages earned in a Transitional Job.[9] This conversion option should be structured so that SSDI recipients—as well as applicants and potential applicants—are always better off economically if they take a Transitional Job or any other job.

Another work incentive involves guaranteeing that under-65 SSDI recipients, applicants, and potential applicants have excellent health insurance. Today, SSDI recipients qualify for Medicare. That should continue. Applicants and potential applicants, meanwhile, would be enrolled in the YoungMedicare program to be described shortly.

For more detail about how the current SSDI and SSI programs work, and what a single, expanded SSDI program with improved work opportunities would look like, visit: www.govinplace.org/content/Disability_Policy_Reform.pdf.

9. Social Security Improvement

The Social Security pension program also does not guarantee retirees a minimum income that is well above the poverty line.

The program should be modified to guarantee that all Social Security recipients 65 to 69 receive a minimum monthly payment that is at least 90% of the amount that a couple needs to "get by," based on what Americans told the Gallup Poll is the least a four-person family needs to "get by."[10] The 90% target creates a modest incentive to work through age 69. At age 70, the payment would rise to 100%. The current Social Security policy would continue under which recipients who contribute more into the Social Security system would receive proportionately higher payments.

For background on the history of Social Security, its dramatic impact in reducing senior poverty, and the need to increase the minimum benefit to address the still-high number of impoverished seniors, visit: www.govinplace.org/content/SocialSecurity.pdf.

10. New Automatic Savings Program for Retirement

Even before the vanishing of employer-based "defined benefit" pension plans, many workers failed to accumulate enough savings to enable them to enjoy a decent living standard in retirement. The near-disappearance of such plans has turned the problem into a crisis. The asset losses than many individuals suffered in their 401(k) plans, IRAs, and other saving vehicles during the Great Recession of 2007-2009 made matters worse. Rapidly rising health care costs have also hurt retirees.

Most American adults know they should save money. They usually want to save, and often try. But ignorance about how much Social Security will provide *vis-à-vis* their true financial needs after retirement inhibits saving. The biggest obstacle is the limited incomes that so many scrape by on, plus the never-ending pressure to pay for today's basic needs with resources on hand.

Another impediment to saving enough money is the complexity of some of the existing mechanisms for doing so. Finally, simple human nature's reluctance to get into the groove of periodically paying into a savings account, IRA, or other retirement vehicle shrinks the percentage of Americans who save what they should. Thus, when far too many Americans retire, they find that Social Security plus the little they have saved does not go nearly far enough.

The good news is that one of the central mechanisms of the New Deal—wage withholding—provides at least a partial, and a very simple, solution: automatic savings. It could be mandatory (as in Australia). It might be "presumptive" (i.e., a fixed percentage of wages is withheld and saved unless the worker reduces the percentage or even opts out of the program, an approach that California, Illinois, and Oregon are testing). Unlike traditional social insurance, however, the amount withheld from each worker's paycheck would belong to the worker, would be invested carefully in an account the worker legally owns and controls, and could be withdrawn in installments once the worker reaches age 62 (or perhaps later) or starts to claim Social Security retirement benefits. When the individual dies, the account balance would be distributed per a valid will or according to law.

For an outline of the automatic savings programs of Australia, California, Illinois, and Oregon that highlights the major design features such a program must resolve, visit: www.govinplace.org/content/Automatic_Savings.pdf.

11. Health Insurance Guarantee for Under-65 Individuals

Whether health insurance is a natural right or not, it is surely a necessity. In the 21st century, at long last, it should become a legal right. A New Deal 3.0 should guarantee every American under 65, regardless of health status, excellent health insurance. A new program, which I call "YoungMedicare," would cover all individuals under 65 who are not receiving SSDI benefits (and thus enrolled in Medicare) or covered by the military, VA, or other special health care systems. YoungMedicare would rely on powerful marketplace incentives to control costs.

All Americans under 65 (unless covered by another federal health care system) would be automatically enrolled in YoungMedicare as individuals—not as poor persons, employees, spouses, or dependents. The program would feature comprehensive medical, hospital, prescription drug, and other benefits as defined in the Affordable Care Act's list of Essential Health Benefits. Enrollees would not pay deductibles or co-pays (except, if a generic drug is available and satisfactory, a co-pay for choosing an equivalent brand-name drug). Pre-existing conditions would be irrelevant. Enrollees would never face an annual or lifetime benefit limit.

To control costs, YoungMedicare would harness the most basic of market forces—choice, competition, and price signals—to align the natural incentive of enrollees to save money with clear incentives for health care plans and providers to control their costs, hold down prices, and improve the quality of care. Specifically, enrollees would pay no premium to enroll in the lowest-bidding, high-quality health care plan in their area (e.g., county). But premiums would otherwise apply. Individuals would be required to pay out-of-pocket (on an after-tax basis) the full extra cost of enrolling in any higher-bidding, qualifying plan.

Enrollees' incentive to enroll in less expensive health care plans—but also high-quality plans—is clear. They save money, yet they do not risk their own or their families' health. The enrollees' incentive in turn creates a parallel incentive for the competing health care plans and their providers. Plans and providers would at last face a powerful and enduring reason to control their costs, hold down prices, and improve their quality of care.

Within the YoungMedicare framework, the plans that submit the lowest premium bid or close to the lowest bid, and that simultaneously improve the quality of the care they deliver, position themselves to attract more customers, generate higher revenue, and earn higher profits. The plans that bid too high, or tolerate poor quality of care, will attract far fewer customers, shed revenue, and become unprofitable.

There are many legitimate ways for the plans to control costs, enhance quality, and produce better health outcomes. One solution stands out. The greatest opportunity lies in squeezing out the high level of error, waste, and inefficiency that character-ize the delivery of health care in the U.S.

Choice is key to the YoungMedicare model. Enrollees would have an annual choice among competing health care plans—including HMOs, PPOs, and fee-for-service alternatives. This would allow them, from year-to-year, a choice of all doctors and hospitals in their communities. During a year, enrollees would be free to switch doctors within their chosen plan, which would be required to offer a wide choice of providers. Individuals could also change health care plans mid-year in special circumstances, such as a move to a different county.

Both Medicaid and Obamacare (to the extent that they provide health insurance to the under-65 population) would be absorbed into YoungMedicare. Because workers, their spouses, and their children are the biggest group of Americans covered, it would be appropriate to operate the new health insurance program—and finance it in large part—as a social insurance program that, akin to Workers' Compensation, is financed largely by an employer mandate. Initially, it would be separate from Medicare. In the long run, it might make sense to merge it with Medicare.

For further discussion of how the YoungMedicare program would cover the under-65 population, reduce costs, and improve quality, visit: www.govinplace.org/content/ReformingHealth Insurance.pdf.

12. Long-Term Care Insurance Guarantee

Today, millions of Americans suffer from severe financial distress, as well as emotional anguish and diminished health, because of their inability to pay for the assisted living and nursing home care they need during their final months of life. The rapid migration of the Baby Boom generation into old age will make matters worse.

The U.S. urgently needs a coherent system that guarantees all Americans the ability to pay for high-quality long-term care. Medicare's nursing home benefit does not last more than a few weeks. It is also conditioned on the "patient" making "progress." But many older Americans are not "patients" making "progress," and they may need long-term care for months or years.

As with Medicare, it is the population of workers who, after retirement, primarily bear the risk of needing long-term care. Thus, either as a part or partner of Medicare, it would ultimately make sense to create a social insurance program that uses payroll-based premiums as the financing mechanism for much—perhaps all—of the long-term care insurance program that is added to a New Deal 3.0.

For additional information about the growing number of older Americans, the increasing need for long-term care, and the logic of a social insurance solution, visit: www.govinplace.org/content/Long-TermCare.pdf.

13. Reform of K12 Education Financing and Organization

The American system of paying for K12 education is a disgrace. Per-pupil spending does not vary based on student need, but rather fluctuates—often wildly—with the property values and overall wealth of the community. Taxpayers in poorer communities often pay higher property and other taxes to finance lower levels of per-pupil spending (which is typically associated with shabbier schools, bigger class sizes, more students with disabilities, and worse educational programming and outcomes). Meanwhile, taxpayers in wealthier communities are often able to pay lower property and other taxes to finance higher levels of per-pupil spending (which typically results in high-end schools, smaller class sizes, and better educational programming and outcomes).

The rule of "where you live, you must learn" underpins these financial inequities. It also locks in racial and economic segregation. For further detail about government's role in creating racially and economically segregated schools in both the south and north, visit: www.govinplace.org/content/Segregated_Schools.pdf.

It is essential to remember that "where you live, you must learn" is not a law of nature. It is a rule imposed by government. There is no reason why government could not establish a different rule for publicly funded K12 schools. For example, the rule that state governments apply to students seeking to attend state-funded public colleges is: "No matter where you live in the state, you may request to attend any publicly-funded K12 school in the state. You will be admitted on the same terms as students who live near the school."

K12 education will always be delivered at the local level. Public K12 school districts need not vanish. But the rigid rule of "where you live, you must learn" should end, along with using local property taxes (and other local taxes) to finance K12 education. Instead, children regardless of their residence within the state should be free to apply to any qualifying, tax-supported school and be admitted on equal terms.

If more students apply to a K12 school than the school initially has room for, the solution is not to reject students but to expand the school's capacity. Conducting the application process well in advance will help avoid the problem of a mismatch between demand and supply.

K12 education should be entirely financed and primarily overseen at the state level. This justifies the elimination of the rule of "where you live, you must learn." It also allows for equalizing per-pupil spending, as well as ensuring consistent quality and accountability. Full financing of K12 schools would be the states' primary contribution to creating a New Deal 3.0.

The main components of reform would thus be:

1) Elimination of the economically and racially discriminatory requirement that local residency determines where a child attends a tax-funded school;

2) A state guarantee of equal per-pupil spending (with equal adjustments for children with disabilities who need special education services and for other purposes);

3) Rigorous standards for safe facilities and qualified teachers, enforced primarily and consistently at the state level;

4) Incentives to school districts and schools to reduce economic and racial segregation; and

5) Shifting the focus of accountability away from how well each class, school, or system does in meeting rigid state or national grade-based benchmarks, and

towards how well individual students are making progress in reading, math, and other subjects.

Getting K12 education right is a matter of economic security, equal opportunity, racial justice, and national productivity.

14. *Free College Education*

Finally, when it comes to paying for college, Bernie Sanders is right. Since the demise of the GI Bill, the nation's system for financing college education has become a mess. For many students and families facing high tuition and mountains of debt, it is now a disaster.

Under a New Deal 3.0, the federal government should guarantee all qualifying high school graduates (or those with equivalent status) the resources to pay the full, reasonable, in-state tuition and fees of any public technical college or public university. The same amount should also be available to defray the cost of tuition and fees charged by an out-of-state public technical college, an out-of-state public university, or an independently accredited (i.e., non-rip-off) private college.

FIXING THE GAPS AND FLAWS IN MARKET REGULATION

While the wide holes and serious defects in America's system of economic security can be fixed by a small number of big policy changes, the challenge faced in reforming the nation's regulatory structure is different in nature. The gaps and flaws in the U.S. system of market regulation are not few: they are numerous. They cannot be fixed by a short list of big policy changes. A longer list of changes, comprised of both big and small reforms, is required.

Improving the regulation of the market—so as to end harmful cost externalization, restore consumer sovereignty, and strengthen the market's overall effectiveness—falls into five broad categories.

1. Prohibition

Lawmakers and regulators should impose new or different restrictions to eliminate cost externalization, and reduce other forms of harm, whenever experience suggests that less restrictive methods will be insufficient. In some cases, the damage and risk will be so dangerous that outright and immediate prohibition is the only option. In other cases, it may be possible to ration and shrink the harm, e.g., allow the emission of a low maximum level of an environmental contaminant, but diminish the maximum each year until the contaminant is no longer emitted at all.

2. Pricing

It is always tempting to prohibit harm outright and immediately. Sometimes, however, the most effective harm-reduction strategy is to impose prices (e.g., taxes or fees) for harmful behavior, with the prices calibrated in proportion to the severity of the harm and on a timetable leading to the harm's steady reduction to a much lower level (if not zero). For example, CO_2 and other greenhouse gas emissions can be taxed based on the volume of emissions, with the tax per unit of emission steadily rising in order to spur steady declines in the amounts emitted.

In some instances, it may make sense to combine prohibition and pricing. For example, the federal government could prohibit the emission of more than X units of CO_2 by an energy-generating plant, factory, or vehicle, *and* simultaneously impose a tax or fee on each unit of emission below X units. To accelerate the pace of pollution reduction, the maximum emission could be steadily lowered each year, while the tax or fee per allowable unit of emission is incrementally raised each year.

The case for a carbon tax is particularly compelling. According to the Carbon Tax Center (CTC):[11]

> The need is dire: the levels of CO_2 already in the Earth's atmosphere and being added daily are destabilizing established climate patterns and damaging the ecosystems on which all living beings depend. Very large and rapid reductions in the United States' and other nations' carbon emissions are essential to avoid runaway climate destabilization and minimize severe weather events, inundation of coastal cities, spread of diseases, loss of forests, failure of agriculture and water supply, infrastructure destruction, forced migrations, political upheavals and international conflict.

The cause of the problem is that the cumulatively catastrophic cost of carbon emission is externalized—that is, paid for by the people of the U.S. and the world as a whole—rather than borne by polluters through the prices they pay or charge. The CTC calls this a "market failure" because it suppresses incentives to design and deploy cost-effective methods of reducing CO_2 emissions:[12]

> Currently, the prices of electricity, gasoline and other fuels reflect little or none of the long-term costs from climate change or even the near-term health costs of burning fossil fuels. This immense "market failure" suppresses incentives to develop and deploy carbon-reducing measures such as energy efficiency (e.g., high-

mileage cars and high-efficiency air conditioners), renewable energy (e.g., wind turbines, solar panels), low-carbon fuels (e.g., biofuels from high-cellulose plants), and conservation-based behavior such as bicycling, recycling and overall mindfulness toward energy consumption.

Like hundreds of economists around the world, the CTC concludes that—in lieu of prohibition or rationing—pricing in the form of a tax is the best solution because it provides a missing economic incentive for polluters to reduce their emissions in order to minimize the tax: "A robust tax on carbon pollution will create powerful incentives inducing policy-makers and individuals to reduce carbon emissions through conservation, substitution and innovation."[13]

In 2017, the CTC gave its support to a proposal by the Climate Leadership Council to enact a national carbon tax starting at $40 per ton of CO_2 and rising each year. By 2030, CTC estimated that a $5 per ton annual increase in the tax would lower annual U.S. CO_2 emissions below their 2005 level (a common baseline year) by 40%. The Climate Leadership Council is not composed of left-leaning tree-huggers. Its proposal for a $40-and-rising tax on CO_2 was co-authored by multiple Secretaries of State, Secretaries of the Treasury, and Chairs of the President's Council of Economic Advisors for Presidents Richard Nixon, Ronald Reagan, George H.W. Bush, and George W. Bush.[14, 15]

To address the concern that a carbon tax would merely lubricate an increase in the size of government spending by generating more tax revenue, CTC supported the Climate

Leadership Council's plan to return the carbon tax revenue directly to the American people. The Climate Leadership Council proposed giving a quarterly "dividend" to all U.S. households.[16]

A combination of tougher restrictions and pollution pricing may also be an effective approach to dealing with another serious environmental problem: agricultural runoff. As mentioned in the previous chapter, the Environmental Protection Agency (EPA) has found that "[a]nimal manure, excess fertilizer applied to crops and fields, and soil erosion make agriculture one of the largest sources of nitrogen and phosphorus pollution in the country."[17] To curtail the "nutrient pollution" that the EPA has defined as "one of America's most widespread, costly and challenging environmental problems," a blend of stronger prohibitions and price signals might be the best way to proceed.[18]

3. Transparency

Regulatory policy can also be improved by requiring consumers and investors to receive more clear, complete, and timely information about the risks they face. Some risks are so severe that their causes should simply be forbidden. But where a risk is allowed, the individuals and businesses that face the risk deserve to have advance, understandable, and repeated notice.

All of us have listened to TV ads that hype the latest on-patent prescription drugs to cure our ailments. The Food and Drug Administration (FDA) requires that the TV ads end with a full disclosure of risks. Sadly, according to researchers at Dartmouth University and the University of Wisconsin-Madison, 60% of claims in prescription drug ads were false or misleading:[19]

Consumers should be wary when watching those
advertisements for pharmaceuticals on the nightly TV
news, as six out of ten claims could potentially mislead
the viewer, say researchers in an article published in the
Journal of General Internal Medicine.
...

Researchers Adrienne E. Faerber of the Dartmouth
Institute for Health Policy & Clinical Practice and David
H. Kreling of the University of Wisconsin-Madison
School of Pharmacy found that potentially misleading
claims are prevalent throughout consumer-targeted
prescription and non-prescription drug advertisements
on television.
. . .

The researchers reviewed 168 TV advertisements for
prescription and over-the- counter drugs aired between
2008 and 2010, and identified statements that were
strongly emphasized in the ad. A team of trained
analysts then classified those claims as being truthful,
potentially misleading or false.

They found that false claims, which are factually false or
unsubstantiated, were rare, with only 1 in 10 claims
false. False advertising is illegal and can lead to criminal
and civil penalties.

Most claims were potentially misleading—6 in 10 claims
left out important information, exaggerated information, provided opinions, or made meaningless
associations with lifestyles, the researchers said.

False or potentially misleading claims may be more
frequent in over-the-counter drug ads than ads for
prescription drugs—6 of 10 claims in prescription drug

ads were misleading or false, while 8 of 10 claims in
OTC drug ads were misleading or false.

The FDA requires that TV ads disclose each drug's risks. But it is virtually impossible to understand what the ads are actually saying about each drug's risks, because the warnings are rattled off rapid fire and *sotto voce*.

Sadly, rather than require truth in advertising and understandable disclosure, the FDA is heading in the wrong direction. The people's guardian is looking to require that TV drug ads disclose fewer risks.[20]

Federal regulatory policy should move in the opposite direction. TV drug ads should disclose all of the risks. The disclosures should be delivered slowly and at the same volume as the main voiceover used in the ad. If this increases the length and cost of each drug ad, so be it. That outcome is exactly the reversal of cost externalization — call it: cost internalization — that should happen.

4. Enforcement

In many cases, there's nothing wrong with Congress's laws or agencies' regulations. They might do an excellent job in counteracting cost externalization if the regulators were not hamstrung by a shortage of resources resulting in weak enforcement.

One might imagine that protecting children and families from eating poisoned food on sale in stores would be the one area of regulatory enforcement that would never be lax or shortchanged. If so, one would be mistaken. Based on an analysis by the U.S. Department of Health and Human Services (DHSS) inspector general, *USA Today* reported—on the day after Christmas 2017—that, even when people are getting sick, "[t]he federal recall process for about 80% of the nation's food is so slow it can take up to 10 months to get unsafe products off all store shelves."[21] The DHHS analysis found:

> Of the 30 recalls reviewed by the inspector general, 23 were [C]lass 1 recalls, which ... means they could cause death [and] irreversible health problems like kidney failure. The other seven were Class 2 which could cause reversible issues that could require up to months-long hospital stays
>
> ...
>
> Of these recalls, it took a median of 29 days and an average of 57 days for the recall to start after FDA became aware of the hazardous condition.
>
> ...
>
> One infant and two fetuses died in the recalls examined between October 2012 and May 2015 and multiple illnesses were reported. Hazards included Hepatitis A in pomegranate seeds, cadmium in frozen spinach and listeria in pistachios.[22]

To appease industry complaints about "overzealous" regulators, Congress may be tempted to cut the resources—particularly, the personnel—that are needed to effectively carry out a sound regulatory program. There are obviously instances where regulators abuse their powers. The same is true for law enforcement officials in other areas. The same solution applies. Stop the abuse, but do not cripple law enforcement.

Regulation is about saving lives and preventing illness, as much as it is about making the market effective. Where life-saving rules are already on the books but take weeks to carry out, government's response should be to strengthen enforcement. In the area where sensible regulation is being thwarted or delayed, Congress should give regulators the tools they need — dollars, personnel, training, equipment, and technology — to do an excellent job.

5. Non-Pricing Incentives

Finally, regulation can in some cases be improved by recognizing (more than is now the case) that violators of regulatory standards are not all equal. Intentional and habitual violators should be treated differently than accidental or occasional violators. One device for doing this would be to create positive incentives for businesses to follow the rules, e.g., by rewarding good behavior with fewer inspections.

RESOLVING THE NEW DEAL'S CONTRADICTIONS

Finally, the two fundamental contradictions that are embedded in the New Deal *writ large* should not be allowed to linger and fester. Both contradictions — (1) the inconsistency between broad-based economic security guarantees vs. means-tested welfare programs, and (2) the conflict between market regulation vs. market manipulation — should be resolved as quickly as possible.

It is essential to the purpose and logic of the New Deal settlement that the United States retain two clusters of New Deal domestic policy: broad-based economic security guarantees and market regulation. Both of these policy clusters lie at the very heart of the New Deal. Their existence is necessary to enabling America to be a just nation, inhabited by secure and safe citizens, and relying on an effective market. The major gaps and serious flaws in both clusters should be fixed—and can be fixed—as described above.

At the same time, we should phase out the two other, incompatible, undermining, clusters of New Deal policy: means-tested welfare programs and market manipulation.

A properly constructed system of broad-based economic security guarantees will eliminate the need to operate and finance means-tested welfare programs. Once economic security policy is enlarged and reformed as proposed in this book—thus virtually ending unemployment and underemployment, driving down poverty to a residual level, raising incomes across the board to an adequate level, providing everyone excellent health insurance and long-term care insurance, and reforming K12 and higher education—there will be no reason to perpetuate means-tested programs that require people to be poor (or nearly so) to get help, create an incentive to hide earnings, discourage work, punish marriage, and fuel racism.

A reformed system of market regulation that aims to ensure an effective free market—a market in which sovereign consumers and investors control the flow of resources—is likewise at odds with market manipulation of consumption and investment. The two approaches to the market, regulate it vs. manipulate it, are not merely in conflict. They are incompatible.

A sound regulatory structure, comprised of what Britain's Conservative Prime Minister Theresa May termed "the right rules and regulations" that interact with private enterprise to create "an open, innovative, free market economy" that advances "collective human progress," should be the goal.[23] Such a regulatory structure has a variety of aims:

1. It protects the environment, workers, consumers, and investors against serious harm and undue risk.

2. It promotes a level playing field that rewards the most productive firms.

3. It prevents economic downturns from descending into economic catastrophes like the Great Depression and Great Recession.

4. It ensures that consumers occupy the position of sovereign commanders of the shape and direction of the market.

The aims of sound market regulation overlap. Together they enhance the economy's capacity to lower consumers' costs, improve the quality of products and services, and enlarge the nation's wealth.

But these desirable aims fundamentally clash with the U.S.'s vast web of market manipulation, which is achieved primarily by means of subsidies (outside and within the tax code) for politically preferred types of consumption and investment. Market manipulation artificially raises — twice — Americans' cost of living. Most of us are compelled to pay higher taxes, sooner or later, to finance the $2.0 trillion or more in subsidies. We are also compelled to pay the higher prices that less productive, otherwise uncompetitive, but heavily subsidized firms are able to get away with.

The greatest harm to Americans that market manipulation inflicts is the way it dethrones consumers and investors as the sovereign commanders of the economy. Instead, it artificially transfers a large portion of the market power of consumers and investors to Congress and Congress's favorite businesses. By doing so, market manipulation tilts the playing field in favor of less productive sectors and firms. This artificial political tilting of the marketplace not only raises the prices of some of the goods and services we buy. It also weakens the overall productivity of the U.S. economy, slowing its capacity to grow and create jobs, curbing our international competitiveness, and weakening the nation's wealth.

There is no middle ground. Market regulation, what Prime Minister May termed "the right rules and regulations," should stay and improve. Market manipulation—that is: cash subsidies, tax subsidies, and other mechanisms that favor specific types of consumption and investment—should be phased out. The sooner the U.S. disenthralls itself from the New Deal's mistaken legacy of market manipulation, the better.

Coda: Eliminating Taxpayers' Subsidies for Roads and Transit

In eliminating taxpayers' subsidies for specific types of consumption and investment, one additional huge subsidy—one that bears only a tangential relation to the New Deal settlement *per se*, but that belongs in the market manipulation policy cluster—should also be eliminated.

Today, local property taxpayers are compelled to pay tens of billions of dollars to subsidize local roads and transit. Getting rid of this government subsidy—and then treating roads and transit as public utilities whose users pay the full cost based on frequency, intensity, and time (i.e., "rush hour") of use—would allow municipal property taxes to be cut by 20% to 50% or more, depending on the jurisdiction.

Under such a utility model, drivers and riders could still take to the roads, or hop on a bus, streetcar, light rail, or train, any time they wished. But the resulting utility fee structure (i.e., variable pricing based on frequency, intensity, and time of use) would encourage more careful decisions about when to use the road grid or utilize transit.

Thus encouraging users via well-calibrated price signals to make more efficient use of the existing infrastructure will have four important effects in addition to permitting massive local property tax cuts. First, it will justify eliminating the special tax on gas imposed primarily by states and the federal government. Second it will end any rational argument for building more, hugely expensive, "freeway" lanes in metropolitan areas. Third, it will spare from demolition thousands of homes and businesses, worth billions of dollars. Finally, a well-calibrated set of price signals will enable traffic to flow more smoothly, reducing congestion and pollution, and thus helping to stop climate change.

For further detail on the reasons for ending property taxpayers' massive subsidy for the roads, and for creating road utilities whose users pay the full cost in ways that reduce congestion and pollution, visit: www.govinplace.org/content/Road_Utilities.pdf.

The same logic applies to transit utilities. Users—all of whose incomes under a New Deal 3.0 would be adequate to pay full fare—should pay full fare for the buses, streetcars, light rail, and trains they ride.

CONCLUSION: BOTTOM LINE

This in sum is what a re-formed New Deal—Version 3.0—would look like. Except where noted, all proposed policy changes are federal.

A Greatly Improved Set of Broad-Based Economic Security Guarantees

A. For workers who are unemployed or underemployed:

1. Transitional Jobs (TJs) providing up to 40 hours of work per week at the minimum wage; and

2. Unemployment Insurance benefits that are voluntarily convertible to wages paid by a TJ.

B. For workers who are employed:

1. A minimum wage of $10-$12 per hour (adjusted for inflation);

2. A new Earnings Supplement (replacing the EITC and CTC) that ensures that full-time work plus the supplement always yields an adequate income far above the poverty line;

3. Stronger collective bargaining;

4. Paid leave while caring for a newborn, newly adopted child, or ailing parent; and

5. Free childcare.

C. For different groups of adults outside the labor market:

1. Disability benefits, consolidated into SSDI, whose minimum payment far exceeds the poverty line and that are voluntarily convertible into TJ wages;

2. Social Security pension benefits that at a minimum far exceed the poverty line; and

3. An automatic savings program that makes it easier for a worker voluntarily to set aside a portion of each paycheck, and conservatively invest the amount in an individually owned, portable savings account that the worker can draw on to boost total retirement income.

D. To protect and improve Americans' health:

1. For the under-65 population (except those receiving SSDI benefits or covered by military, VA, or other special federal health insurance programs), a new federal program, called Young Medicare, that would replace Medicaid, Obamacare, and individual and employer-sponsored health insurance with the following features:

- Excellent health insurance benefits, with no deductibles and very limited co-pays;

- Annual choice of high-quality health care plans and providers; and

- Costs controlled via basic market forces, i.e., by providing enrollees with a base amount that covers the full premium of the lowest-bidding, high-quality health care plan, with enrollees free to join but paying the full extra cost of any higher-bidding plan;

2. For the SSDI and 65+ population: Medicare; and

3. A new long-term care insurance program that provides additional resources for 65+ seniors who need long-term care at home, in an assisted living setting, or in a nursing home.

E. To ensure our children get an excellent education:

1. For K12 education, equalized per-pupil funding within each state, with local taxes replaced by state

governments' taking on full responsibility for the cost and oversight of K12 schools that receive public funds, based on the following features:

- Elimination of student residency requirements (the "where you live, you learn" rule), so that K12 students are free to enroll in any qualifying school in the state;

- An equal base payment, e.g., $10,000 per year, for each pupil;

- Per-pupil funding uniformly adjusted upwards for students with special education needs and to promote more economically diverse — thus, more racially integrated — student bodies; and

- Requirements — strongly enforced — that all schools receiving public funds must meet high standards of safety, administrative and financial competence, teacher quality, and yearly progress by the vast majority of students.

2. For higher education, qualifying college students to receive full federal support to pay for up to four years of reasonable in-state tuition and fees at their home state's public technical colleges and public universities, with the following additional features:

- The same dollar amounts also made available to help defray the cost of tuition and fees charged by out-of-state public technical colleges and public universities, as well as by qualified (i.e., non-ripoff) private colleges; and

- All colleges receiving such funds to be accredited by the Council for Higher Education Accreditation or another reputable accrediting body.

In addition, the system for delivering economic security should be fundamentally transformed. Given the giant leaps that have already taken place in web-based information technology and that the future promises, all American individuals should be set up (unless they demur) with an Individual Progress Portfolio: a single, simple, speedy, online, user-friendly system of accounts for the purpose of delivering the improved model of economic security guarantees.

The Individual Progress Portfolio would do the following for enrollees:

1. Inform them about all available programs;

2. Determine quickly individuals' eligibility or ineligibility for each program;

3. Enroll eligible individuals in all the programs they qualify for;

4. Help them make decisions about how best to use those programs; and

5. Deliver the dollar amounts or other help they have chosen.

For further detail about how the Individual Progress Portfolio would work to help deliver economic security with greater accuracy, impact, and speed, visit: www.govinplace.org/content/Individual_Progress_Portfolio.pdf.

Replacement of Means-Tested Welfare Programs

All means-tested welfare programs would be phased out.

The creation of a comprehensive, "universal," economic security foundation for all Americans, as spelled out above, will end the need for means-tested programs that require poverty (or near-poverty) as a precondition of help. Once no longer needed, there is no good reason to perpetuate TANF, SSI, Food Stamps, LIHEAP, WIC, housing subsidies, Medicaid, CHIP, WIC, etc.

Means-tested programs require poverty or near-poverty as a condition of eligibility. Thus, by definition, they fail to lift the poor and near-poor anywhere close to an adequate level of income. Such programs subject the poor and near-poor to eligibility requirements that perversely create incentives to hide earnings, reject work, and avoid marriage. They are prone to error. Means-tested welfare programs also brand their recipients with a stigma. Recipients tend to dislike them, and many other Americans scorn them.

With a comprehensive set of broad-based economic security guarantees in place that interact to virtually end unemployment and underemployment, eliminate poverty, and raise incomes across the board to an adequate level, the rationale for perpetuating means-tested welfare programs disappears. It is true that, with welfare gone, a tiny fraction of Americans will still "fall through the cracks." But today far more Americans fall through much wider cracks. The proposed New Deal 3.0, by filling the holes and fixing the flaws in today's inadequate system of broad-based economic security guarantees, will sharply reduce the count of those left out and left behind to a small, residual number.

In addition, the families, friends, religious organizations, and non-profit groups that historically have helped the poor will be far better positioned to assist the individuals who do fall through the cracks. To begin with, under a New Deal 3.0, the absolute number of indigent persons in the future will be dramatically smaller. At the same time, precisely because of the economic security policies of the New Deal 3.0, the remaining poor's families, friends, and communities will have much higher incomes, more stable housing, and other resources for providing aid. The religious organizations and non-profit groups that serve the much diminished indigent population will likewise have greater resources to draw on in providing help.

A Universal Basic Income (UBI)—that is: giving every American, or at least every dependent child, a fixed dollar payment per month—has recently become fashionable as an alternative to the means-tested welfare system. But a UBI is a deeply flawed policy. For poor adults without a job, giving them $500 or $1,000 each per month (for these are the UBI payments in the news) still leaves the unemployed poor below the poverty line and even further below a truly adequate income. A UBI limited to children, meanwhile, offers no help to impoverished childless adults, including most of the poor persons who rely on disability benefits and Social Security retirement payments. At the same time, most UBI proposals are extremely expensive, typically costing over $1.0 trillion annually.

Further, a UBI fails to tackle the pressing problems that the proposed New Deal 3.0 addresses: the need for paying jobs, higher wages, a better earnings supplement *per se*, paid leave, free childcare, excellent health insurance for all, long-term care insurance, equalized funding for K12 schools, and free college tuition. The New Deal 3.0 is not a perfect choice. There is no perfect choice. But the proposed expansion and reform of broad-based economic security guarantees described in this chapter as part of a New Deal 3.0 is by far the better choice.

Enhanced Market Regulation

The proposed New Deal 3.0 would also greatly enhance regulation that prevents damage or undue risk to the environment, workers, consumers, and investors. This could involve additional prohibitions. But if more effective, regulation should rely on price signals (e.g., a carbon tax), greater transparency, stronger enforcement, and non-price incentives.

No Market Manipulation

Finally, a New Deal 3.0 would phase out all subsidies (including both direct spending and tax expenditures) that manipulate the market to promote specific types of consumption and investment.

This includes subsidies for agriculture, energy, housing, and transportation (both streets, highways, and bridges, as well as transit). The free choices of consumers and investors—both individuals and corporations—as to whether and how to spend much greater disposable income on products and services would entirely replace government manipulation in allocating resources to the agriculture, energy, and housing sectors.

To the extent tax subsidies are eliminated for utilities like roads and transit, user fees (which lower-and-middle income Americans could afford, thanks to the proposed economic security policies) would function to keep the utilities in business.

Subsidies and special treatment would also be eliminated for capital gains, dividends, and all other politically preferred types of income, property, and sales. All property, sales, and income would be subject to taxation, but at lower rates (except for sales of harmful products like alcohol and tobacco).

One consequence of creating a truly free market—one in which sovereign consumers allocate greater disposable income without political manipulation in the form of direct subsidies or tax expenditures for politically favored consumption and investment—will be a huge reduction in property taxes, as well as cuts in sales taxes and income taxes. Such tax reductions should be concentrated on greatly lowering the tax burdens of lower-income and middle-class Americans. But the wealthy and corporations should also see reductions in their pre-subsidy tax liabilities.

It is altogether fitting and proper (to borrow one of Abraham Lincoln's favorite expressions) to follow up on this chapter's outline of the contours of a transformed New Deal by taking a deeper dive into the numbers. Will a New Deal 3.0 work in fiscal terms? What will the new design cost? What will happen to revenue? Will government budgets balance or move towards balance? How will the responsibilities of different levels of government—local, state, and federal—change?

The preceding outline of a New Deal 3.0 is essential. Without an outline of the logic and structure of its interwoven policy changes, the resulting numbers may seem randomly cobbled together.

But with only an outline, the absence of detailed spending and revenue estimates may leave the impression that, as Gertrude Stein quipped, "There's no there *there*."

The big picture and the fiscal detail go together, like a picture's frame and the canvas's dots of paint. Without both, the argument for a New Deal 3.0 is incomplete. Read on.

CHAPTER 6

RUNNING THE NUMBERS

A GOOD WAY TO TEST WHETHER THE proposed New Deal 3.0 makes fiscal sense is to imagine that its major features took effect a dozen years ago. Let us suppose its shakedown cruise ended a decade in the past. What, in retrospect, would its costs and revenues have looked like, a few years ago, in 2015?

I picked 2015 for several reasons. It was a fairly typical year for the U.S. economy. It was neither one of the bust years of the Great Recession of 2007-2009, nor one of the boom years of 2016-2018. In addition, fiscal data for 2015 are available for all levels of government. Other years might also work well for drawing a fiscal map of a New Deal 3.0. But 2015 seems suitable.

Let us assume that the New Deal 3.0's redesign of American government was in place by 2015. Let us then estimate — backwards in time — the fiscal impact. Would the numbers have worked? Do the resulting budgets make sense?

The answer is: Yes. And since the numbers work for 2015, there is no particular reason to doubt that the costs and revenues of the proposed New Deal 3.0 will make fiscal sense in the future.

In this chapter, I outline the big picture of how the proposed redesign of government would have changed 2015 direct spending, tax expenditures, taxes, fees, and revenue for all levels of government. The details appear in Appendix D, "How a New Deal 3.0 Changes Government Budgets." The appendix lays out the data, assumptions, methodologies, and formulas I used, as well as the specific estimates I made for spending and revenue.

The big fiscal picture now follows. I first present an overview. I then summarize, based on my thinking of how a New Deal 3.0 would have be implemented as of 2015, what its fiscal impact would have been that year on the major components of governmental budgets. I also explain why I locate YoungMedicare outside the regular structure of the federal government, and summarize its costs and revenue. To make the estimates easier on the eye, I round off the numbers in this chapter to the nearest $25 billion. In Appendix D, the estimates are broken down in much greater detail and specified to the nearest $100 million.

Finally, in this chapter's conclusion, I compare the estimated costs of a New Deal 3.0 with its benefits.

FISCAL OVERVIEW

Had the proposed New Deal 3.0 been in force in 2015, direct local spending would have dropped sharply. Direct state spending, too, would have fallen. Within the regular federal budget, direct spending would also have declined. Large cost increases for new and expanded federal economic security guarantees would have been more than offset by cost reductions due to phasing out federal means-tested welfare programs.

Governmental spending via the tax system—that is: tax expenditures—would remain in place under a New Deal 3.0. By 2015, however, the nature and number of tax expenditures would have dramatically altered. At the federal level, two new tax expenditures for workers—an Earnings Supplement Tax Credit and a YoungMedicare Tax Credit—would be the only significant survivors. Virtually all other tax expenditures would have been phased out.

Taxes in 2015 would have fallen overall at the local, state, and federal level. The broad taxes—on property, sales, individual income, and corporate income—would have fallen by greater amounts than several narrow taxes would have increased. Thus, net taxation would have declined.

Offsetting this overall decrease in taxes, a New Deal 3.0 would have resulted in 2015 increases in fees at every level of government. The interaction of lower taxes and higher fees, however, would have resulted in a net reduction in total revenue collections for localities, states, and the federal government.

The YoungMedicare program would occupy a unique place in the 2015 fiscal landscape and beyond. This program, created to guarantee that the entire under-65 population has excellent health insurance, would be organized outside the structure of the federal government. Akin to what typically happens with Workers' Compensation, employers of all sizes would be required to carry Young Medicare coverage by remitting payroll-based premiums. (Since YoungMedicare would be a purely federal program, however, the premiums paid by self-employed persons and small firms may need to be treated as taxes, rather than mandatory payments, in order to satisfy the U.S. Supreme Court's narrowing vision of what regulations of commercial activity are allowed under the Commerce Clause of the Constitution.)

YoungMedicare would be run by a new Government-Sponsored Enterprise (GSE): the National YoungMedicare Corporation (NYMC). Employers' premium revenue would be used immediately to enable the under-65 population— overwhelmingly workers, workers' spouses, and workers' children—to purchase an excellent health insurance plan. All funds would flow into and out of the NYMC's independent trust fund.

YoungMedicare would of course be expensive, but in 2015 it would have cost workers and employers less than what either group spent that year for worse health insurance. Going forward, the cost of the YoungMedicare model would fall further and further below the cost that our existing dysfunctional health care system would otherwise impose on individuals and firms.

Let us now take a closer look at how a New Deal 3.0 in 2015 would have altered direct spending, tax expenditures, taxes, fees, and total revenue.

DIRECT SPENDING

The proposed New Deal 3.0 would have reduced direct spending by localities, states, and the federal government.

Local Governments: Local governments in 2015 would no longer have paid for K12 schools, since the financing of K12 education would have been entirely shifted to state government. Local spending on colleges would also have declined, thanks to the federal assumption of responsibility for paying college tuition and fees. Finally, local governments would have been freed from the burden of financing bits and pieces of means-tested welfare programs, which by 2015 would have phased out. As a result, I estimate that local spending would have dropped sharply by close to $600 billion.

State Governments: State governments in 2015 would have taken on the full cost of financing K12 education. But they would have been freed of the responsibility for financing most of the cost of college education, due to the federal pickup of the cost of college tuition and fees. In addition, states would have shed their obligation to pay for a large slice of federal means-tested welfare programs, which would be gone. As a result, I estimate that net state spending would have dropped by about $100 billion.

Federal Government: The federal story is more complex. Overall, the proposed New Deal 3.0 would have reduced regular federal spending. But there would be a mix of very large increases and very large decreases.

New and enlarged federal economic security guarantees— for Transitional Jobs, childcare, and higher minimum payments for SSDI and Social Security—would have substantially increased spending at the federal level. Together with greater funding for long-term care, I estimate that total direct federal spending for broad-based economic security guarantees in 2015 would have grown by approximately $750 billion. A major share of this increase would go to poor, near-poor, and other low-income persons, even though the programs in question would not be means-tested. (It would temporarily be necessary to apply a means-test to long-term care, but that would fade away as it evolves into a social insurance program.)

These large increases in direct federal spending for broad-based economic security guarantees would have been entirely offset by spending decreases due to the winding down of means-tested welfare programs. By 2015, TANF, SSI, SNAP (Food Stamps), LIHEAP, WIC, housing subsidies, Medicaid, CHIP and other means-tested welfare programs would have been phased out. Also, direct federal spending on the EITC and CTC (i.e., spending on those programs not treated as a tax expenditure) would have been displaced by 2015 due to the operation of the new, larger Earnings Supplement Tax Credit, which (as the next section discusses) would be entirely treated as a tax expenditure. I estimate that the removal of these pieces of the federal budget would have meant in 2015 a drop in direct federal spending of $800 billion.

In short, if the proposed New Deal 3.0 had been in place in 2015, direct federal spending in that year would have declined by nearly $50 billion.

This does not mean that the low-income population in 2015 would have lost $50 billion in federal support. On the contrary, low-income individuals and families in 2015 would have gained tens of billions more in income. The poor, near-poor, and other low-income individuals would have been major beneficiaries of the proposed guarantees of Transitional Jobs, free childcare, and minimum SSDI and Social Security payments that far exceed the poverty line.

Beyond the regular federal budget, the low-income population would also disproportionately benefit from raising the federal minimum wage from $7.25 per hour to an assumed $10.00 per hour for 2015. Of equal importance, the low-income population in 2015 would have greatly benefited from the two new federal tax expenditures discussed in the next section: the $650 billion refundable Earnings Supplement Tax Credit, and the $350 billion YoungMedicare Tax Credit. If low-income individuals would have received only 20% of these two refundable credits, that's more than $200 billion.

Finally, low-income individuals in 2015 would have benefited from YoungMedicare. They would have paid no premiums out-of-pocket to enroll in a health care plan, unless they chose to enroll in a more expensive plan. They would have paid no deductibles for their health care, and rarely paid any co-pays.

TAX EXPENDITURES

The proposed New Deal 3.0 does not assume the elimination of tax expenditures. Ultimately, their total elimination may be desirable. In the short-to-mid term, however, it would badly distort regular governmental budgets if their spending totals were swollen by tax expenditures. There is also a case to be made that some spending is actually better administered through the tax system if the amounts thus allocated depend on calculations that must be made as part of filing income tax returns.

Following is an estimate of the fiscal impact of the New Deal 3.0's two proposed tax expenditures.

Earnings Supplement Tax Credit: The proposed federal Earnings Supplement Tax Credit would be refundable, i.e., filers would receive the full amount even if it exceeds their tax liability. The credit would depend on individual earnings (rather than the combined earnings of spouses), rise as a percent of earnings up to a maximum, but not phase out. These changes largely eliminate the current EITC's marriage penalty and work disincentive. Chapter Five spells out the formula for the proposed Earnings Supplement.

The per-person amounts laid out in Chapter Five, however, are gross credit amounts. The Earnings Supplement Tax Credit would be reduced by the same percentage as the filer's highest marginal tax rate. Low-income and middle-income workers would thus receive a larger final credit than high-income workers.

The estimate for 2015 is that approximately 150 million adult workers would have claimed the credit. I estimate that its gross cost would have been nearly $850 billion. All claimants would have seen the credit reduced, however, by their top marginal tax rate. Assuming an average 20% reduction, I estimate that the net amount that the Earnings Supplement Tax Credit would have provided workers in 2015 — and thus the net cost of this tax expenditure to the federal government — would have been approximately $650 billion.

YoungMedicare Tax Credit: The YoungMedicare Tax Credit is somewhat easier to estimate. It is a refundable amount for workers equal to 70% of their share (if any) of the premium for Young Medicare — that is: 70% of the 0%-to-50% worker's piece of the total premium that each employer would be permitted (but not required) to deduct from a worker's earnings rather than bear as a direct expense to the employer. Any portion of the premium for YoungMedicare that is not shifted to the worker would be paid by the employer.

I estimate that the entire cost of the YoungMedicare program in 2015 would have been approximately $1,300 billion. Employers would thus have been permitted (but not required) to dock their employees' paychecks by up to $650 billion.

Assuming that in 2015 the full half-share—that is: $650 billion—was deducted from employees' paychecks, workers would have been able to claim a refundable federal YoungMedicare tax credit whose gross value at 70% would have been roughly $450 billion. As with the Earnings Supplement Tax Credit, however, the YoungMedicare tax credit for each employee would be reduced by the filer's top marginal tax rate.

Again assuming an average 20% reduction in the credit, the net benefit to workers of the YoungMedicare tax credit—and thus the net cost of this tax expenditure to the federal government—would have been over $350 billion. Thus, the ultimate cost to employees, should they have been obliged in 2015 to see their paychecks docked by half of their employer's YoungMedicare premium, would not have been the $650 billion charge but rather $650 billion minus the net credit of $350 billion, or roughly $300 billion.

The role of the federal YoungMedicare Tax Credit in financing YoungMedicare in this 2015 scenario is summarized below. Taxpayers, via the federal government, can be seen as ultimately bearing the cost of the YoungMedicare tax credit. The other groups paying for YoungMedicare are workers and employers.

- YoungMedicare Tax Credit: $350 billion
- Workers' true cost $300 billion
- Employers' cost $650 billion

If workers in 2015 (or any year) were required by their employers to pay less than half of the employers' total premium, the cost of both the tax credit and the workers' true cost would decline, while the employers' total cost would rise.

Bottom Line: Under the proposed New Deal 3.0, tax expenditures would remain, but their purpose and allocation in 2015 would have dramatically changed. Tax expenditures that help workers attain a sufficient income, and that pay for a large part of their potential health insurance costs, would predominate. Both of these new tax expenditures would tilt in favor of lower-income and middle-class filers of federal income tax returns, because the value of the two credits for these filers would be reduced by relatively low marginal tax rates. Higher-income filers would benefit, but less, because their tax credits would be reduced by their relatively high marginal tax rates.

Otherwise, existing tax expenditures would have almost entirely been phased out. A core aim of a New Deal 3.0 is to eliminate subsidies for politically favored types of consumption and investment. As a result, by 2015, virtually all of today's tax expenditures would have vanished. However, three of the items that economists like to define as a tax expenditure would continue:

1) The exclusion from employees' taxable income of employers' required payment of YoungMedicare premiums;

2) The exclusion from homeowners' taxable income of the imputed "rent" that homeowners receive from "leasing" — to themselves — their own homes; and

3) The exclusion from capital gains treatment of the profit from the sale of a principal residence.

Perhaps because I am not an economist, I do not view these three as real tax expenditures.

REVENUE: TAXES, FEES, AND TOTAL

The New Deal 3.0's emphasis on improving economic security requires that, when government spending is not necessary and taxes can appropriately be cut, broad taxes paid by lower-income and middle-class taxpayers should fall. By broad taxes, I mean taxes on property, sales, individual income, and corporate income. Lower-income and middle-class taxpayers should benefit the most. All income groups should nonetheless share in the savings that result from justifiable spending cuts and associated tax cuts.

Broad taxes should also fall to offset tax increases that are justified in two circumstances: (1) where it is appropriate to raise narrow taxes on harmful products (e.g., alcohol and tobacco products) or activities (e.g., CO_2 emissions) in order to safeguard the public's health and discourage harmful business practices, and (2) when taxpayer-financed subsidies for a governmental service should end because it is both possible and appropriate to require instead that the users of the service pay for the service's full costs, as is the case with roads, bridges, tunnels, transit, and other transportation services. Here again, the resulting cuts in broad taxes should primarily benefit lower-income and middle-class taxpayers. But all income groups should see lower taxes as the result of imposing higher "harm taxes" and switching to user fees.

The logic of a New Deal 3.0 would thus simultaneously lower broad taxes, raise taxes on harmful products and activities, and increase user fees, at all governmental levels.

My estimate is that if the proposed New Deal 3.0 had been in effect in 2015, local, state, and federal taxes would have decreased in total by nearly $400 billion. Packed into these totals are a blend of large decreases in broad taxes, the elimination of some excise taxes, and significant increases in "harm taxes." At the same time, the logic of the New Deal 3.0's approach to user fees would have resulted in 2015 in an increase in such fees in the amount of nearly $350 billion. Thus, total revenue would have dropped by a net of $50 billion.

Following is a quick summary. The details appear in Appendix D.

Tax Decreases

Broad Tax Cuts: Local, state, and federal taxes on property, sales (in general), individual income, and corporate income would have been reduced by over $425 billion.

Excise Tax and License Fee Cuts: The gas tax, the portion of vehicle license fees not needed to issue and enforce valid licenses, and the federal airway tax would have been eliminated, saving taxpayers nearly $125 billion.

Added together, the two preceding sets of tax decreases would have rounded off in 2015 at $550 billion.

Tax Increases

Impact of Existing Taxes: Subjecting motor fuel sales to normal sales tax rates, and treating Transitional Jobs earnings as taxable income for the purposes of the Unemployment Insurance tax and federal payroll taxation, would have increased 2015 revenue by an amount that rounds up to $50 billion.

"Harm Tax" Increases: The taxation of alcohol, tobacco, and CO_2 emissions would have increased local, state, and especially federal revenue by well over $100 billion.

Added together, these two sets of tax increases would have rounded off in 2015 at $150 billion.

Overall Tax Impact

Thus, had the proposed New Deal 3.0 been in effect in 2015, the overall impact of decreasing most taxes by $550 billion, but increasing a smaller number of taxes by $150 billion would have been a reduction in net taxation of nearly $400 billion.

Fee Increases

A New Deal 3.0 would have resulted in higher fees at all levels. The total increase I have estimated for 2015 would have been approximately $350 billion. The largest portion of the fee increase would have involved requiring the users of the road grid (local streets, state highways, and the "I" system) to pay fees to cover the repair and maintenance of the new road utilities that would be created. The next largest portion would have involved requiring the users of transit utilities to pay fees to cover the full cost of transit.

Bottom Line: Revenue Decreases

When the balance is struck between taxes and fees, the impact of New Deal 3.0 revenue policy for 2015 would have been a substantial decline in regular governmental revenue. At each level of government, the estimated overall cut in taxation would have been greater than the estimated rise in fees. The combined governmental net decrease in taxes, approximately $400 billion, would have exceeded the combined governmental increase in fees, approximately $350 billion. The bottom line for 2015 would have been a drop in governmental revenue of approximately $50 billion.

The numbers are a bit mind-numbing. It is important, however, not to lose sight of the big picture. The meaning of a New Deal 3.0 is that the overwhelming majority of Americans in 2015 would have had more money in their wallets, purses, and bank accounts.

Lower-income and middle-class Americans would be especially better off. With greater economic security, lower taxes, and the two new refundable tax credits discussed earlier, they would be well positioned to live in greater comfort. They would also be able to afford the user fees they would be obliged to pay to use the new road utilities and existing transit utilities.

But higher-income Americans would not necessarily be worse off. Only if their high incomes and wealth depended heavily on taxpayer-funded subsidies for particular types of consumption and investment would the wealthy likely see an increase in their taxes.

YOUNGMEDICARE

Finally, the New Deal 3.0 calls for creating, outside of the formal structure of the federal government, a new kind of Government-Sponsored Enterprise (GSE) to operate the YoungMedicare program for most individuals under age 65. This section explains why the proposed National YoungMedicare Corporation (NYMC) should be organized in this way, what its functions would be, and how it would be financed.

Several factors justify placing YoungMedicare beyond the realm of the formal structure of the federal government.

First—Consistency with Precedent: To begin with, there is ample precedent for placing outside of the structure of government a large social insurance program that provides workers with health insurance and requires employers to pay a payroll-based premium to finance the coverage. For over a century, this has been how the nation's oldest social insurance program, Workers' Compensation, has operated.

Almost all employers are mandated to participate in Workers' Compensation. In many states, all it takes is a single employee to trigger the employer's obligation to "carry" Workers' Comp insurance.[1] In addition, one of the mandates that employers must meet is a requirement to spend a specific amount of money based on their payroll (as well as other factors) when they purchase a Workers' Comp insurance policy.[2,3]

While Workers' Compensation is a mandatory social insurance program that is financed by payroll-based premiums, in most states the government's role is limited to enforcing the employer mandate and overseeing the integrity of the commercial insurers that sell Workers' Comp policies. In 20 states, however, the government itself competes with private commercial firms in selling Workers' Comp coverage. And in a handful of states the government functions as the exclusive Workers' Comp insurer.[4,5]

The proposed YoungMedicare program would resemble Workers' Compensation in many respects. As with Workers' Comp, a primary aim of YoungMedicare would be to provide pre-65 workers with health insurance. The main difference is that Workers' Comp limits coverage to workers themselves. YoungMedicare would extend coverage to most of the rest of the under-65 population, based on the reality that most of the rest of the under-65 population is connected to the workforce. They are workers' spouses, workers' children, ex-workers, and future workers.

Another similarity is that, as with Workers' Compensation in most states, YoungMedicare would require that all employers must pay for health insurance, and that the premium must be based on payroll. The Workers' Comp pattern in some states of designating state government as the exclusive insurer also provides a precedent for YoungMedicare's policy of requiring employers to remit their payroll-based premiums to a single entity, the National YoungMedicare Corporation.

There are important differences of course. But the Workers' Compensation model provides a strong precedent for both creating a new social insurance program to coordinate the financing and purchase of health insurance, and for locating the operator of that program outside the regular structure of government.

Second — Self-Service. Our two largest social insurance programs, Social Security and Medicare, transfer revenue from one group of taxpayers to distinctly different group of beneficiaries. There is nothing wrong with this approach. It faces actuarial challenges and other difficulties, but those can all be tackled. The social value is enormous.

But because Social Security and Medicare do involve transferring revenue between different groups, it makes sense to include both programs within the framework of the regular federal government. Congressional oversight, debate, and action, we can hope, will fairly balance the valid interests of younger taxpayers who are financing a large part of Social Security and Medicare with the legitimate claims of seniors to the income stream and health insurance that they deserve (and that they helped to finance for their own parents and grandparents).

By contrast, YoungMedicare would be fundamentally different in its revenue inflow and cash outflow. The workers who would finance most of the program—whether directly or in the form of reduced compensation that enables their employers to pay the required premiums—would not be helping out a different, older cohort of Americans. Nor would they be placing in reserve a sum of money to help themselves down the road.

Rather, YoungMedicare would be a vehicle for enabling the vast majority of under-65 adults in the U.S. to pool their resources *today* and obtain health insurance *today* for themselves and their families. Far more effectively than our current dysfunctional health insurance system, YoungMedicare would enable those under 65 to immediately provide themselves, their spouses, and their children with excellent coverage within a framework that relies on market forces—choice, competition, and incentives—to lower premiums, enhance quality, and improve outcomes.

In essence, YoungMedicare would be a pooling mechanism whose in-flow and out-go of money would be in almost real-time equilibrium. The under-65 adults paying into the program, both directly and in the form of reduced compensation, would by and large be financing their own and their families' virtually simultaneous acquisition of health insurance coverage for the month in question.

It is true that there would be some slippage. Or, better put, there would be a measure of forgiveness in allowing unemployed adults to retain eligibility. The unemployed (and their families) should not be thrown out of the program on both humane grounds and practical grounds. They may need health care to return to work and thus return to paying into the system. Indeed, the unemployed should still be seen as workers in the full meaning of the term. They may be unemployed now, but the odds are high that they worked in the past and will work again in the future. They are likely to have previously paid in, and they will likely pay in again. Throwing them out of YoungMedicare for a few months because of a typically short-term layoff, and then reinstating them after they are back on a payroll, is not only cruel. It also imposes needless administrative cost and complexity.

A second type of slippage involves adults whose spouses and children are younger than 65, but who themselves reach age 65. When that happens, their earnings would be excluded from payrolls for the purpose of calculating their employers' payroll-based premiums for YoungMedicare. They themselves would obtain coverage from "regular" Medicare.

Again, both humanitarian and practical reasons argue against removing the spouses and children from YoungMedicare. The spouse may separately be working and separately paying into YoungMedicare; or the spouse may in the future find employment and start paying in. The same holds true for children. Tracking down the under-65 spouses and children of workers who turn 65; then figuring out which ones are unemployed vs. working (and constantly revisiting the question); and then dis-enrolling and re-enrolling them; is more trouble than it is worth.

A third issue involves whether it is fair to require that certain workers' earnings be counted towards employers' YoungMedicare premium payments if those workers are covered as SSDI recipients through Medicare, or if they are using TRI-CARE (the military health system), the VA system, or other specialized health care systems (e.g., Indian Health Services). But here, too, the complexity of real life provides an answer. A worker's spouse or children may be covered by YoungMedicare even if the worker gets coverage elsewhere. Indeed, the worker may even be using both YoungMedicare and another health care system at the same time.

Exempting such workers' earnings when calculating the payroll used to assess YoungMedicare premiums might not significantly hurt the program's financing. But even if such an exemption had only a modest fiscal impact, it would pose a significant administrative burden for businesses. Employers know if their workers are under age 65 or 65+, but they may have no idea if their workers are covered via SSDI under Medicare, or by TRICARE, the VA, or other health care systems.

In the case of military personnel on active duty overseas, the case for exempting earnings is more compelling. The only health care system they are likely to use overseas will be the military's system. The task of administering the exemption for this group would also be easy. Even for members of this group, however, some of the arguments against a carve-out should be considered. They may have spouses and children back in the States who are using YoungMedicare or will soon rely on it.

In wrestling with these issues, it is important not to lose sight of the big picture. In the main, YoungMedicare would involve the overwhelming majority of under-65 workers in financing the immediate provision of health insurance to themselves, their spouses, and their children. In the main, it will be the only health insurance that such workers, their spouses, and their children have. This immediate link between payment and provision, which I have labeled "self-service," is another reason why YoungMedicare is fundamentally different from other governmental health insurance programs. It is a major justification for locating YoungMedicare outside the regular structure of the federal government.

Third—True Fiscal Independence: YoungMedicare would be fiscally independent of the regular federal budget in name and deed. Its revenues and spending would be under the sole control of independent trustees, the members of the board of directors of the National YoungMedicare Corporation. The program would neither provide funds to the U.S. Treasury for general purposes, nor receive general funds from the U.S. Treasury to support its operations.

The trustees of YoungMedicare might reasonably decide to pay a fee for specified administrative services to the federal agency that runs the Medicare program, the Centers for Medicare and Medicaid Services, or CMS. The trustees might also appropriately arrange to pay a fee to the U.S. Treasury to collect, deposit, and invest YoungMedicare's revenue. But with respect to the rest of the federal government, YoungMedicare would follow Polonius's advice to Laertes to "neither a borrower nor a lender be." The complete independence from the federal government of YoungMedicare's revenues is yet another reason the program can appropriately be situated outside the government's regular structure.

Fourth—The Distorting Alternative: Another reason for placing YoungMedicare outside the government's regular structure is that the other choice—folding its spending and revenue into the federal budget—would badly distort the federal budget.

Fifth—Replacing Private With Private: A final argument for placing YoungMedicare outside the regular structure of the federal government is that most spending on behalf of the under-65 population for health care already takes place outside of the control of the regular federal government. YoungMedicare's role is not to take over that spending so much as to reorganize its use *within* the private sector so that it actually produces the health care outcomes we desire. Apart from YoungMedicare's role in pooling resources and structuring competition, its most important function will be to facilitate the effective deployment *inside* the private health insurance system of private market forces—choice, competition, and incentives— so as to drive down health insurance premiums, improve the quality of health care delivery, and strengthen population health outcomes.

Adding YoungMedicare to government's regular structure could undermine this essential task. Keeping the program outside of the regular structure will enable it to remain focused on helping the private sector to do what, in theory, the private sector does best: mobilize powerful incentives to reward low-cost, high-quality products and services.

In the distant future, it may become desirable to add YoungMedicare to the regular structure of the federal government, and even incorporate its spending and revenue into the federal budget. Let us debate this in 2050. In the meantime, the operation, financing, and health insurance purchasing mechanism of YoungMedicare is so different from other federal social insurance programs that positioning it outside the regular structure of government makes sense.

Chapter Five has already explained how individuals participating in YoungMedicare would select a health care plan from among competing options. They would pay nothing to join the lowest-bidding (but high-quality) health care plan in their area (e.g., county). They could opt to enroll in any more costly plan, provided they paid out-of-pocket the full extra cost.

I estimate that YoungMedicare in 2015 would have enrolled approximately 250 million persons under age 65. Its cost, as noted above, I estimate would have been over $1,300 billion. Let us conclude this section by discussing the financing of YoungMedicare. Where does the money come from?

The simplest and fairest approach would be to follow the example of the Workers' Compensation program. YoungMedicare would be funded by imposing a mandate — not on individuals — but on all employers to "carry" health insurance by remitting a payroll-based premium to the National YoungMedicare Corporation. For constitutional reasons, the employer mandate's application to the self-employed and the smallest employers may need to be designated as a tax. For larger employers, describing it as a mandatory premium should pass constitutional muster. The ACA now imposes an employer mandate that applies only to bigger firms. Its constitutionality has so far not been denied in any federal court.

Rather than replicate the complicated Workers' Comp premium formula, however, I favor an approach that is much easier to understand and implement. Under the proposed New Deal 3.0, YoungMedicare would be financed by a mandate that employers must remit quarterly to the National YoungMedicare Corporation a premium equal to 17.5% of Medicare taxable earnings.

Workers could be required to share in the cost—up to a point—if the employer insists. But no worker's earnings could experience a deduction of greater than 8.75% per week. Subject to that fixed limit, a business could charge its employees a flat amount or a percentage of earnings. The business could also vary the employee deduction based on pay, family size, or seniority. (It would of course be illegal to vary any charge to a worker based on the worker's age, sex, race, religion, sexual orientation or any other improper type of discrimination.) Employers would of course be free to charge their workers very little, or nothing at all, thus absorbing the full cost.

Despite YoungMedicare's great cost, the program would save money for both workers and businesses. Let's first look at workers. As explained above in the discussion of tax expenditures, even if workers in 2015 would have been required by their employers to pay half of the cost—that is: roughly $650 billion— the proposed federal YoungMedicare Tax Credit would have absorbed about $350 billion of that. Thus, workers' true cost would have been the balance of roughly $300 billion. According to the Centers for Medicare and Medicaid Services, however, this is roughly $20 billion less than the "household contributions" to private health insurance premiums that workers actually paid in 2015.[6] In addition, the YoungMedicare benefit design would free workers from the tens of billions they now spend each year for deductibles, co-insurance, and co-pays.

Now let's turn to employers. Assuming they chose to impose on their workers half of the premium they are required to remit to YoungMedicare, their cost would be roughly $650 billion. But according to CMS, this is nearly $30 million less than what employers actually spent in 2015 for private health insurance.[7]

Appendix D explains in greater detail the cost of YoungMedicare, the suggested approach to financing the program, and the savings that would result for workers and business.

CONCLUSION: THE BENEFITS OF A NEW DEAL 3.0

The primary purpose of this chapter has been to give the proposed New Deal 3.0 a price tag and show that the cost is reasonable.

Might the reforms embedded in a New Deal 3.0, if in effect in 2015, have cost less than I have estimated? Or more than my estimates? Of course. Might those reforms have triggered different outcomes for taxes and fees? Again: of course. Any number of changes in assumptions, methodology, and policy details would have resulted in different figures.

But under almost any set of assumptions, methodological choices, and policy refinements, I would argue that the "complete change of concept" in government functions that underpins a New Deal 3.0 would produce more-or-less the same fiscal outcome. If by 2015 American government had rested on ...

1) a major expansion of broad-based economic security guarantees of the kind I describe in Chapter Five,

2) the phase-out of means-tested welfare programs,

3) enhanced market regulation, and

4) the elimination of market manipulation,

... we would end up with something that closely resembles the picture of spending and revenue that I paint in this chapter.

Alternatively, even if the assumptions and methodology used were different, a handful of policy elements could be fine-tuned so as to yield virtually identical spending and revenue totals. Budgets are a human creation. There are dozens of legitimate ways to remain true to their broad policy aims, yet gently reshape the contours of specific formulas, in order to produce the same fiscal outcome.

The most essential question to ask about the proposed New Deal 3.0, therefore, is not whether the numbers work, but is the cost justified by the benefit? No discussion of the cost of reforming government can be complete without an examination of the resulting benefits. "Cost/benefit analysis" is not a cliché. It has meaning. It is important. Would the net cost of the New Deal 3.0 yield worthwhile, justifying benefits?

The starting point of this cost/benefit analysis is of course the fact that the proposed New Deal 3.0 (at least as I have structured it, and using my assumptions and methodology) would actually shrink the regular costs of American government.

Contrary to what some might expect, direct spending, tax expenditures, taxes, and revenue will decline across all levels of government. Since the number of government programs would also shrink, especially at the federal level, the size of government's bureaucracy would also decrease.

Only outside the regular structure of the federal government, under the aegis of the National YoungMedicare Corporation, can it be said that a cost increase would occur. The YoungMedicare program would indeed be very expensive. But in addition to reducing administrative costs, YoungMedicare would reduce the total amount spent to provide the under-65 population with health insurance, compared to what workers and business now are obliged to spend for worse coverage.

For the sake of this comparison of costs and benefits, however, let us stipulate that the proposed New Deal 3.0 will increase what might be labeled "government-required" spending. Let us then look at the benefit side of the New Deal 3.0 ledger. Are the resulting benefits worth it? One of Oscar Wilde's characters quipped that only a cynic knows the price of everything and the value of nothing. In exchange for the dramatic reforms that a New Deal 3.0 would put in place, does its cost/benefit ratio make it a value proposition for America's residents, businesses, and policymakers?

Following is a rundown of the benefits that a New Deal 3.0 would have purchased in 2015 and would continue to finance in the future.

Economic Security Without Means-Testing: The single greatest benefit of a New Deal 3.0 would be its guarantees of broad-based economic security to America's adults (and, thus, their children) without imposing a means test.

There are three main sources of economic insecurity in the U.S. today:

1) *Work Insecurity*: Unemployment, underemployment, unstable work, and volatile hours;

2) *Income Insecurity*: Insufficient earnings, disability benefits, and retirement income that make it impossible to afford the routine costs of food, clothing, shelter, utilities, transportation, and other basics; and

3) *Extraordinary Cost Insecurity*: Inability to pay for several extraordinary costs that even a stable and adequate yearly income is frequently too small to cover: the costs of childcare, health insurance, long-term care, and higher education.

The proposed New Deal 3.0 corrects for all three types of economic insecurity.

Work Insecurity

Mass unemployment—indeed, even modest levels of unemployment—would belong to the past. The new Transitional Jobs program would function in a counter-cyclical manner to provide all unemployed adults with up to 40 hours of paid work to the extent that the private labor market suffers from a job shortage. The TJ program would also be calibrated to offer part-time jobs to the underemployed and provide "fill-in" employment to those with unstable work or volatile hours.

Income Insecurity

Poverty would drop dramatically to a residual level. A New Deal 3.0 would in fact go well beyond driving the poverty rate down to 2-3%. Virtually all adults would have an income, well above the poverty line, that nears or exceeds the level that Americans (according to the Gallup Poll) believe is the minimum amount needed to get by. The near-disappearance of poverty and across-the-board gains in income security would be the result of a "policy package" that, in addition to offering 40 hours of paid work to all adults who want it, would:

- Raise the minimum wage in 2015 to $10 per hour (on a rapid path to $12 per hour, with future increases for inflation);

- Provide workers with an Earnings Supplement that is much larger than the current EITC and CTC combined, and has been shorn of the current marriage penalty and work disincentive;

- As a result, guarantee that all full-time work yields an income—based on earnings plus the new Earnings Supplement—that far exceeds the poverty line and crosses the threshold of income adequacy;

- Guarantee paid leave, so that if workers need temporarily to leave their jobs to care for a newborn or newly adopted child, or an ailing parent, they will receive a replacement income until they return to work;

- Guarantee for adults with a serious disability, all of whom would be able to enroll in SSDI, a minimum benefit that far exceeds the poverty line;

- Guarantee for seniors who retire on Social Security a minimum income that far exceeds the poverty line; and

- Also set up an automatic savings program that makes it easier for workers voluntarily to set aside a portion of their earnings for retirement.

Extraordinary Cost Insecurity

Finally, the proposed New Deal 3.0 would help tackle the third type of insecurity that arise when individuals and families must grapple with extraordinary costs. Even an adequate income will prove insufficient for tens of millions of Americans to absorb the high costs of childcare, health insurance, long-term care, and higher education. To tackle these extraordinary costs, the New Deal 3.0 would guarantee:

- Free childcare for all young children when their parents are working;

- Enrollment of the bulk of the pre-65 population in YoungMedicare, enabling enrollees at no cost or modest prices to obtain excellent health insurance benefits from their choice among competing health care plans and providers;

- Expanded access to long-term care services, ultimately in the form of a social insurance program that covers all elderly seniors; and

- Free tuition and fees at in-state public technical colleges and public universities, which could also be used to help pay for out-of-state public schools of higher education and accredited private colleges.

These measures, taken together, would dramatically reduce poverty, and (going beyond poverty reduction) enable virtually all Americans to achieve a much greater level of economic security. A much smaller version of these measures, according to the Urban Institute, would have sharply cut the U.S. poverty rate (using a more realistic Supplemental Poverty Measure) between 50% and 58%.[8] It is plausible to believe that poverty in the U.S. could be reduced by 90%, and economic security greatly enhanced across the board, if all of the proposed policies — together with certain non-fiscal policies, such as stronger collective bargaining — were put into effect.

Another benefit that would flow from a New Deal 3.0 would be its phasing out of means-tested welfare programs. The proposed broad-based economic security guarantees, once put in place, will make it unnecessary to continue the current patchwork of means-tested programs. Winding down "welfare" would liberate the poor from its inadequate help, harmful incentives, and racially biased stigmatization.

Other benefits packed into a New Deal 3.0 would flow from stronger and smarter regulation to protect the environment, workers, consumers, and investors from cost externalization by the market. A carbon tax would help slow down climate change. It and other anti-pollution efforts would help to clean the air, water, and land. Improvements in other branches of regulation would also save workers' lives and protect their health, spare consumers from injury and cartels, and help shield investors from swindles and deception.

Finally, a major benefit of the New Deal 3.0 would be the liberation of the market from political manipulation, enabling the market to allocate resources more efficiently and generate greater national wealth. The elimination of subsidies for specific types of consumption and investment will no doubt annoy the subsidized, but the economy will be greatly strengthened. Of equal importance, ending these kinds of subsidies will make America's consumers and investors the undisputed sovereigns of the U.S. economy. Putting individual consumers and investors in charge of a well-regulated economy's direction and shape—in lieu of government control and producer control—is the vital source of the wealth of the nation.

Taken together, the changes that flow from a New Deal 3.0 would produce far more winners than losers.

The unemployed and underemployed would win: they would be offered jobs. The overwhelming majority of the poor would win: they will stop being poor. Low-income and middle-class families would win: their incomes will rise to more adequate levels, and they will get free childcare, free health care, eventually free long-term care, and free college tuition for their children.

Of course, these "free" benefits are not literally free. (They are no more free than "freeways" are free.) Low-income and middle-class families would pay their fair share of the cost. But for the most part under a New Deal 3.0, their taxes will fall compared to today. The increase in their incomes, combined with the decline in their taxes, will enable them to afford the new fees needed to finance an improved road and transit infrastructure.

For high-income individuals and families, the story would be mixed. They will live in a better country—one largely free of economic insecurity, cost externalization within the market, and a distorted economy. Some of the wealthy will personally be better off. Others will see their taxes rise. This would not be due to higher income tax rates. All broad tax rates—whether applied to property, sales, individual income, or corporate income—would fall for every income group. Rather, to the extent wealthy individuals end up worse off, it will be because the subsidies that government previously handed to them through the tax system and other devices will be gone.

Those subsidies today overwhelmingly flow to the wealthy. When the subsidies for the rich dry up, the rich will at last have to do what they should have been doing all along: pay their fair share of taxes. Even so, a rational tax policy should leave members of the upper class with over half of their income. Creating a New Deal 3.0 does not require the U.S. to return to the days when (with all taxes taken into account) the top tax rate exceeded 50%. The wealthy should keep most of their earnings and most of their other income. It is not tolerable, however, that they should get favorable treatment for certain types of income, get to claim special deductions and credits, and pay far less than their fair share.

It is comforting—it is more than comforting: it is essential—that the benefits of a New Deal 3.0 outweigh its costs. This fact, however, tells us little about how we get from here to there. What is the path forward to actually putting in place the proposed New Deal 3.0? What are the "politics" that would allow this next change of concept in government's functions to advance into actual laws? These questions—and proposed answers—are the subject of this book's next and final chapter.

CHAPTER 7

THE PATH TO REFORM

"The arc of the moral universe is long, but it bends toward justice."
— Reverend Theodore Parker, 1853
— Dr. Martin Luther King, Jr., 1965

"All this will not be finished in the first 100 days. Nor will it be finished in the first 1,000 days, nor in the life of this Administration, nor even perhaps in our lifetime on this planet. But let us begin."
— President John F. Kennedy, January 20, 1961

FUNDAMENTALLY RESTRUCTURING America's domestic policy will not be easy or quick. It will be necessary to enact partial (some will say: piecemeal) reforms. It will be necessary to compromise.

But it is foolish to imagine that dramatic changes in the functions, financing, and form of our government cannot happen. Skeptics will always delight in the frustration of reformers. But history makes clear that sweeping reform can happen.

IMPOSSIBLE REFORMS THAT HAPPENED

American history is in large part a saga of big reforms—scoffed at by defenders of the status quo as impossible, and sneered at by "practical people" as naively ambitious—that in fact became law.

The creation of a new nation "conceived in liberty and dedicated to the proposition that all men are created equal" was

America's first exercise in impossibility. A disorganized cabal of discontented colonials could not possibly overcome their rivalries, maintain discipline, muster an army, negotiate treaties with Great Britain's rivals in Europe, and win independence from one of the most powerful nations on earth.

Yet the colonials succeeded. They declared independence. They rebranded their 13 colonies as "free and independent states" in 1776. They created a disciplined army at Valley Forge in the winter of 1777-1778. They negotiated an alliance with France in 1778. They won a decisive victory at Yorktown in 1781. They completed a peace treaty with Great Britain in 1783. The impossible happened.

The abolition of slavery in the United States was equally impossible. Until Lincoln issued the Emancipation Proclamation in 1863, and Congress passed the 13th Amendment and enough states ratified it in 1865

Women would never get the right to vote. Until they did.

A national system of economic security could never get through Congress or be ratified by the Supreme Court. Until it was.

Farm workers would never get the right to organize unions and bargain collectively for better wages and working conditions. Until they did.

National health insurance was also impossible. Until, with Obamacare, a version of it became the law.

Americans are used to recognizing that we achieve the impossible when it involves exploration and engineering. The Lewis and Clark expedition, the Transcontinental Railroad, and the Panama Canal are familiar examples. Few expected when

JFK took office in 1961 that Americans would walk on the moon by the end of the decade. But in 1969, the Apollo 11 spaceship landed, and Neil Armstrong took a giant leap for mankind.

It may be harder to discern, but it is equally true, that the history of American government is the history of impossible reforms. Usually, those impossible reforms become more than law. They become so embedded in the affection of the American people and the fabric of American life — think of abolition, votes for women, Social Security, civil rights, and Medicare — that they will never be undone.

FROM HERE TO THERE

So how do we begin to put government in a much better place? What are the steps Americans need to follow to create a New Deal 3.0?

Let us first recap the four fundamental changes that the U.S. should make in redesigning the New Deal settlement.

First — Complete the New Deal's System of
Broad-Based Economic Security Guarantees

The existing cluster of "universal" economic security guarantees needs major improvement. The premise of America's economic security system — that is: the value of legally ensuring that the unemployed, employees, disabled workers, and retired workers have a stable economic foundation that provides an adequate level of income and good health insurance, despite the "hazards and vicissitudes" of the U.S. labor market and life in general — is sound. The heavy reliance on social insurance and labor market regulation as the vehicles for guaranteeing economic security is also sound. But there are huge gaps and serious flaws in the architecture of U.S. economic security policy and labor market regulation that need to be fixed. The following major changes are needed.

1) *Transitional Jobs:* Unemployed, underemployed, and erratically employed individuals should be given the right to wage-paying Transitional Jobs (TJs), at the minimum wage and affording up to 40 hours of paid work per week when all work is combined, if they cannot find sufficient regular unsubsidized employment after a reasonable job search.

2) *Minimum Wage:* The federal minimum wage should be raised to between $10-$12 per hour (and adjusted for inflation).

3) *Earnings Supplement:* The nation's earnings supplements — the Earned Income Tax Credit (EITC) and Child Tax Credit (CTC) — should be consolidated, simplified, expanded to more workers, increased in amount, and (to avoid significant marriage and work penalties) based on each individual worker's earnings and no longer phased out.

4) *Collective Bargaining:* Workers' rights to form unions and bargain collectively should be strengthened.

5) *Paid Leave:* Workers should get paid leave so they can care for a newly born or adopted child, or attend to the needs of an ailing parent, without financial hardship.

6) *Childcare:* Free and quality childcare should be guaranteed so that parents can safely take care of their young children while they work for a living.

7) *Disability and Retirement Benefits:* The federal government's disability insurance program and pension insurance program—what we think of as the heart of Social Security—should be reformed to ensure that all adults who truly have a severe disability, or who retire at age 65 or older, have an income that far exceeds the poverty line.

8) *Automatic Savings:* In addition, a modest portion of each paycheck prior to age 65 should be automatically saved and conservatively invested (unless the worker opts out) to help seniors retire in comfort.

9) *Health Insurance:* Pre-65 Americans should be guaranteed health insurance, excellent benefits, and an annual choice among competing health plans and providers, as part of a new YoungMedicare program that uses competition and price signals to incentivize lower premiums, better quality, and improved outcomes. Medicare should be preserved and strengthened.

10) *Long-term Care:* The health insurance system should be augmented by creating a new national system of long-term care insurance, ensuring that seniors who need assisted living or nursing home care can afford it.

11) *K12 Education:* We should end the K12 education rule of "where you live, you must learn," equalize K12 per-pupil financing within each state, and have states take over full funding of K12 education.

12) *College Education:* We should provide qualifying college students with free tuition and fees for in-state public colleges (or a corresponding amount to help cover tuition and fees at out-of-state public colleges or accredited private schools). Higher education should not mean a mountain of debt.

Second – End Means-Tested Welfare Programs

While government economic security policies should be carefully crafted to ensure that low-income individuals rise well above the poverty line, this should no longer be achieved through means-tested welfare programs that narrowly target the poor and near-poor. Filling the gaps and correcting the flaws in the New Deal's cluster of broad-based economic security guarantees, in the specific ways spelled in Chapter Five, will virtually eradicate poverty in the U.S. Then, remembering FDR's call to "quit this business of relief," we should phase out the New Deal settlement's means-tested welfare programs.

Bill Clinton talked about "ending welfare as we know it," but that is insufficient. The U.S. should aim to end welfare – what FDR called "relief" – period.

Third – Enhance the System of Market Regulation

While the overall design of market regulation that the New Deal *writ large* has put in place is sound, there are major shortcomings in policy and enforcement in each type of regulation. We should substantially improve environmental protection, and do our part in stopping and reversing climate change. We need to strengthen safeguards for workers, consumers, and investors. Particularly in the area of environmental regulation, there are opportunities to supplement rules with price signals (e.g., carbon pricing) to create incentives for firms to reduce their pollution of air, water, and land.

Fourth – Eliminate Government Subsidies that Manipulate the Market

One of the New Deal's worst design flaws is the vast array of government subsidies that manipulate the market in order to promote politically favored types of consumption and investment. We should eliminate these kinds of subsidies, whether paid out directly or embedded in the tax code as tax expenditures. They impose a high cost on U.S. taxpayers. They badly distort the operation of the nation's market. As a result, they undermine the economy's productivity and weaken the nation's wealth. As with means-tested welfare programs for the poor, market-manipulating subsidies that primarily provide welfare for the wealthy and corporations should be ended, period.

The billions spent on means-tested welfare programs, and the much larger amount spent on subsidy welfare, should be used to finance the new economic security model and reduce taxes in a fair way. This multi-dimensional policy change will allow individuals and firms—with a great deal of additional money in hand for the vast majority of Americans—to fully control the direction and shape of the American economy and culture.

So how do we actually achieve these major structural reforms of the New Deal settlement? What's the roadmap to getting to a New Deal 3.0?

PROCEEDING PRAGMATICALLY, STEP BY STEP

It might be desirable to enact, all at once, this entire redesign of American government. On occasion, unique historical moments create a window of opportunity for quickly putting put in place, as a package, large reforms that dramatically extend the reach of economic security and effective markets. Such is the story of the original New Deal of 1933-1938.

But it is wise to recognize the general necessity of a piece-meal, step-by-step approach that steadily (if messily) phases in the new model as small doors and cracks open in the policy-making process. Pragmatic experimentalism is the hallmark of America's democratic experience. It often means that the U.S. is slower to do the right thing. But when our pragmatic approach is harnessed to a larger vision of freedom such as a New Deal 3.0, we generally move in the right direction.

Pragmatism, of course, does not always work. In ending slavery, pragmatism utterly failed. The U.S. descended into a bloody civil war before the triumph of the Union's armies and navy allowed the political process to deliver abolition. Pragmatism did not prevent the near-extermination of Native Americans, the *de facto* re-enslavement of black Americans once Reconstruction ended, the wholesale imprisonment of Japanese Americans during World War II, the abuse of numerous ethnic groups, the subjugation of women, or the mistreatment of gay individuals. All of these dismal episodes in U.S. history cast a deep shadow over our national commitment to freedom.

Yet America's pragmatic approach to reform, and the slow bending of our values and the arc of our history towards freedom, has also helped avoid the kind of catastrophic revolution that, in pursuit of mirages of social perfection, can wipe out millions of innocent human beings. The French Revolution, Russian Revolution, and Chinese Revolution each annihilated an *ancien régime* and substituted a top-to-bottom vision of perfection. Each unleashed unspeakable terror and slaughter. The myriad checks and balances that slow down U.S. progress, and impel our reforms to be pragmatic and piecemeal, also make it harder to create a living hell for the country as a whole.

And as often as not, the pragmatic approach that is the hallmark of U.S. policy reform has succeeded over time in producing good results. Such progress, however, has almost always occurred step-by-step over long stretches of time. Almost no good public policy in the United States has achieved its final form in a single act.

Most notably, the abolition of slavery took place in phases, divided by long intervals of inaction. First, several northern states abolished it. Second, as a result of the Northwest Ordinance, Congress outlawed slavery in the Midwest. Then, thanks to the Emancipation Proclamation, President Lincoln abolished it in the ten southern states in rebellion. Finally, with the 13th Amendment, Congress and the requisite number of states ended slavery in the U.S. as a whole.

Even after slavery was legally abolished, "slavery by another name" continued. Following Reconstruction, thousands of black Americans were arrested on trumped-up charges, falsely imprisoned, and sold to mines and factories. Illegal peonage lasted until World War II, when the U.S. Justice Department finally cracked down.[1]

Similarly, it took decades for federal minimum wage legislation (first enacted in 1938) to apply to:

- Workers in the air transport industry (1949);

- Certain retail trade employees (1961);

- Employees in public schools, nursing homes, laundries, the entire construction industry, and big farms (1967); and

- Many domestic workers (1974).

The same step-by-step process recurs in policy after policy. Even the Medicare we know today was not enacted all at once. The original Medicare legislation was enacted by Congress, and signed by President Lyndon B. Johnson, in 1965. It was not until nearly 40 years later that President George W. Bush proposed, Congress enacted, and the President signed into law Medicare Part D's coverage of prescription drugs. Both Obamacare (2010) and Trump-era legislation to prevent the shutdown of the federal government (2018) improved Medicare's drug benefit by closing its so-called "donut hole."

Following are three pragmatic approaches to phasing in the proposed design of a New Deal 3.0. Each approach should be pursued whenever an opening for action arises.

Gradual Expansion of Coverage

Gradually extending coverage of an economic security guarantee or market regulation to more and more individuals or organizations—group by group—is one of the easiest pragmatic ways to phase in a new policy.

For instance, eligibility for the proposed national Transitional Jobs program could gradually be expanded based on the duration of an individual's unemployment or underemployment. TJs might initially be offered to jobless workers who have been unemployed for over ten weeks. Eligibility could then steadily be extended to increasingly larger numbers who have been unemployed for over eight weeks, then over six week, and finally over four weeks.

Or gradual expansion could be based on age. Consider free childcare. It could initially be limited to the youngest children, e.g., ages 0-3. (The proposed recalculation of the 2015 federal budget assumes this limit.) The ceiling could over time be lifted, one year at a time, to extend free childcare to four-year-olds, five-year-olds, etc., to age 13.

Gradual expansion could also be based on income. This involves temporary use of means-testing. But if means-testing is truly temporary, it poses less of a problem. Thus, for example, long-term care could initially be limited to lower-income persons. Means-testing would be phased out as long-term care evolves into a social insurance program, the preferred vehicle, that steadily accumulates sufficient funds to cover all qualifying persons. Long-term care would thus steadily be extended over time to seniors with higher and higher incomes as the program attains fiscal maturity. Eventually, the income cap would be lifted altogether. (The 2015 budget recalculation increases federal funding for long-term care, but it assumes that a means-test would still be in effect. By 2015, the proposed long-term care social insurance program would not yet have built up sufficient funds.)

Ramping Up of Benefits

Another type of gradual expansion shifts the focus from who gets help to the amount of help. Thus, for policies that use formulas to provide money based on a percentage of earnings or a maximum sum, the policy could periodically increase the percentages and maximums.

For instance, the proposed Earnings Supplement tax credit for so-called "childless" adults could be ramped up from the EITC's current level of 7.65% of earnings with a maximum of just over $500 and a phase-out starting at roughly $8,400 of earnings to: (1) 10% of earnings, maximum of $1,500, phase-out starting at $10,000; (2) then 15% of earnings, maximum of $2,250, phase-out starting at $15,000; (3) and finally 20% of earnings, maximum of $3,000, with the phase out gone. (The latter is the ultimate earnings supplement policy proposed in Chapter Five for workers regardless of the number of dependent children. The 2015 budget recalculation assumes that, by that year, the ramping up will have been completed.)

Phasing Out of Subsidies

Finally, another pragmatic approach is the reverse of the ramping up a benefit: the gradual phasing out of a subsidy.

For many who receive market-manipulating direct payments or tax breaks for their particular forms of consumption or investment, it may be too much of a shock to lose the entire subsidy all at once. To cushion the impact, it may be appropriate to steadily phase out such subsidies, perhaps eliminating them over a five-year period.

CONCLUSION

A proverb should guide the pragmatic process of achieving large-scale reform: "Do not let the perfect become the enemy of the good." Much as it would be desirable to enact the proposed redesign of American government all at once, a practical step-by-step approach to phasing in a New Deal 3.0 should be embraced whenever the opportunity arises.

At the same time, advocates of reform should be on the lookout for unique moments to go further and faster. As Abraham Lincoln and Thaddeus Stevens showed in 1865 with the 13th Amendment, and as Franklin Roosevelt and Frances Perkins showed in 1935 with the Social Security Act, a big push at precisely the right moment in American history can sometimes turn a slow crawl into a rapid sprint to justice.

In most eras, however, such rapid sprints are rare. No one grasped this better than Franklin Roosevelt himself.

FDR understood at a deep level that the new and terrible crisis that the U.S. faced in 1933 required the opening of a brand new chapter in the role of American government. But he also recognized that the "complete change of concept" that he envisioned would require an experimental and pragmatic approach.

As part of this experimental and pragmatic approach, Roosevelt frequently compromised, often accepted partial measures, at times changed his mind, and occasionally backtracked. Here is just one example. In 1933, FDR replaced much of the existing "relief" system (created by his predecessor, Herbert Hoover) with a new program that provided the unemployed with wage-paying jobs: the Civil Works Administration (CWA). In 1934, he ditched the CWA and returned to "relief." Then, in early 1935, he urged Congress to "quit this business of relief."

That spring, FDR moved most of the people on "relief" into a rebranded CWA, the Works Progress Administration (WPA). A few months later in signing the Social Security Act, however, he authorized a new "relief" program: Aid to Dependent Children (ADC), the parent of Aid to Families with Dependent Children (AFDC) and the grandparent of Temporary Assistance to Needy Families (TANF). The program distributed cash payments for the most part to women whose husbands had died or abandoned them. WPA jobs and ADC's "relief" payments operated in tandem.

Roosevelt's openness to experimentation was no accident. Early in his 1932 campaign, in a speech at Oglethorpe University in Georgia, FDR had declared: "The country needs and, unless I mistake its temper, the country demands bold, persistent experimentation. It is common sense to take a method and try it: If it fails, admit it frankly and try another."[2]

FDR's pragmatic approach during the original New Deal was indeed a core feature of his personality. It was in his bones to be pragmatic. As Joseph Lelyveld emphasizes in his history of Roosevelt's final year in office and in life, "first and foremost he was a pragmatist."[3] FDR was obsessed with his predecessor Woodrow Wilson's failure to be pragmatic, according to Lelyveld, and explicitly distanced himself from Wilson on that dimension: "'I am not a Wilsonian idealist,' he once said in what was probably his most apt self-characterization on this point. 'I have problems to solve.'"[4]

Had Roosevelt lived another 20 or 30 years, he might well have approved of the need for yet another sweeping "complete change of concept" in the functions of government, this time involving an even broader experiment that included fixing the gaps, flaws, and mistakes of both the original New Deal 1.0, and its successor as the post-war era evolved, New Deal 2.0. As FDR had made clear in his 1932 speech at Oglethorpe University, the essence of America's democracy is experimentation: "bold, persistent experimentation."

But FDR would equally have insisted that any effort to reform the New Deal take place in a pragmatic manner, proceeding step-by-step unless a rare moment arose for large-scale change. Nonetheless, Roosevelt would have never lost sight of the end goal. In Lelyveld's words: "he was at once calculating and visionary."[5]

We should of course be cautious — very cautious — in making guesses about what Franklin Roosevelt would think or do about the New Deal *writ large* if, by some miracle, he returned to life today. No one expressed this caution more forcefully than one of FDR's closest observers, his ally and champion Frances Perkins: "One cannot predict," Perkins wrote, "what Roosevelt would have said or done in the postwar world."[6]

But Perkins also recognized how open and willing FDR was to see things in a new light and pursue change. "He was essentially adaptable to new circumstances," she added, "always quick to understand the changing needs and hopes of the people and to vary his action to meet changing situations."[7]

I like to think that, if Roosevelt miraculously returned to life today, he would view with sympathy this book's analysis, recommendations, and strategy as a logical next step in the great American experiment. He would be open to, and perhaps endorse, a New Deal 3.0.

One thing we can be sure of. Roosevelt would have been impatient with the current pace of change in reforming American government. His byword was "action, and action now." If alive today, FDR would demand action again.

APPENDICES

APPENDIX A

THE GOVERNMENT QUIZ

TO GET ANOTHER PICTURE OF HOW American government is both pervasive and hidden—and to help you assess what you really think it should do—take the Government Quiz.

It's fun and simple. Just record the number of times you answer "Yes" to the government activities—or potential activities—listed below.

The quiz does not ask about local and state government. To keep the list of questions short, it deals only with the federal government's role.

Do you believe the federal government should:

A. Maintain an army?   Yes [ ]   No [ ]

B. Maintain a navy?   Yes [ ]   No [ ]

C. Maintain an air force?   Yes [ ]   No [ ]

D. Maintain the Marine Corps?   Yes [ ]   No [ ]

E. Maintain the Coast Guard?   Yes [ ]   No [ ]

F. Maintain a border patrol?   Yes [ ]   No [ ]

G. Maintain the Centers for Disease Control, to detect the threat of epidemics and other health hazards, and to work with the medical community to protect the U.S. population from illness?

Yes [ ]   No [ ]

H. Fund the National Institutes of Health, the National Science Foundation, and NASA, in order to pay for biomedical research, basic scientific research, and space exploration?

Yes [ ]   No [ ]

I. Operate an Unemployment Insurance program, under which workers who have lost their jobs can receive a cash payment for 26 weeks while they look for a new job?

Yes [ ]   No [ ]

J. Establish a Transitional Jobs program that offers unemployed workers the ability to work in a temporary job at the minimum wage until they find regular employment?

Yes [ ]   No [ ]

K. Require all employers to pay a minimum wage?

Yes [ ]   No [ ]

If you answered "Yes," what do you feel the federal minimum wage should be?.
[ ] Current level: $7.25 per hour
[ ] $10.00 per hour
[ ] $12.00 per hour
[ ] $15.00 per hour
[ ] Higher than $15.00 per hour

L. Limit to 40 hours per week the number of hours that an employer can require a worker to work (unless the worker is paid extra for overtime)?

Yes [ ]   No [ ]

M. Provide low-wage workers a higher income by giving them, based on their total earnings, an Earnings Supplement?

Yes [ ]   No [ ]

If "Yes," should the amount of the Earnings Supplement increase depending on the number of children?

Yes [ ]   No [ ]

N. Operate a disability insurance program, providing adults a monthly payment if they have a severe disability that prevents them from working?

Yes [ ]   No [ ]

O. Maintain the Social Security program, under which workers who have paid Social Security taxes during their working years, and then retire at 62 or later, are entitled to receive monthly Social Security payments?

Yes [ ]   No [ ]

P. Maintain the Medicaid program, under which poor and near-poor individuals can receive free health insurance?

Yes [ ]   No [ ]

Q. Maintain the portion of the Affordable Care Act (Obamacare) under which uninsured individuals between 100%-400% of the poverty line pay only part of the premium—because the rest is subsidized—when they choose a health insurance plan?

Yes [ ]   No [ ]

R. Maintain the Medicare program, under which seniors who paid Medicare taxes during their working years are entitled, at age 65, to receive hospital, medical, and prescription drug benefits?

Yes [ ]   No [ ]

S. Maintain the program known as Temporary Assistance to Needy Families (TANF), under which very low-income, often non-working, parents of dependent children receive a monthly cash payment?

Yes [ ]   No [ ]

T. Maintain the Food Stamps (SNAP) program, under which low-income individuals, both non-working and working, receive funds they can use to buy food?

Yes [ ]   No [ ]

U. Maintain subsidized housing programs that provide some low-income individuals with low-rent public housing and give others vouchers to pay part of the cost of renting private housing?

Yes [ ]   No [ ]

V. Regulate businesses to make sure that they:

(1) Do not pollute the air, water, and land?

Yes [ ]   No [ ]

(2) Do not operate workplaces that endanger employees' safety?

Yes [ ]   No [ ]

(3) Do not sell products that injure consumers when used as intended?

Yes [ ]   No [ ]

(4) Do not form monopolies or fix prices?

Yes [ ]   No [ ]

W. Regulate banks to ensure that the banks are solvent, funds are prudently invested, and deposits are insured?

Yes [ ]   No [ ]

X. Regulate the stock market, bond market, and financial sector in general to ensure that investors get accurate, complete, and timely information about potential investments, and prohibit certain high-risk activities from taking place?

Yes [ ]   No [ ]

Y. Provide cash subsidies or tax breaks that encourage consumers to buy more of a designated product or service than they might normally do?

Yes [ ]   No [ ]

Z. Provide cash subsidies or tax breaks that encourage investors to make larger investments in designated assets than they might normally do?

Yes [ ]   No [ ]

The maximum possible number of "Yes" answers is 30. If you answered "Yes" more than 25 times, it's fair to say that you believe in a far-reaching federal government (whether you admit it or not).

APPENDIX B
THE U.S. JOB SHORTAGE

A COMPARISON OF BUREAU OF LABOR Statistics (BLS) data on the number of unemployed Americans vs. the number of job openings (as reported since 2000 in the Job Openings and Labor Turnover Survey, JOLTS) indicates that, most of the time, the United States faces a significant job shortage.

A NOTE ON SUBJECTIVE MEASURES AND OUTCOMES

It is important to note that BLS's data on unemployed individuals and job openings is unbalanced, in the sense that a great deal of subjectivity is involved in counting an adult as "unemployed" while the count of a job "opening" is more objective.

Franklin Roosevelt's Secretary of Labor, Frances Perkins, questioned whether it was even possible to count the unemployed. Reflecting on her time as FDR's Industrial Commissioner in New York State before both moved to Washington, Perkins wrote: "It became clear that one could never count the unemployed—one could only count the employed. A count of people not doing something at a particular time has no significance. If one is trying to find out the degree of cigarette smoking in the community one counts the smokers."[1]

Located within the U.S. Department that Frances Perkins ran for 13 years, BLS nonetheless does its best. In counting the unemployed, however, BLS has unavoidably been compelled to ask subjective questions and make arbitrary choices.

To begin with, the adult Americans who are asked about their relationship to the labor market are instructed to answer subjective questions about whether they "currently want a job," are "available for work," and have "actively looked for work" during the prior four weeks.[2] Individuals can objectively reveal their ages (it's a number). They can objectively disclose their earnings (it's the dollar amount in their paychecks). There is always fudging and forgetting, but most people get the facts right and it is possible to verify.

The choice of whether an individual "currently wants a job" or is "available for work," however, is subject to personal feelings and interpretation about what it means to "want" and be "available." While some of the tests for "actively looking for work" are objective (e.g., answering a Help Wanted ad), others are highly subjective. One of the tests for "actively looking for work," for example, is "contacting friends or relatives." Have you met this test if you say "Heard about any jobs?" to your softball league teammates over beers, or Uncle Joe and Aunt Sue during Thanksgiving dinner?

In addition, the BLS has set an arbitrary boundary in making its distinction between those who are *outside* the labor market (and, thus, cannot be counted as officially unemployed) vs. *inside* the labor market (and, thus, are counted as either unemployed or employed):[3]

- Adults 18-65 who want a job now, are available to work now, and may even have searched for work during the past 12 months — but have *not* searched for work during the prior four weeks — are placed *outside* the labor market, and thus cannot be counted as unemployed.

- But if the same group of adults *did* search for work during the prior four weeks, or if they worked (even an hour), they are placed *inside* the labor market. (Only a subset of this group is counted as "officially" unemployed — that is: those who did not work at all. This dividing line will be discussed shortly.)

Why use active job search within the past four weeks as the test that sets apart those outside the labor market who cannot be counted as unemployed vs. those inside the labor market who may be counted as "officially" unemployed? Why not three weeks? Or five weeks? BLS's choice is not wrong; but it is arbitrary.

Finally, in drawing the distinction within the labor market between those who are "officially" unemployed vs. those who are employed, BLS counts everyone who earns a wage, regardless of how many hours worked or wanted, as being employed. Thus, only a person with zero hours of work can be "officially" unemployed. A person who has only a few hours a day of work, feels unemployed, wants a lot more hours of work, is available, and has searched for extra work is entirely removed from the "officially" unemployed category.

BLS might have drawn a different line. It might have decided that the "officially" unemployed category also includes part-time workers with fewer than 12 or 16 hours of weekly work if they want more work, are available to do it, and have actively searched for it within the last four weeks. Once again,

BLS was not wrong to select zero hours of work as the absolute boundary between the "officially" unemployed vs. the employed. But the decision was subjective; and the result is arbitrary.

By contrast, the JOLTS methodology for determining whether a job opening exists is much more objective. According to BLS, a job is "open" only if it meets all three of the following conditions:[4]

1) A specific position exists and there is work available for that position. The position can be full-time or part-time. It can be permanent, short-term, or seasonal.

2) The job could start within 30 days, whether or not the establishment finds a suitable candidate during that time.

3) There is active recruiting for workers from outside the establishment location that has the opening.

What is "active recruiting?" Active recruiting means the establishment is taking steps to fill a position. It may include advertising in newspapers, on television, or on radio; posting Internet notices; posting "help wanted" signs; networking with colleagues or making "word of mouth" announcements; accepting applications; interviewing candidates; contacting employment agencies; or soliciting employees at job fairs, state or local employment offices, or similar sources.[5]

The complexity of the BLS definition of a job "opening" creates room for error. There is also a degree of subjectivity in the definition of "active recruiting" (e.g., "word of mouth" announcements). But in contrast to the essential role played by a responding individual's personal, subjective feelings in self-determining that the individual "wants" a job, is "available" for a job, and is "searching" for a job in categorizing the individual as "officially" unemployed, the BLS definition of a job opening depends far less on the responding employer's subjective feelings and far more on objective facts.

The BLS definition of a "job opening" also includes an element of arbitrariness. For instance, a job is "open" if it could start within 30 days. Why not 20 days or 40 days? The choice of 30 days is arbitrary. But compared to the number of arbitrary choices BLS makes in defining who is inside the labor market and (within the labor market) who is "officially" unemployed, the number of arbitrary choices BLS makes in defining a job opening are fewer (and, I would argue, of less consequence).

Because the definition of an "officially" unemployed adult is so highly subjective and relies on so many arbitrary definitions, the count of "officially" unemployed jobseekers is subjective and arbitrary. In turn, the comparison between the number of "officially" unemployed jobseekers vs. the number of job openings—that is: the existence and extent of a job shortage—is subjective and arbitrary.

DIFFERENT MEASURES OF A CONSTANT JOB SHORTAGE

These difficulties nonetheless do not prevent us from reaching a conclusion about whether the U.S. has a job shortage. Under both the "official" and several alternative measures of the unemployed, a comparison with the number of job openings reveals that more unemployed jobseekers than job openings—thus, a job shortage—is the norm. Switching from one to another definition of the unemployed—thus, from one to another comparison .between the number of unemployed jobseekers vs. the number of job openings—simply alters the job shortage's frequency and magnitude.

Decades ago, BLS recognized the subjectivity of its official definition of who is unemployed. The agency then fashioned several alternative—albeit equally subjective—definitions of who could be described as an unemployed jobseeker:[6]

> Each month, the Bureau of Labor Statistics publishes various measures of unemployment and other labor market difficulties. There are six "alternative measures of labor underutilization," known as U-1 through U-6, that provide insights into a broad range of problems encountered by workers in today's labor market.
>
> ....
>
> Each of the six measures rose at the onset of the 2001 recession and continued to trend up before declining in mid-2003. They all began increasing again at or slightly before the onset of the 2007–2009 recession, the longest and deepest recession of the post-World War II era. The measures continued to rise sharply during the recession and steadily increased afterwards until beginning to trend down in 2010.

Thus, there are alternative subjective counts of how many Americans, at any point in time, add up to the total in the unemployed jobseeker column. But whether we use BLS's measure of the "officially" unemployed, or add in other groups that BLS recognizes might reasonably be defined as unemployed, the comparison with the supply of job openings reveals that most of the time a substantially larger number of unemployed Americans would like paid work than the U.S. labor market has jobs on offer. In short, several of the ways you put together BLS data on the unemployed typically reveal a job shortage.

Let us begin with one of the most conservative comparisons: "officially" unemployed jobseekers vs. job vacancies. As Table B-1 shows, both during and for several years after the Great Recession (December 2007 through June 2009) the official count of those 16 and older who wanted a job now, were available to work now, and had actively searched during the prior four weeks far exceeded the number of job openings.[7]

The largest gap between jobseekers vs. job openings occurred after the recession's formal end in October 2009. In December of that year, approximately 15.1 million unemployed jobseekers were staring at somewhat over 2.4 million job vacancies. In other words, there was a shortage of 12.7 million jobs.[8]

Of greater significance, during several of the five years before the Great Recession, through most of the Great Recession, and for several years after the Great Recession ended, the ratio of jobseekers to job vacancies was greater than 2:1. Even in the absence of a formal recession, the U.S. economy saw a large mismatch between the supply of "officially" unemployed adults vs. the number of jobs available.[9]

At the same time, it is correct that the U.S. labor market has also experienced significant periods of time, including 2017-2018 (and beyond), when the number of "officially" unemployed jobseekers has roughly equaled the number of job vacancies. Since 2009, the "official" job shortage has steadily shrunk. In June 2018, fewer than 6.6 million jobseekers (less than half of the Great

Table B-1: US Job Shortage: 2000-2018
Count of "Officially" Unemployed v. Number of Job Openings
(in thousands)

Year	Officially Unemployed	Job Openings	Job Shortage
Dec. 2000	5,634	4,736	898
Dec. 2001	8,258	3,385	4,873
Dec. 2002	8,640	2,943	5,697
Dec. 2003	8,317	3,214	5,103
Dec. 2004	7.934	3,650	4,284
Dec. 2005	7,279	4,064	3,215
Dec. 2006	6,762	4,278	2,484
Dec. 2007	7,645	4,123	3,522
Dec. 2008	11,286	2,830	8,456
Dec. 2009	15,098	2,407	12,691
Dec. 2010	14,348	2,857	11,491
Dec. 2011	13,093	3,369	9,724
Dec. 2012	12,298	3,570	8,728
Dec. 2013	10,404	3,783	6,621
Dec. 2014	8,704	4,820	3,884
Dec. 2015	7,907	5,395	2,512
Dec. 2016	7,502	5,486	2,016
Dec. 2017	6,576	5,667	909
Jun. 2018	6,564	6,662	(98)

Recession peak) were looking at approximately 6.7 million job vacancies. The "official" job shortage had vanished.[10]

Yet the bottom line is that since 2000, the year when BLS began to generate the job vacancy data that lets us compare "officially" unemployed jobseekers v. job openings, a substantial job shortage—typically a ratio of 2:1 or more—has been the norm. The absence of a job shortage has proven the exception.

The severity of the "official" job shortage problem becomes more serious when we recall that, when adding up available jobs, BLS counts all job openings: seasonal as well as year-round, and part-time as well as full-time, regardless of the wage and regardless of the benefits.[11] Thus, to the extent that unemployed jobseekers—whether in bad times or good times—join the ranks of the employed, they may not be employed for long, may not work 30-40 hours per week, may not earn a good wage, or may not have health insurance or other important benefits.

When we examine the BLS data that contrast a broader measure of unemployed jobseekers vs. job vacancies, the U.S. job shortage worsens at all points in time. Table B-2 compares BLS's count of all those 16 years of age or older who want a job now, are available for work, and have searched anytime during the past 12 months (as opposed to only the prior four weeks) vs. BLS's count of job vacancies:[12]

Near the peak of unemployment, just after the Great Recession ended, this broader definition of unemployment meant in December 2009 that 17.6 million jobseekers (not 15.1 million) were looking at 2.4 million jobs. The job shortage was about 15.2 million jobs (not 12.7 million). As of June 2018, the ratio of seekers/vacancies stood at a much improved but still

Table B-2: US Job Shortage: 2000-2018
Broader Count of Unemployed Jobseekers v. Number of Job Openings
(in thousands)

Year	"Officially" Unemployed *Plus others* Wanting Job Now Available for Work Searched Last 12 Months	Job Openings	Job Shortage
Dec. 2000	6,820	4,736	2,084
Dec. 2001	9,589	3,385	6,204
Dec. 2002	10,080	2,943	7,137
Dec. 2003	9,823	3,214	6,609
Dec. 2004	9,424	3,650	5,774
Dec. 2005	8,883	4,064	4,819
Dec. 2006	8,190	4,278	3,912
Dec. 2007	9,006	4,123	4,883
Dec. 2008	13,180	2,830	10,350
Dec. 2009	17,612	2,407	15,205
Dec. 2010	17,045	2,857	14,188
Dec. 2011	15,688	3,369	12,319
Dec. 2012	15,004	3,570	11,434
Dec. 2013	12,923	3,783	9,140
Dec. 2014	11,038	4,820	6,218
Dec. 2015	9,782	5,395	4,387
Dec. 2016	9,200	5,486	3,714
Dec. 2017	8,176	5,667	2,509
Jun. 2018	7,977	6,662	1,315

troubling 8.0 million jobseekers (not the official count of under 6.6 million) vs. approximately 6.7 million openings. For roughly 1.3 million jobseekers, no job would be available even if every opening were filled. And as already noted, some of the job vacancies were seasonal, part-time, paid low wages, and lacked benefits.

There is yet another group that could arguably be defined as unemployed that I have not added in here. BLS also tallies persons 16 years and older who state they want a job, but who do not say they are available to work now and who have not searched for work (during the prior 12 months, much less the past four weeks).[13] They are arguably unemployed, but they are not jobseekers. For this reason, I do not include them here in my comparisons of jobseekers vs. job openings.

All of the prior measures of unemployed jobseekers share the premise that an unemployed jobseeker is an individual who has no paid work at all. Zero hours. But there is a significant body of workers counted by BLS who are employed part-time "for economic reasons" even though many of them presumably want full-time work and, in many cases, are available to take a full-time job and have recently searched for one.

BLS's definition of this category explains that it encompasses "those who worked 1 to 34 hours during the reference week for an economic reason such as slack work or unfavorable business conditions, inability to find full-time work, or seasonal declines in demand."[14] (BLS distinguishes this group from "persons who usually work part time for noneconomic reasons such as child-care problems, family or personal obligations, school or training, retirement or Social Security limits on earnings, and other reasons."[15]) During the Great Recession, the group of part-time workers for economic reasons climbed to over 9.1 million. In recent years, it has dropped substantially. In June 2018, the number stood at approximately 4.7 million.[16]

It would be highly subjective to attempt to divide the population of those who are employed part-time "for economic reasons" into (A) those who are not available to do additional work vs. (B) those who, akin to the "officially" unemployed, want more work, are available to do it, and have searched during the last four weeks (or perhaps the prior 12 months) for either additional part-time work or a full-time job. But for the purposes of fully understanding the U.S. job shortage, it is helpful to compare the sum of unemployed jobseekers *plus* part-time workers "for economic reasons" vs. job vacancies.

Table B-3 adds together (1) the "officially" unemployed, (2) the jobless (not double-counting "the officially" unemployed) who want a job now, are available to work now, and searched during the prior 12 months (but not the prior four weeks), and (3) all part-time workers "for economic reasons." The table then contrasts this total with the official JOLTS measure of job openings.

Even if, in addition to the "officially" unemployed, only 50% of (2) + (3) were in fact "active" jobseekers—that is: wanted work, were available to work, and earnestly sought work during a recent period—comparing them with the number of job openings leads to a clear conclusion. Most of the time, far more unemployed and underemployed Americans desire paid work than the U.S. labor market makes available. In bad times, the gap is enormous. In good times, the job shortage is still typically large.

Table B-3: US Job Shortage: 2000-2018
More Comprehensive Count of Unemployed v. Number of Job Openings
(in thousands)

Year	"Officially" Unemployed *Plus others* Wanting Job Now Available for Work Searched Last 12 Months *Plus others* Working Part-Time For Economic Reasons	Job Openings	Job Shortage
Dec. 2000	10,063	4,736	5,327
Dec. 2001	13,982	3,385	10,597
Dec. 2002	14,401	2,943	11,458
Dec. 2003	14,573	3,214	11,359
Dec. 2004	13,851	3,650	10,201
Dec. 2005	12,998	4,064	8,934
Dec. 2006	12,377	4,278	8,099
Dec. 2007	13,624	4,123	9,501
Dec. 2008	21,209	2,830	18,379
Dec. 2009	26,710	2,407	24,303
Dec. 2010	25,980	2,857	23,123
Dec. 2011	23,859	3,369	20,490
Dec. 2012	22,947	3,570	19,377
Dec. 2013	20,750	3,783	16,967
Dec. 2014	17,855	4,820	13,035
Dec. 2015	15,809	5,395	10,414
Dec. 2016	14,754	5,486	9,268
Dec. 2017	13,091	5,667	7,424
Jun. 2018	12,720	6,662	6,058

CONCLUSION

No matter how you slice the BLS data, you get what economists call a "demand deficiency" and ordinary folks call "not enough jobs to go around." With occasional exceptions, far more adult American jobseekers without work or without enough work want jobs than the labor market can provide. The U.S. job shortage is real. It is occasionally gigantic. It is frequently big. Its size fluctuates. Occasionally, the most conservative measure of the job shortage shrinks to a residual level or even vanishes. But most of the time, the BLS data confirm that a significant aggregate job shortage exists, whatever the conventional wisdom may be.

APPENDIX C

DEFINING AN ADEQUATE INCOME

How much is an adequate income? What is the target that full-time work at a higher federal minimum wage *plus* a single, simpler, and bigger earnings supplement ought to reach? Any answer will be subjective and subject to debate. That fact, however, should neither terminate the discussion nor prevent us from picking dollar amounts.

The poverty line is clearly not the answer. It would simplify things if we could use the poverty line as the beginning of an adequate income. But neither its history nor its structure justifies the use of the poverty line as the start of income adequacy.

The official federal poverty line, hastily constructed by Mollie Orshansky in the early 1960s, piles a stack of questionable decisions and outdated assumptions on top of one another to calculate a series of "poverty thresholds" for different family sizes. Orshansky constructed the official poverty line in 1964 by starting with the U.S. Department of Agriculture's cost for USDA's nutritionally deficient "economy food plan." She then multiplied that cost times three based on a one-time, out-of-date USDA survey showing that low-income families in 1955 spent one-third of their income on food.

The "economy food plan" piece of the formula involved far fewer dollars than a family truly needed even in 1955 to achieve a basic nutritional diet. The USDA had arbitrarily pegged the "economy food plan" at 20% less than the USDA's "low-cost food plan." The latter, Orshansky explained, had "long been used as a guide for families who must watch food expenses."[1] The 20% lower "economy food plan" by January 1964, with respect to a four-person family, was 23¢ per person per meal, 70¢ per person per day, and $4.60 per person per week. There was no allowance for meals away from home, between-meal snacks, or food for guests.

As Orshanky noted, the USDA's "economy food plan" was "designed for short-term use when funds are extremely low." She further explained: "If a family follows this plan exactly, adequate nutrition is attainable, but in practice nearly half the families that spent so little fell far short: of families spending at this rate in 1955, over 40% had diets that provided less than two-thirds the minimum requirements of one or more nutrients."[2]

Meanwhile, the second part of the formula for the poverty line—the 1:3 ratio of food costs to total income—was no longer true in the early 1960s and grew less true over time. According to a 2016 report by the Pew Charitable Trusts, food typically consumed 10% of family pre-tax income—nowhere close to a one-third—during the nearly two decades from 1996 through 2014. Families' primary expense was housing, which typically accounted for over 20% of pre-tax income during the 1996-to-2014 period. Over the past two decades, spending on housing increased for Americans in all income tiers. By 2014, the typical lower-income household spent far more on housing as a share of income (40%) than those in the middle (25%) or at the top (17%).

Lower-income renters (as opposed to homeowners) spent close to 50% of their pre-tax income on rent.[3]

If using the one-to-three ratio of food costs to total income made some sense in the early 1960s, the decision to continue to bake that ratio into the construction of a poverty line for over 50 years has made less and less sense over time. It makes no sense today.

Defining the U.S. poverty line by multiplying the cost of a 60-year-old, nutritionally deficient food plan times a hopelessly outdated and insufficient 1:3 ratio of food costs to total income, and then multiplying the product each year by the Consumer Price Index, is not merely subjective. It is irrational (except as a way keeping track, and measuring change, by applying the same yardstick).

Even if the official federal poverty line retains a shred of validity as a poverty line—that is: a sensible border between penury and want—it has no validity as a boundary between an inadequate income and an adequate income, i.e., enough to maintain a minimally decent standard of living. Orshansky acknowledged early on that the poverty thresholds indeed produced an "underestimate of poverty" and should not be taken as yardsticks for defining an adequate income.[4] She later wrote of her creation: "The best you can say for the measure is that at a time when it seemed useful, it was there."[5]

What, then, about the emerging successor to the official federal poverty line, the Supplemental Poverty Measure (SPM)?

In response to the shortcomings of estimating poverty in the U.S. by using the official poverty line, a group of experts joined with the Bureau of Labor Statistics and the Census Bureau to formulate a new and better poverty measure, the SPM.[6] One departure from the official poverty measure is the opposite of subjective and arbitrary. The official poverty measure counts only cash resources. It fails to take into account the non-cash resources that millions of low-income Americans actually receive, e.g., refundable tax credits like the EITC and SNAP (Food Stamp) benefits. The SPM, in contrast, was fashioned and has been deployed to count both the cash and major non-cash resources that low-income individuals actually have at their disposal.

In counting this broader set of resources, the SPM deducts from the total "necessary expenses for critical goods and services." This offset adds an element of subjectivity. What are "necessary" expenses? What is a "critical" good or service? Reasonable people will differ. But on the whole the SPM's approach towards counting resources moves in the direction of objectivity and accuracy.

But the SPM's methodology for calculating its new poverty thresholds, while less odd than the methodology used in setting the official poverty line, is still quite subjective and arbitrary. The SPM takes the 33rd percentile of Americans' expenditures for a "basic set of goods" — food clothing, shelter and utilities (FCSU) — and multiplies it by 120%. It then adjusts the product for family size. But why does the "basic set of goods" exclude transportation, even though virtually all families must incur vehicle or transit costs to go to work, shop, and live their lives? Why, given the arbitrary decision to limit the "basic set of goods" to FCSU, is the 33rd percentile of the cost of FCSU the most appropriate choice of a percentile? Why not the 25th percentile, or the 40th percentile? Finally, why multiply the chosen 33rd percentile by 120% to account for needs other than FCSU? Why not multiply by 115% or 125%? All of the choices that feed into the SPM's thresholds (as opposed to the counting of resources) are subjective and arbitrary.

It is also essential to remember that the SPM, despite its technical differences from the official poverty measure, nonetheless has the same purpose. As its name makes clear, the SPM measures poverty. Its aim is to determine how many Americans are poor by setting and applying a more credible series of boundaries between penury and want. Like Mollie Orshansky's original poverty thresholds, however, the SPM's thresholds were never meant to define a minimally adequate income needed to maintain a decent level of comfort in the U.S.

In the end, the official poverty line and the SPM produce similar thresholds and results. Tables C-1 and C-2 show the similarity between (A) the official poverty line in 2017 vs. SPM's thresholds in 2017 for a four-person family, and (B) how many Americans counted as poor in 2017 using the two different yardsticks. The fact that both the official poverty line and the

Table C-1: Official vs. SPM Poverty Thresholds—Two Adults with Two Children: 2017	
Measure	**Threshold Amount**
Official Poverty Line	$24,858
SPM: SPM: Owners With Mortgages	$27,085
SPM: Owners Without Mortgages	$23,261
SPM: Renters	$27,005

Table C-2: Percentage of Poor Americans: Official Measure vs. SPM: 2017		
	Official Measure	SPM
All people	12.3%	13.9%
Under 18 years	17.5%	15.6%
18-64 years	11.2%	13.2%
65 years and over	9.2%	14.1%

SPM thresholds end up with roughly similar dollar amounts for a four-person family—coupled with the fact that the total percentage of Americans living in both official poverty and SPM poverty are similar (although differences exist, particularly between subgroups)—underscores the conclusion that, like the official poverty line, the SPM can only be used to gauge poverty, not how many Americans have enough resources to maintain an adequate living standard. [7]

The preceding critique of the official poverty line and the SPM should not be understood as a criticism of the integrity, good faith, honorable intentions, hard work, or creativity of Mollie Orshansky, her colleagues in the 1960s, or the more recent authors of the SPM. They did the best they could in trying to turn an abstraction—poverty—into a ladder of specific dollar thresholds. No matter how they approached the task, however, the result would inevitably be subjective and arbitrary. And as Orshansky noted in the 1960s, no matter how we define poverty, the resulting thresholds remain borderlines between poverty and just-above-poverty within the territory of income inadequacy. They distinguish penury from want. They do not represent what either experts or the American people would consider to be the minimally adequate income needed to provide a decent level of comfort in the United States.

Because both the official poverty line and the SPM are subjective and limited in purpose to marking the boundary between penury and want, a better way to define a minimally adequate income for the U.S. is to ask the American people themselves what they believe is a minimally adequate income. The public's "gut-feeling" answers will also be subjective and arbitrary. But public opinion on this matter has several advantages. It reflects the lived experience of the U.S. population, i.e., the public's day-to-day, year-to-year judgment about the cost of maintaining what they perceive is a minimally adequate living standard. Using the American public's real-life judgment about how much income is required to "get by" may also make it easier for the nation's voters and policy-makers to accept the use of a specific set of fixed income goals in formulating public policy.

Before proceeding, let us restate the primary policy question we are tackling in this appendix. How large — atop a full-time job at a higher minimum wage that rises to $12 per hour — should a single, simpler, bigger U.S. earnings supplement be in order to ensure that the sum of (1) full-time, year-round earnings at the new minimum wage, plus (2) the revised earnings supplement, produces a minimally adequate income for American families of different sizes?

The policy question can be further quantified. With the earnings piece of the equation fixed — 40 hours/week x 52 weeks/year x $12/hour = gross income of $24,960 — how many additional dollars should the earnings supplement provide to reach (or get a bit over) the minimum amount needed, on average across the country for families of different sizes, to attain a minimally adequate income and living standard?

Fortunately, we have data about what Americans as a whole think is enough money to maintain a minimally adequate standard of living. Several times over the past decades, most recently in 2013, the Gallup Poll has asked a cross-section of Americans to specify "the smallest amount of money a family of four needs to make each year to get by."[8] The lower-income group in the Gallup Poll's 2013 sample (i.e., those with less than $30,000 per year) indicated on average that "the smallest amount of money a family of four needs to make each year to get by" was $43,600. The entire cross-section of Americans polled by Gallup stated that an annual income of $50,000 per year and $58,000 per year were, respectively, the median and mean amounts needed by a four-person family to "get by."[9]

Relying on the Gallup survey, and based on a few simple assumptions, I have calculated the amounts shown in Table C-3 as the 2017 income levels that U.S. families of different sizes needed in order to have a minimally adequate income.

Here are the assumptions made in creating the 2017 adequate income thresholds listed in Table C-3:

- Accept the amount chosen by the lower-income group (those with household incomes below $30,000 annually) that Gallup polled in 2013 as the minimally adequate annual income needed for a family of four to "get by": i.e., $43,600 per year;

- Account for inflation between 2013 and 2017, and settle on a round number, by adjusting the 2017 threshold for a four-person family to $44,000;

- Recognize that, as family size rises from one person to four persons (with its adequate income threshold of $44,000 per year)—and then rises further from four persons to eight persons—achieving a minimally adequate income for each family size will require an extra per-person increment of income. Each increment's dollar amount will decline as family size grows. Assume the following increments:

  - *Single Person vs. Two-Person Family*: Compared to a lower-income single person who often has one or more roommates to split the cost of a rented apartment, a two-person family— especially when the second person is a child— is likely to need to rent an entire apartment. This typically entails a large increase in cost. Rent, utilities, and other housing costs will all be substantially higher. Food, clothing, and other costs will increase sharply. The increment in going from one person to two persons is assumed to be $6,000.

  - *Two-Person Family vs. Three-Person Family*: Going from a two-person household to a three -person household often means going from a smaller to a larger apartment, which often involves a substantial increase in rent. However, some of the housing costs will be fixed. For example, there will be no need for a more costly stove, cooktop, microwave, or washer/ dryer. Other costs will increase, but modestly, e.g., utilities. Yet other costs will rise significantly, such as food and clothing. The increment in going from two persons to three persons is assumed to be $5,500.

  - *Three-Person Family vs. Four-Person Family*: Going from a three-person to a four-person household, thus bringing us to our "target" four-person family, would still involve a significant increase, but again a smaller one. Housing costs would not increase substantially if the number of bedrooms remains unchanged. Some clothing can be passed on from older to younger children. The increment in going from three persons to four persons is assumed to be $5,000.

- *Additional Family Members:* For each additional family member, the marginal increase in housing costs will be modest. The opportunities to share bedrooms, pass on clothing, share toys, reuse books, etc. will increase. The increment for each additional family member is assumed to be $1,750.

The preceding adjustments result in the per-family thresholds for an adequate income shown in Table C-3. The adjustments are consistent with the methodology that the existing Earned Income Tax Credit (EITC) uses to steadily taper the growth in its maximum credit increments in going from a single person to two-person, three-person, and four-person families (i.e., families with one, two, and three or more dependent children). The 2017 declining EITC increments, coupled with the constant Child Tax Credit (CTC) increment, were $3,890 in going from a single person to a two-person/one-child family; an additional $3,216 in going to a three-person/two-children family; and an extra $1,702 in going to the "target" four-person/three-children family. The EITC itself provides no additional increment beyond three dependent children. The increment for the CTC is the same for each dependent child.

Table C-3: Adequate Income Based on 2013 Gallup Poll for 2017	
Family Size	**2017 Adequate Income**
1 Adult *plus* following number of Children	Based on 2013 Gallup Poll Question and this appendix's Assumptions and Methodology
0	$27,500
1	$33,500
2	$39,000
3	$44,000
4	$45,750
5	$47,500
6	$49,250
7	$51,000

Table C-4 compares the official federal poverty line for 2017 vs. the higher proposed amounts that, based on the Gallup Poll and this appendix's just discussed assumptions and methodology, I use in this book as the thresholds for an adequate income. As the last two columns in Table C-4 show, the proposed adequate income amounts are much greater than the poverty line for all family sizes.

Based on the recommended amounts for an adequate income, calculating the maximum earnings supplements for different family sizes is simple. The maximum earnings supplement is approximately the amount needed to fill the gap between full-time, year-round work at $12 per hour, i.e., $24,960, and the higher 2017 amounts shown in both Table C-3 and Table C-4 as the threshold for an annual adequate income for different family

Table C-4: Comparison of Poverty Line and Adequate Income Thresholds: 2017				
Family Size	Poverty Line	Adequate Income	Change: Adequate Income Over Poverty Line	
1 Adult *plus* following number of Children:	Amount	Amount	Dollar Increase	Percent Increase
0	$12,060	$27,500	$15,440	228%
1	$16,240	$33,500	$17,260	206%
2	$20,420	$39,000	$18,580	191%
3	$24,600	$44,000	$19,400	179%
4	$28,780	$45,750	$16,970	159%
5	$32,960	$47,500	$14,540	144%
6	$37,140	$49,250	$12,110	133%
7	$41,320	$51,000	$ 9,680	123%

sizes. Table C-5 shows what those maximums would be. The maximum earnings supplement amounts have been rounded off to simpler numbers to make them easier to understand and compare.

The maximum earnings supplement amounts shown in Table C-5 are used in Chapter Five in constructing the full earnings supplement formulas spelled out in detail in that chapter. As noted, this appendix calculates the maximum earnings supplements for the year 2017. The maximums would

Table C-5: Maximum Earnings Supplement: 2017			
Family Size	Full-Time Earnings	Adequate Income	Proposed Maximum Earnings Supplement
Worker Alone	$24,960	$27,500	$3,000
Worker + 1 Child	$24,960	$33,500	$9,500
Worker + 2 Children	$24,960	$39,000	$15,000
Worker + 3 Children	$24,960	$44,000	$19,500
Worker + 4 Children	$24,960	$45,750	$21,300
Worker + 5 Children	$24,960	$47,500	$22,025
Worker + 6 Children	$24,960	$49,250	$24,675
Worker + 7 Children	$24,960	$51,000	$26,250

have been somewhat lower in 2015, the year selected for the budget recalculation summarized in Chapter Six and explained in detail in Appendix D. The earnings supplement maximums would, of course, be slightly higher in 2018 and (assuming inflation) in future years.

Table C-6 confirms that the sum of (A) full-time, year-round earnings at $12 per hour, i.e., $24,960 (shown in the 2nd column) plus (B) the proposed earnings supplement maximums (shown in the 3rd column) do indeed produce (C) an annual income (shown in the 4th column), that somewhat exceeds (D) the proposed adequate income thresholds for different family sizes (listed in the 5th column), typically by (E) 1% or 2%, as shown in the final column.

Table C-6: Earnings Plus Earnings Supplement Compared to Adequate Income: 2017					
Family Size	Annual Earnings	Maximum Earnings Supplement*	Annual Income	Adequate Income**	Annual Income as a % of Adequate Income
1 Adult plus number of Children:	Full-Time Year-Round Work at $12/hour	Per Year	Earnings plus Supplement		
0	$24,960	$3,000	$27,960	$27,500	102%
1	$24,960	$9,500	$34,460	$33,500	103%
2	$24,960	$15,000	$39,960	$39,000	102%
3	$24,960	$19,500	$44,460	$44,000	101%
4	$24,960	$21,300	$46,260	$45,750	101%
5	$24,960	$22,025	$47,985	$47,500	101%
6	$24,960	$24,675	$49,635	$49,250	101%
7	$24,960	$26,250	$51,210	$51,000	100%

* As proposed in Table C-5 and Chapter Five
** Based on Gallup Poll and this appendix's assumptions and methodology

For every family size, the resulting annual income is greater than the corresponding adequate income thresholds by $200 to $900 per year. The final column of Table C-6 expresses this result in percentages. For every family size, annual income is slightly higher than 100% of the adequate income benchmarks.

Finally, it should be noted that the proposed earnings supplement formula spelled out in Chapter Five is federal. A state or locality would be free to top up the supplement if it felt more was needed to reach the state's or locality's higher income target.

Appendix D
How a New Deal 3.0
Changes Budgets

AN IMPORTANT TEST THAT THIS proposed reform of American government must meet is the Numbers Test. This is especially true because the proposed redesign is so large in scope, encompassing at least a dozen big interwoven policy changes and scores of smaller ones.

What will the new policies cost and save? Will they raise or lower total spending, and by how much? What will happen with taxes and fees? How will total revenue change? Will the resulting budgets balance? Do the resulting budgets consume a reasonable but not an excessive share of individuals' income and corporate profits?

The 2015 budget recalculation summarized in Chapter Six ("Running the Numbers"), and detailed in this appendix, confirm that, if the proposed New Deal 3.0 had been a done deal as of 2015, the resulting government budgets would either balance or move towards balance. Regular spending, taxes, and total revenue would fall. Broad taxes (on property, sales, and income) would fall for lower-income and middle-class Americans, thus raising their disposable incomes. The YoungMedicare program, which (akin to the Workers' Compensation social insurance program) would operate outside the structure of regular government, would be expensive. But the premiums necessary to finance it would lower health care costs for both workers and business.

All dollar amounts for local, state, and federal spending and revenue (unless otherwise noted) come from Christopher Chantrill, usgovernmentspending.com.

A FEW WORDS ABOUT GOVERNMENT BUDGETS

Before digging into the numbers, I would like to explain the process followed in recalculating government budgets.

The heart of Chapter Six and this appendix is a budget "redo." It starts with the actual 2015 budgets of all local governments, all state governments, and the federal government. It then recalculates these budgets to show what they would look like if they were not based on current policies, but instead carried out the "complete change of concept" of the proposed New Deal 3.0 and implemented its major policy reforms.

It would be pleasant if this 2015 budget recalculation were a simple process, like 2+ 2 = 4. But just as the task of fashioning the governmental budgets we actually had in 2015 was a complex and messy business, so the task of reconstituting those budgets to carry out the aims and policies of the New Deal 3.0 (or, for that matter, any other sweeping reform) is rather complex and a bit messy.

There are several reasons why it is tough and untidy work to unpack, then repackage, the budgets of all levels of American government. Here are the main sources of difficulty.

First: Government budgets do not fall from outer space. They are crafted on earth by human beings. In the U.S., they ultimately depend on hundreds of choices by hundreds of elected officials. They thus rest on thousands of human judgments—many of which are equally plausible and equally responsible—about where to spend, how much to spend, and how to raise revenue.

Second: The guts of any government budget—exactly how much money to allocate to a program in a year, and exactly how much revenue to raise from taxes vs. fees in the same year—seldom depend on absolute formulas (like $a^2 + b^2 = c^2$). Occasionally, formulas come into play. But most of the big decisions depend not only on data but also on preferences, priorities, hunches, precedents, and feel-good percentages. At times, key budget choices seem—perhaps they are—entirely subjective and arbitrary. Here are just a few examples of policy choices that have profound impacts on today's government budgets but include a large degree of subjectivity and arbitrariness:

- Why is 26 weeks the duration of basic Unemployment Insurance benefits? Why not 20 weeks or 30 weeks? Does it have to do with the convenient fact that 26 weeks is half of the 52 weeks in a year, and half a year "feels like" the right length of time to give the unemployed a cash benefit?

- Why is the federal minimum wage $7.25 per hour? Why not $7.00? Or $7.50?

- Why does Medicare eligibility start at age 65? Why not 62 (when Social Security benefits first become available)? Why not 70 (when the Mandatory Minimum Distribution from an IRA begins)?

Third: Budgets inherently involve compromises and tradeoffs. A major driver of compromises and tradeoffs is the need to produce balanced budgets at the local and state level and the on-and-off pressure at the federal level to hold down deficits.

At the local and state level, all direct expenditures are supposed to add up to all revenue (including both "own-source" revenue and intergovernmental revenue). At the federal level, there is usually a deficit; but some sort of consensus eventually emerges as to how big the federal deficit will be. It should come as no surprise, however, that initial drafts of local and state government budgets usually result in far greater total spending than total revenue. At the federal level, early budget drafts usually produce "too high" a deficit to swallow. Furthermore, once mayors, governors, and presidents submit their formal budget proposals, city councils, state legislatures, and Congress often want to spend more and raise less.

Thus, as the process reaches endgame for formulating official executive budget proposals or cobbling together final legislative budgets, what seems like random game-playing with numbers, programs, and policy inevitably takes place. Compromises and tradeoffs become the order of the day. Thus:

- If the House wants to spend $125 billion more on Medicaid, but the Senate only wants to spend $65 billion more, the final result may end up at $95 billion simply because it's the midpoint. Both $125 billion and $65 billion were probably arbitrary figures to begin with. Splitting the difference is not really any more arbitrary. But it often seems so.

- If the House desires programs A and B to get more funding, and the Senate wishes to cut spending on X and Y, the result could be more money for A, less money for X, and no change for B and Y. Again, the two bodies' initial preferences may have been less the result of "good public policy" than the preferences of powerful committee chairs. But the compromise somehow seems more artificial.

- If spending exceeds revenue by 10%, the final outcome could be 2.7%, 6.9%, and 11.3% cuts in major spending programs, and 5.8% and 13.1% increases in taxes and fees. Why? Simply because those particular percentage changes yield a final bill that a legislative majority will pass and a chief executive will sign. The outcome seems utterly random. It gives support to the witticism, mistakenly attributed to Bismarck, that "laws, like sausages, cease to inspire respect in proportion as we know how they are made." But I prefer the sage comment of the president of a nine-member city council who remarked: "Five votes is policy." In the end, getting enough votes to settle arbitrarily on certain fiscal details may be the only way to complete the big policy picture.

This 2015 budget recalculation rests on hundreds of personal judgments that I made in translating the proposed New Deal 3.0 into fiscal reality. It reflects a large number of my individual preferences, priorities, and hunches. It channels as well my thinking about what precedents to apply and my instincts about going with certain feel-good numbers.

As part of the process, the budget recalculation also incorporates many compromises and tradeoffs (with myself) between competing objectives. Some of these compromises and tradeoffs are arbitrary at the granular level of "which number to pick." But I had to make them to achieve the five fiscal goals that I felt needed to be met to demonstrate that a New Deal 3.0 could achieve budgetary reform in a responsible manner.

Those overarching goals include:

1) less direct spending at all levels of government;

2) lower taxes at all levels;

3) despite raising fees, lower net revenue at all levels;

4) truly balanced local and state budgets that no longer run *de facto* deficits but instead achieve balance between local spending and "own source" revenue; and

5) a smaller federal deficit.

Despite the individual imprint, and notwithstanding the many compromises and tradeoffs, I believe that the following recalculation of 2015 government budgets is a reasonable effort to implement the major policies of the proposed New Deal 3.0 and honor the preceding five fiscal goals. Is it the only possible way to get that job done? Of course not. There are hundreds of other options. But what follows is a plausible estimation of what it would take to make a New Deal 3.0 come alive in a fiscally responsible manner.

THE BIG PICTURE

Tables D-1, D-2, D-3, and D-4 illustrate the changes proposed for 2015 for each level of government—local, state, federal—and for all governments combined.

Table D-1: Local Government Spending and Revenue: 2015 *(amounts in billions)*			
	Local Actual 2015	Local Proposed 2015	Local Change
Spending	$ 1,762.2	$ 1,172.8	$ (589.4)
All Revenue	$ 1,206.2	$ 1,180.5	$ (25.7)
Taxes	$ 694.5	$ 454.2	$ (240.2)
Utility Fees	$ 257.8	$ 472.3	$ 214.5
Other	$ 253.9	$ 253.9	$0
(Deficit) / Surplus	$ (556.0)	$ 7.7	$ 563.7

Table D-2: State Government Spending and Revenue: 2015 *(amounts in billions)*			
	State Actual 2015	State Proposed 2015	State Change
Spending	$ 1,634.1	$ 1,534.7	$ (99.4)
All Revenue	$ 1,554.9	$ 1,537.0	$ (17.9)
Taxes	$ 1,195.6	$ 1,107.8	$ (87.8)
Utility Fees	$ 36.5	$106.4	$ 69.9
Other	$ 322.8	$ 322.8	$ 0
(Deficit) / Surplus	$ (79.2)	$2.3	$ 81.5

Table D-3: Federal Government Spending and Revenue: 2015 (amounts in billions)			
	Federal Actual 2015	Federal Proposed 2015	Federal Change
Spending	$ 3,688.4	$ 3,616.2	$ (72.2)
All Revenue	$ 3,249.9	$ 3,246.5	$ (3.4)
Taxes	$ 3 ,153.4	$ 3,095.5	$ (57.9)
Utility Fees	$ 0	$ 54.5	$ 54.5
Other	$ 96.5	$ 96.5	$ 0
(Deficit) / Surplus	$ (438.5)	($ 369.7)	$ 68.8

Table D-4: All Governments' Spending and Revenue: 2015 (amounts in billions)			
	All Actual 2015	All Proposed 2015	All Change
Spending	$ 6,461.5	$ 6,323.7	$ (137.9)
All Revenue	$ 6,011.0	$ 5,964.0	$ (47.0)
Taxes	$ 5,043.5	$ 4,657.5	$ (386.0)
Utility Fees	$ 294.3	$ 633.3	$ 339.0
Other	$ 673.2	$ 673.2	$ 0
(Deficit) / Surplus	$ (450.5)	$ (359.7)	$ 90.0

SPENDING CHANGES

The table that follows, D-5, lays out the spending changes that would have occurred in government budgets in 2015 if a New Deal 3.0 had been in place.

Table D-5: 2015 Actual v. New Deal 3.0 Proposed Budgets: Estimated Spending Changes *(amounts in billions)*				
	Local	State	Federal	Total
2015 Actual	$ 1,762.2	$1,634.1	$ 3,688.4	$ 6,461.5*
Economic Security *Add:*				
+ Transitional jobs			$ 78.7	
+ Childcare program			$ 97.6	
+ Expanded SSDI			$ 117.1	
+ Improved Social Security			$ 37.1	
+ YoungMedicare purchase of services			$ 1.0 **	
+ Long-term care support during transition to LTC insurance			$ 125.0	
Transfer:				
K12 Education	$ (604.2)	$ 652.5	$ (39.5)	
Higher Education	$ (21.2)	$ (192.7)	$ 297.1	
Subtract:				
– Support for EITC/CTC			$ (80.7) ***	
– Means-tested welfare programs (including TANF, SSI, SNAP, LIHEAP, Medicaid, CHIP, ACA)	$ (58.6)	$ (519.1)	$ (621.1)	
– Subsidies for health programs			$ (5.7)	
Subsidies for Specific Economic Activity			$ (34.1)	
Public Safety, Health, Resources, Infrastructure	$ 93.5	$ (40.1)	$ (44.7)	
2015 Revised Total	$ 1,172.8	$ 1,534.7	$ 3,616.2	$ 6,323.7
Change from 2015 Actual*	$ (589.4)	$ (99.4)	$ (72.2)	$ (137.9)

Notes to *, **, and *** on following page

NOTES to Table D-5

* Sum of 2015 Actual local, state, and federal spending ($7,084.7 billion) exceeds 2015 Actual total ($6,461.5 billion) because double-counted local/federal and state/federal spending ($623.1 billion) has been subtracted from 2015 Actual total. This double-counting of spending for localities and states of 2015 Actual federal spending also explains why the Change From 2015 Actual sum of net local, state, and federal spending reductions exceeds the ($137.9) net total spending reduction shown in the final column. Numbers may not always add up exactly due to rounding.

** This assumes that the trustees of the YoungMedicare program would purchase administrative services from the U.S. Treasury and CMS to, respectively, collect the revenue required for the program and operate the program. This expense would be reduced or eliminated if the trustees of YoungMedicare chose other mechanisms to collect revenue and administer the program.

***Replacing the EITC and CTC, the much larger proposed Earnings Supplement (net estimate of $669.9 billion) would be paid for entirely as a refundable U.S. individual income tax credit.

NOTE: The proposed two broad, refundable, individual income tax credits—i.e., YoungMedicare tax credit ($455.2 billion) and the Earnings Supplement tax credit ($669.9 billion) — would be offset by the elimination of an equivalent amount of tax expenditures for specific types of consumption and investment.

Very large increases and decreases in spending are estimated at every level of government, but the net impact at every level would be less spending.

SNAPSHOT OF MAJOR SPENDING CHANGES

Following is a snapshot of each of the spending changes shown in Table D-5. To distinguish increases vs. decreases in this section, I highlight estimated *increases* in *italics*, while I show estimated decreases in regular typeface. After the snapshot, the spending estimates are explained in greater detail.

Transitional Jobs: The take-up of Transitional Jobs (TJ) by a large share of the nation's unemployed and underemployed adults, under the umbrella of a new federal program that guarantees TJs for jobless adults or part-time workers who seek additional hours of paid employment, is estimated to increase federal spending by *$78.7 billion.* (It is assumed that, in 2015, the federal TJ program has not yet evolved into a social insurance program.)

Childcare: Utilization of a new federal guarantee of childcare is estimated to raise federal spending by *$97.6 billion.* (It is assumed that, in 2015, the federal childcare program has not yet evolved into a social insurance program.)

Expanded SSDI: The additional federal cost of expanding the existing Social Security Disability Insurance (SSDI) program so that it covers all adults with a serious disability, and ensures each covered person a benefit that substantially exceeds the poverty line, is estimated to cost *$117.1 billon.*

Improved Social Security: The additional federal cost of raising the minimum Social Security benefit, so that retirees at 65 or older are guaranteed a minimum payment that substantially exceeds the poverty line, is estimated to cost *$37.1 billion.*

YoungMedicare: A *$1.0 billion* increase in spending by the U.S. Treasury and Centers for Medicare and Medicaid Services (CMS) reflects the assumption that the trustees of the National YoungMedicare Corporation would purchase services from those federal agencies to collect the revenue required for the program and help administer it.

Long-Term Care: Additional federal spending of *$125.0 billion* reflects the creation of a new program to provide frail seniors (for the most part) with needed long-term care support. (This represents a step in a longer process of transitioning to a new, federal, long-term care social insurance program. It is assumed that, in 2015, the federal long-term care program has not yet begun to operate as a social insurance program.)

K12 Education: More than offsetting the elimination of (1) local spending for K12 education (including state "school aid" transfers) in the amount of $604.2 billion plus (2) federal spending for K12 schools in the amount of $39.5 billion, state spending for K12 schools would increase by *$652.5 billion.*

Higher Education: More than offsetting large reductions in local and state funding for higher education (local spending would fall by $21.2 billion, while state spending would drop by $192.7 billion), federal spending for higher education would increase by *$297.1 billion* as part of the movement towards making in-state public college tuition free, reducing the cost of attending out-of-state public colleges, and lowering the cost of attending qualifying (i.e., non-ripoff) private colleges.

EITC/CTC: On-budget support for the federal Earned Income Tax Credit (EITC) and Child Tax Credit (CTC), totaling $80.7 billion, would end. This reduction, plus the simultaneous elimination of the larger portion of the EITC and CTC that is now treated as a tax expenditure, would be far more than offset by the creation of new, *$669.9 billion,* refundable, federal Earnings Supplement that is fully treated as a tax expenditure. (This reform is also discussed in the subsequent snapshot of how federal tax expenditures in general would be fundamentally reformed.)

Means-Tested Welfare Programs: Multiple means-tested welfare programs would be phased out. The programs in this category include:

1) Temporary Assistance to Needy Families (TANF);

2) Supplemental Security Income (SSI);

3) The Supplemental Nutrition Assistance Program (SNAP, aka Food Stamps);

4) The Low-Income Home Energy Assistance Program (LIHEAP);

5) Medicaid;

6) The Children's Health Insurance Program (CHIP, aka SCHIP); and

7) The subsidies provided through the Affordable Care Act (Obamacare) for persons below 400% of the poverty line.

Ending these means-tested programs by 2015 would have resulted in lower local spending of $58.6 billion, cuts in state spending of $519.1 billion, and reductions in federal spending of $621.1 billion.

Health Programs: A series of smaller categorical health programs, largely made unnecessary by the creation of YoungMedicare, would be eliminated. The federal savings would be $5.7 billion.

Subsidies for Specific Types of Economic Activity: To the extent these subsidies—and the government agencies that distribute them—appear "on budget," they would be eliminated. For example, federal agriculture subsidies in 2015 totaled $13.5 billion. The 2015 total amount of federal subsidies for what appear to be specific types of economic activity—that is: meant to favor a politically preferred type of consumption or investment—is estimated to be $34.1 billion. In this 2015 recalculation, those costs are removed from the federal budget.

Because of the quirks of federal budgeting, federal subsidy programs are grouped together with federal "businesses" like the U.S. Postal Service and deposit insurance. Such businesses in any particular year may make a profit or suffer a loss. To the extent a federal agency has a valid governmental purpose—such as delivering the mail, or insuring bank deposits—its revenues over time should cover its costs.

Strong oversight by Congress, the Governmental Accountability Office (GAO), and the Office of Management and Budget (OMB) should continue. But, like the finances of the Federal Reserve, the finances of unsubsidized government businesses that properly remain in operation should in time be moved "off-budget," i.e., handled outside of the regular federal budget process.[1]

Infrastructure: At the local level, spending on repairing and maintaining existing roads and bridges, as well as on transit systems, would be raised by *$93.5 billion*. State and federal spending, which largely focuses on building more freeway lanes, would be reduced: at the state level by $40.1 billion, and at the federal level by $44.7 billion.

Altogether, the 2015 budget recalculation would result in infrastructure spending going up by *$8.8 billion*.

DETAILS OF MAJOR SPENDING CHANGES

Let us now examine in much greater detail the major spending changes that, in implementing a New Deal 3.0, would have occurred in 2015 in government budgets.

Transitional Jobs: The recalculated federal budget would involve the creation of a new federal jobs-guarantee program, called Transitional Jobs (TJ), that would cost *$78.7 billion*. In 2015, according to BLS, the number of "officially" unemployed adults was 8.3 million.[2] Another group of adults not in the labor force, but who were available to work, wanted a job now, and had searched work (but not within the "official" timeframe of the prior four works) came to 2.0 million.[3] In addition, the number of adults employed part-time for economic reasons, i.e., who may have wanted and sought additional work, was as much as 6.4 million.[4] Thus, in 2015, a total of 16.6 million can be seen as the universe of U.S. adults who were unemployed in one form or another, and either wanted a wage-paying job or may have wanted additional paid work.

Different percentages of each group are likely to be willing to take up the offer of a minimum wage Transitional Job. It is reasonable to assume that the "non-officially" unemployed who have been jobless for five weeks or more would be the most likely to take up the offer of a TJ. At the other end of the spectrum, the "officially" unemployed who have been idle for fewer than five weeks may be less likely to be attracted to a TJ. They may have access to Unemployment Insurance benefits, and if so may have many additional weeks of UI benefits to go. They may have sufficient savings to justify holding off on a TJ as they explore higher-paying options in the regular labor market.

It is also reasonable to assume that those who already have part-time paid work will be less likely to be attracted to a TJ. In addition to possibly having a relatively less pressing need for income, they may be disinclined to work in a TJ for the minimum wage if their current part-time employment pays more than the minimum wage.

Table D-6 shows, for 2015, BLS's count of the number of unemployed in each group, the assumed percentages in each group that would take up a TJ offer, and the resulting number of estimated TJ workers. The estimate for 2015 of the total number of unemployed and underemployed who would work in a TJ is 4.2 million.

The following assumptions apply to the estimate of the cost of each TJ slot:

1) A minimum wage of $10 per hour (since the budget exercise is for 2015, prior to the full rise of the proposed hourly wage increase to $12 per hour);

2) A 40-hour workweek for the fully unemployed who are hired for full-time TJs and a 20-hour work week for those with part-time jobs who are hired for part-time TJs;

3) Each TJ slot would be filled an average of 48 weeks as the slot would be unoccupied for several weeks between when a TJ worker leaves it and a different TJ worker fills it; and

4) A 15% add-on to wage costs to cover the expense of employer payroll taxes (FICA, Medicare, and UI, as well as Workers' Compensation) and administration.

Based on these assumptions, the estimated cost in 2015 for each annual TJ slot would be $22,080 for full-time work and $11,040 for part-time work.

Table D-6: Estimate of Unemployed and Underemployed Who Would Work in a Transitional Job (TJ)			
		Estimated	TJ Participants
	Total in Category	*Percent*	*Number*
"Officially" Unemployed Adults:			
15 weeks and over	3,593,583	40%	1,437,433
5 to 14 weeks	2,308,250	40%	923,300
Less than 5 weeks	2,405,833	10%	240,583
Subtotal	**8,307,666**		**2,601,317**
Other Unemployed Adults:			
Not in labor force, searched for work and available, discouraged, want job now	664,417	20%	132,883
Not in labor force, searched for work and available, not discouraged, want job now	1,291,250	15%	193,688
Subtotal	**1,955,667**		**326,571**
Underemployed Adults:			
Employed part-time for economic reasons	6,373,330	20%	1,274,666
Total Unemployed & Underemployed Adults	16,636,663		4,202,553

Assuming the take-up rates shown in Table D-6 and the estimated cost in 2015 for each full-time TJ ($22,080) and part-time TJ ($11,040), Table D-7 presents the estimated 2015 cost of the overall TJ program: $78.7 billion.

Table D-7: 2015 Estimate of Cost of Transitional Job (TJ) Program			
	Assumptions		
	Number of TJ Participants	Cost Per TJ	Total Cost
"Officially" Unemployed Adults:			
15 weeks and over	1,437,433	$ 22,080	$ 31,738,525,056
5 to 14 weeks	923,300	$ 22,080	$ 20,386,464,000
Less than 5 weeks	240,583	$ 22,080	$ 5,312,079,264
Subtotal	2,601,316		$ 57,437,068,320
Other Unemployed Adults:			
Not in labor force, searched for work and available, discouraged, want job now	132,883	$ 22,080	$ 2,934,065,472
Not in labor force, searched for work and available, not discouraged, want job now	193,688	$ 22,080	$ 4,276,620,000
Subtotal	326,571		$ 7,210,685,472
Underemployed Adults:			
Employed part-time for economic reasons	1,274,666	$11,040	$ 14,072,312,640
Total Unemployed & Underemployed Adults	4,202,553		$ 78,720,066,432

Childcare Program: The recalculated federal budget would involve a new, free, federal childcare guarantee that is estimated to cost $97.6 billion. In 2015, according to the Census Bureau, the total number of U.S. children who were less than 1 year old, 1 year-olds, and 2-year-olds — *plus* half of 3-year-olds and half of 4 -year-olds — was 15,929,999.[5] (The other half of the 3- and 4-year-old population is assumed to be primarily enrolled in pre-school programs or kindergarten to the extent described in a subsequent section on K12 education.)

Not all of the parents or guardians of these 15.9 million children, even if there is no out-of-pocket cost for childcare, will choose to enroll their children in childcare. The assumption made here for 2015 is that 60% of the children, or 9,557,999 children, would be enrolled.

According to a 2016 report, the national average cost for one child at a childcare center was $196 per week, which (assuming 50 weeks a year) totals $9,800 per year.[6] To account for quality assurance and administrative costs, the 2015 budget assumption for the cost of childcare is $10,210 per child per year. Thus, the program's cost is estimated to be $97.6 billion.

The number of parents who decide to use childcare may well be less than 60%, although the percentage could be higher. Even if enrollment reaches 60%, some parents would not use childcare full-time or full-year. Also, since no means test would apply to eligibility for childcare, administrative costs would be limited. These factors would all tend to lower the program's cost. On the other hand, if a much higher percentage than 60% of children were enrolled, the program's cost would be higher.

As the minimum wage rises, the cost of the childcare program would increase over time. Also, if more parents opt for High-Quality Early Childhood Education, the average cost per child per year would also rise. In addition, experience may indicate that quality assurance and administrative costs need to be greater to ensure that all childcare meets high standards of safety, quality, and program integrity. Thus, while the $97.6 billion figure is a plausible estimate of the cost of the program for 2015, the actual cost could be different in either direction in that year and is likely to rise in the future.

It should be remembered that the $97.6 billion figure is the gross cost estimate for 2015 of a new, free, federal childcare program that would be available to all U.S. children from 0-4 regardless of family income. In 2015, however, the federal government already spent $5.1 billion on means-tested childcare programs. That expenditure and program would be eliminated. The assistance it provides to low-income parents would be absorbed by the new universal program. The net cost of the new program would thus be $92.5 billion.

Some children older than 4 years of age will need childcare if their parents work second-shift or third-shift jobs (or attend school at night), but no responsible older sibling, parent, or trusted relative or friend is able to care for the children until their parents return. Arguably, the eligibility rules of the childcare program for 0- to 4-year-olds should be modified to free up a portion of its cost ($97.6 billion in 2015) to provide free childcare for some of these older children.

Alternatively, it may be reasonable to ask parents—almost none of whom, under a New Deal 3.0, will be poor or even have less than adequate incomes if they work (as explained in Chapter Five)—to pay out-of-pocket for a portion of the cost of placing their older children in childcare if they work a late shift and can find no responsible child-minder.

With a dramatic increase in the federal investment in childcare (i.e., the additional $92.5 billion in 2015), it is reasonable to expect that the challenge of providing free-to-affordable childcare can be met. Major adjustments and much fine-tuning, however, are likely to be necessary along the way.

Expanded SSDI: The recalculated federal budget would involve a major revision of the current federal Social Security Disability Insurance Program (SSDI). The gross cost of the new program is assumed to increase spending by $117.1 billion.[7]

The following assumptions were made in reaching this estimate:

- The existing means-tested Supplemental Security Income (SSI) program, which cost $56.3 billion in 2015, would be absorbed into SSDI. The SSDI social insurance program, which cost $146.3 billion in 2015, applies no means test but is now available solely to qualifying workers based on prior work effort.

- As a result of this absorption, SSI would be eliminated. Government spending on means-tested programs would thus be reduced by the cost of the SSI program, i.e., a reduction of $56.3 billion in 2015.

- However, the cost of SSDI would be greatly expanded as part of a two-part 2015 budget recalculation. First, as noted above, the $56.3 billion that the federal government spent in 2015 on SSI would be added to the $146.3 billion that the federal government spent in 2015 on SSDI benefits and administration. Second, the resulting sum — $202.6 billion — would be further increased by 30%, or $60.8 billion, to create an SSDI program that costs a total of $263.4 billion.

- The total increase in funding for SSDI—that is: the sum of the $56.3 billion transferred from SSI plus the additional $60.8 billion, for a total of $117.1 billion—is intended to provide resources sufficient to ensure that all U.S. adults between 19-65 whose disabilities truly prevent them from working would receive an adequate income that is well above the poverty line and between 75-90% of what Americans define as the adequate income needed to "get by." (See Appendix C, "Defining an Adequate Income.")

The additional expenditure actually needed to achieve this policy goal could be less or more than an extra $60.8 billion. The decision to increase the combined 2015 baseline (i.e., existing SSI plus existing SSDI spending) by 30% is arbitrary. The intent of the percentage is to signal a very big increase in spending. The actual percentage increase could be 20% or 40% or some other percentage.

Standing alone, the increase in SSDI eligibility and benefits will create an incentive to seek to enroll in the program. On the other hand, the combination of the following policies will create an incentive to give up disability benefits and, more importantly, refrain from applying for them in the first place:

1) making Transitional Jobs easily available to disability benefit recipients, applicants, and potential applicants;

2) raising the minimum wage; and

3) substantially increasing the Earnings Supplement.

A possible side-effect may be to increase the cost of the TJ program and Earnings Supplement.

Making it crystal clear that persons with a disability will get excellent health insurance regardless of their status as a disability recipient, unemployed worker, employed worker, or retiree (either through Medicare or YoungMedicare) may also constrain the cost of the restructured SSDI program. How the incentive to enroll in a more generous disability program would interact with incentives to exit or avoid the program is an important question, but the current state of evidence is probably insufficient to justify even a ballpark fiscal prediction.

Expanded Social Security: The recalculated federal budget would involve the expansion of the core Social Security retirement program. In 2015, the assumption is an added cost of $37.1 billion. The estimate is based on the simple assumption that overall Social Security payments in 2015 would have been 5% higher, or $37.1 billion more, rising from the 2015 actual of $741.5 billion to an estimated $778.5 billion.[8]

Higher benefits would be concentrated on—indeed, limited to—the lowest-income recipients. The goal is to guarantee, as quickly as possible, that all Social Security recipients get a payment that not only exceeds the poverty line, but also raises them to at least 90% of the minimally adequate income that Americans say is the least needed to "get by." (See Appendix C, "Defining an Adequate Income.")

Will 5% of the current Social Security base be sufficient to achieve this goal? Perhaps not. If not, the percentage should be steadily increased.

How to pay for the higher minimum benefit is a fair and essential question. The current panic in some quarters about the future "insolvency" of Social Security, however, is nonsense. The program faces fiscal challenges, but it is not in crisis. Social Security's fiscal pressures should not be allowed to prevent a grown-up discussion about how best to improve the program to ensure that no beneficiary is poor or near-poor. Nor should Social Security's fiscal challenges dampen thoughtful discussion about how to keep the program's revenues and expenses in sync over the long actuarial term. This is not the place to elaborate the many potential tools available to create a stable future for Social Security. But as Franklin Roosevelt, the patron saint of Social Security, might have said: "the only thing to fear about Social Security's future is fear itself."

Purchase of Services by YoungMedicare: The recalculated 2015 federal budget allocates $1.0 billion to the new YoungMedicare program. This amount is a relatively small placeholder to reflect the assumed decision by YoungMedicare's trustees to purchase specific services from two branches the federal government. It is assumed that the National YoungMedicare Corporation would contract with the U.S. Treasury to collect the revenue needed to finance the program. It is assumed that the Corporation would also contract with CMS to help administer the program.

There are practical reasons for making these assumptions. The U.S. Treasury already collects payroll taxes from employers for Social Security and Medicare, so adding a payroll-based premium to collect from employers would be relatively simple. Likewise, CMS has more experience than any other federal agency in administering a nationwide health insurance program, Medicare, that now provides enrollees with considerable choice. But it should be emphasized that both of these purchase-of-service arrangements would be voluntary on both sides.

Whether $1.0 billion is a correct estimate of the cost of both services is unknown. It is a "guesstimate." The final cost could be lower or higher.

Long-Term Care Funding in the Transition to LTC Insurance: The recalculated federal budget for 2015 allocates $125.0 billion to pay for long-term care, primarily for low-income adults, during what will necessarily be a lengthy transition from Medicaid's existing support for long-term care for low-income persons to a situation where a universal federal Long-Term Care (LTC) Insurance program takes over.

In 2015, according to Centers for Medicare and Medicaid Services (CMS) National Health Expenditure Data, Medicaid (including local, state, and federal funds) spent a total of $545.1 billion. Of that, Medicaid allocated $49.7 billion to nursing care facilities and continuing care retirement communities, $32.0 billion to home health care, and $92.4 billion to "other health, residential, and personal care."[9] Not all of the sum of the last three figures — that is: $174.1 billion — was for long-term care.[10]

According to the Kaiser Family Foundation (KFF), during overlapping Federal Fiscal Year 2016, out of Medicaid's total expenditure of $553.5 billion, 21.4% or $118.5 was spent on what KFF classified as "Fee-for-Service Long-Term Care."[11] Applying the same percentage to CMS's 2015 total for Medicaid spending (i.e., $545.1 billion x 21.4%) results in an estimate of 2015 Medicaid spending on long-term care of $116.7 billion.

As discussed in Chapter Five, the proposed New Deal 3.0 would eliminate Medicaid and other means-tested welfare programs. The budgetary impact of this fundamental change is detailed shortly. Accompanying the absorption of most of Medicaid's health insurance function by YoungMedicare, the proposed $125.0 billion addition to the recalculated 2015 federal budget would replace Medicaid payments for long-term care (at all levels of government). On top of the approximately $117 billion that Medicaid already spent in 2015 for long-term care, an additional amount—roughly $8 billion—would be added. The resulting $125.0 billion is intended as a temporary federal fill-in that would fade away over time.

The fill-in would continue, slowly shrinking, during a lengthy transition to a fully funded federal LTC Insurance program for all Americans. Over time, more and more adults who paid into the new LTC Insurance program would come to rely on that program for any long-term care they needed.

Eventually, the temporary program would terminate. During its lifetime and winding down, it will need to be means-tested, so as to use its limited resources for those most in need. Notwithstanding the defects of means-testing spelled out in this book, those problems can be tolerated for a temporary program that is phasing out. Once the temporary program ends, every American—regardless of means—would be a participant in the LTC Insurance program, which would operate on social insurance principles.

K12 Education: The recalculated 2015 budget would involve a fundamental transfer of responsibility as to which government pays for K12 education. In 2015 and going forward, local and federal spending would virtually disappear. States would assume almost the entire financial responsibility.[12]

Local government (i.e., primarily school board) spending for K12 education in the amount of $604.2 billion would end. Local governments could of course continue to operate K12 schools. But they would no longer levy taxes to fund them.

Federal spending for K12 education, mostly in the form of various grant programs, would be reduced by 99% from $40.0 billion to $0.5 billion, a $39.5 billion drop. A small amount of federal spending would be used to collect data, disseminate studies, and convene educators to share best practices.

In contrast, direct state government spending for K12 education would be increased by $652.5 billion—more than the sum of both reductions—from $6.6 billion to a total of $659.1 billion. (Note that local spending on K12 education that is now funded by state government is treated in this budget exercise as local spending, not state spending, to avoid double-counting the same expenditure as both local and state. Going forward, it would be entirely treated as state spending. Thus much of the increased state spending on K12 education is a bookkeeping exercise, although a significant portion of the increase is real.)

Overall, under the 2015 budget recalculation, spending on K12 schools would rise by $8.8 billion, from $650.9 billion to $659.6 billion.

The 2015 budget exercise's proposed $659.1 expenditure by states on K12 education results from the interaction of the following:

1) Estimates of the overall 2015 number of pre-school-age and school-age children;

2) Assumptions about the percentages who will enroll in pre-school programs and K12 schools, require special education services, and need help in learning English; and

3) Assumptions about the annual cost per student for each category of education.

Table D-8 pulls together the estimates I make about student enrollment and cost by category, i.e., (1) all pre-school and K12 students, (2) those who require special education, and (3) those needing ESL services.

My estimate of the total number of students enrolled in pre-school and K12 schools (59.9 million) is somewhat greater than the total number that the national Center for Education Statistics (NCES) reported as actually enrolling in K12 schools in 2015 (55.5 million).[13] I assume that a larger number of younger children would attend pre-school programs and kindergarten, and that fewer students would drop out, because of the reforms in school finance and accountability proposed in Chapter Five.

I assume an average "core" cost of $10,000 per student. This amount is based on data from both the Center for Education Reform and the National Center for Education Statistics.[14]

The estimate of the number of pre-school and K12 students with disabilities (6.9 million) is similar to the NCES count for

Table D-8: Estimated State Spending on K12 Education					
Age Groups	Total Children	Education Category	% Enrolled	Number of Students	Cost Total
US Children <19					
50% of 3 –4	3,982,500	Pre-School	75%	2,986,875	$ 29,868,748,500
5-9 years	20,481,130	K12	100%	20,481,130	$ 204,811,300,000
10-14 years	20,605,579	K12	100%	20,605,579	$ 206,055,790,000
15-17, 75% of 18	15,813,533	K12	100%	15,813,533	$ 158,135,325,000
Subtotal	60,882,741			59,887,116	$ 598,871,163,500
US Children <19					
Under 5	19,912,499	Special	4%	796,500	$ 5,575,499,720
5-9 years	20,481,130	Special	15%	3,072,170	$ 21,505,186,500
10-14 years	20,605,579	Special	11%	2,266,614	$ 15,866,295,830
15-17, 75% of 18	15,813,533	Special	5%	790,677	$ 5,534,736,375
Subtotal	76,812,741			6,925,960	$48,481,718,425
US Children <19					
Under 5	19,912,499	ESL	5%	995,625	$ 1,991,249,900
5-9 years	20,481,130	ESL	10%	2,048,113	$ 4,096,226,000
10-14 years	20,605,579	ESL	10%	2,060,558	$ 4,121,115,800
15-17, 75% of 18	15,813,533	ESL	5%	790,677	$ 1,581,353,250
Subtotal	76,812,741			5,894,972	$ 11,789,944,950
TOTAL					$ 659,142,826,875

2015 (6.7 million).[15] Because of the higher assumption about total enrollment (discussed in the previous paragraph), it is appropriate to assume a higher number of children with disabilities will receive special education services.

The 2015 budget recalculation assumes additional annual spending for students requiring special education services (i.e., in addition to the "core" amount of $10,000 per student) at an average of $7,000 per student. This is roughly a $1,000 per student increase from a calculation made in 2004.[16]

The estimates and cost assumptions for ESL Learners—that is: students who need help in learning English so they can succeed in school—are placeholders. The 2015 budget recalculation assumes additional annual spending for ESL learners at an average of $2,000 per student. Lowering or raising this set of figures will not appreciably affect the overall level of estimated K12 spending.

College Education: The recalculated 2015 budget for a New Deal 3.0 also involves a fundamental—but different—transfer of responsibility as to which government pays for college education. In the case of college education, from 2015 onwards, both local and state spending would drop by 50% or more. Federal spending, in sharp contrast, would increase nearly sixfold.

Local government spending on college education would be reduced by $21.2 billion, an approximately 50% decrease from $41.2 billion to $20.0 billion.

State government spending on college education would also be reduced. It would decline by $192.7 billion or 83%, from $232.7 billion to $40.0 billion.

The federal government's spending for college education would rise—by more than the sum of the local and state reductions—by $297.1 billion. The federal expenditure on college education would climb by 580%, from $51.3 billion to $348.4 billion.

Overall, spending on college education would increase by 26% or $83.1 billion. It would go from $325.3 billion to $408.4 billion.

For the most part, the large increase in federal spending on college education would involve providing qualifying college students with the resources they need to pay all or most of the cost of college tuition and fees. The funds would not be given to students in cash. Rather, students' Individual Progress Portfolios would be credited with resources sufficient to pay for full in-state tuition and fees at a public two-year or four-year college. The credited amount could also be used to defray a large share of out-of-state tuition and fees at a different state's public college, or pick up a portion of tuition and fees at an independently accredited (i.e., non-ripoff) private college. (For an explanation of the Individual Progress Portfolio, visit: www.govinplace.org/content/Individual_Progress_Portfolio.pdf.)

Following are the estimates and assumptions made in the 2015 budget recalculation about the number of young adults attending college and the amount of tuition the federal government would finance:

- The 2015 pool of potential college students is estimated to be 30,555,102.[17] The pool is comprised of:

    - 30% of 18-year-olds: 1,265,083

    - 80% of 19-year-olds through 24-year-olds: 21,527,974

    - 25% of 25-year-olds through 29-year-olds: 5,600,292

    - 10% of 30-year-olds through 34-year-olds: 2,161,753

- Of this pool of potential students, 75% are assumed to attend college. This is somewhat higher than the 69.2% college attendance rate for 2015 high school graduates.[18] An attendance rate exceeding 70% would be probable, however, given the proposed New Deal 3.0 policy of paying the cost—full or in large part—of college tuition and fees. The estimate for students who would actually have attended college in 2015 is thus 22,916,327.

- The number of students attending college is split 34%/66% between two-year colleges and four-year colleges, i.e., 7,863,445 students in two-year colleges and 15,052,881 in four-year colleges. The ratio is approximately the same as the historic division of students between two-year colleges and four-year colleges.[19]

- For the 2017-2018 school year, the College Board estimated tuition and fees at two-year colleges to be $5,000 per year and at four-year colleges to be $10,000 per year.[20] For convenience's sake, the same estimates are used for this 2015 budget recalculation. An additional $5,000 is provided in this estimate to defray a portion of the cost of room, board, books, transportation, and other expenses.

Multiplying the estimated number of students in two-year and four-year colleges by an estimated annual cost of $10,000 for two-year colleges and $15,000 for four-year colleges, the 2015 total amount that would have been credited to students' Individual Progress Portfolios for the purposes of paying for tuition, fees, and other expenses would have been $304.4 billion. This amount would comprise the largest part of the expanded federal investment in higher education, which (as explained earlier) would total $348.4 billion. The balance would provide funding for graduate students in those areas where the federal government determines financial support is needed to avoid shortages in research or workers.

The proposed drop in local and state spending of higher education does not mean a diminution in enrollment in local and state colleges. Localities and states would continue to operate an extensive mix of two-year and four-year colleges. Nor does the proposed change mean a reduction in total spending on higher education. As noted above, spending on higher education in the 2015 recalculated budget would have increased by 26% or $83.1 billion.

What would change, in this 2015 recalculation and going forward, is that the primary source of income for higher education—at least for the instructional component of colleges—would no longer come from a blend of local and state taxes and charges. Rather, of the total 2015 estimate of $408.4 billion for college education, the new approach calls for the federal government to fund approximately 85% of the total. Most of that would be directed by qualifying students, through their Individual Progress Portfolios, to their choice of accredited colleges.

Earned Income Tax Credit (EITC) and Child Tax Credit (CTC): The recalculated 2015 federal budget assumes the elimination from the regular federal budget of the cost of the refundable portions of the EITC and CTC, which in 2015 totaled $80.7 billion.

While the EITC and CTC in their current form would be eliminated, they would be replaced by a new, single, simpler, bigger, refundable federal Earnings Supplement Tax Credit. The estimated 2015 cost of this Earnings Supplement, including both the refunded portion and the non-refunded portion that would henceforth both be handled as a tax expenditure, would have been $669.9 billion.

The gross amount of the Earnings Supplement Tax Credit would be higher: $837.4 billion. However, the tax credit would be reduced by the filer's highest marginal tax rate. Assuming that the gross amount of the Earnings Supplement Tax Credit is reduced at an average rate of 20%, resulting in a reduction in the credit of $167.5 billion, its net cost would be $669.9 billion.

A later section on tax expenditures explains in detail the assumptions that result in these estimates for the proposed Earnings Supplement Tax Credit (as well the assumptions that underpin the proposed YoungMedicare Tax Credit).

Means-Tested Welfare Program: The recalculated 2015 budget assumes the phasing out by 2015 of spending on means-tested welfare programs. This means:

- A reduction of $58.6 billion in local spending;
- A reduction of $519.1 billion in state spending; and
- A reduction of $621.1 billion in federal spending.

Thus, the total reduction in 2015 government spending on means-tested welfare programs would be $1,198.8 billion.

The following programs would be eliminated: Temporary Assistance to Needy Families (TANF), Supplemental Security Income (SSI), SNAP (Food Stamps), Low-Income Home Energy Assistance Program (LIHEAP), public housing subsidies, Medicaid, Children Health Insurance Program (CHIP), Affordable Care Act subsidies, and others.

Subsidies for Health Programs: The federal government operates over a score of smaller health programs that either would no longer be needed, or would cost less, once the delivery of excellent health insurance to the under-65 population was guaranteed by YoungMedicare. The 2015 federal expenditure for these programs was $23.0 billion.[21]

The assumption made here is that approximately 25% of the cost of this set of programs, i.e., $5.7 billion, can be eliminated in light of the replacement of Medicaid, CHIP, and a large part of the ACA with the proposed new federal YoungMedicare health insurance program for the under-65 population. Medicare would not be affected.

Subsidies for Specific Economic Activity: Consistent with the New Deal 3.0 core policy of eliminating government subsidies for specific types of consumption and investment, the 2015 budget recalculation ends the federal government's subsidies in the following areas: farm subsidies; disaster relief and insurance; community development; and regional development.

The 2015 effect of eliminating these subsidized programs would to reduce federal spending by $34.1 billion:[22]

- $13.4 billion in farm subsidies;
- $9.0 billion subsidy for disaster relief and insurance;
- $7.8 billion subsidy for community development;
- $3.9 billion subsidy for area and regional development.

There are a number of other programs at the local, state, and federal level that historically received subsidies. These programs, however, operate as "businesses" whose expenses sometimes exceed, but at times come in below, their revenues. The question of whether parking facilities, the U.S. Postal Service, deposit insurance, and other activities that qualify as businesses should be owned and operated by government is an important question. Addressing it lies beyond the scope of this book. But whether such businesses remain under government control or not, the subsidies they receive should be eliminated. Like other businesses, they should be self-supporting. The fees they charge their customers should be made sufficient to cover their expenses.

It is important to stress that ending federal subsidies for the economic activities mentioned above does not mean ending the activities themselves. In 2015, as is true today and will be true in the future, we need farms to produce the long list of currently subsidized crops: barley, chickpeas (small and large), corn, cotton, oats, peanuts, dry peas, lentils, rice, sorghum, soybeans, and wheat. We likewise need disaster insurance, parking facilities, mail and parcel delivery, and deposit insurance.

What is not necessary—what is harmful—is to require taxpayers to subsidize these specific economic activities. If we want to ensure that farm families attain an adequate income, we should address that problem directly. The New Deal 3.0 does so by creating a mechanism—the Earnings Supplement Tax Credit—for raising workers' incomes to the level that the American people define as enough to get by. The same mechanism should be adapted to farm families. And assuming that we continue to want a society that provides disaster relief, parking facilities, mail and parcel delivery, and deposit insurance, we should expect the users of these services to pay the full cost.

Infrastructure: Finally, the recalculated 2015 budget assumes major changes in transportation spending.[23] Spending on roads and transit combined would rise from $242.7 billion to $318.7 billion. Packed into this aggregate $76.0 billion increase, however, is a major shift in spending priorities.

Roads: With respect to roads, there would have been a $17.2 billion increase in spending from the 2015 actual total of $172.3 billion to this recalculation's level of $189.5 billion. But how road dollars would have been spent in 2015 would have dramatically altered:

- Local spending would have risen to 65% of total road spending; state spending would have fallen to 30% of the total; and federal spending would be limited to 5% of the total.

- Maintenance of existing streets and other roads in their current configuration—that is, fixing potholes, cracks, and uneven road surfaces, and repairing at-risk bridges—would have taken 95% of all spending at all levels.

- The remaining 5% would have been used to demolish unneeded roadways, as well as pay for the very few new roads actually needed in the U.S.

These spending changes would be accompanied by treating all road systems as utilities, ending tax subsidies for roads, and requiring drivers to pay for the full cost of the roads, bridges, and tunnels they use. The elimination of subsidies for roads, and the obligation of drivers to pay user fees for the roads they make use of (with fees rising based on vehicle weight and the times of day when roads become congested) will create a strong economic incentive for drivers to modify their driving patterns, avoid congestion, and possibly switch to other means of transport.

Transit: With respect to transit, there would have been a $58.8 billion increase in spending, from a 2015 actual total of $70.4 billion to a recalculated $129.2 billion:

- Local spending would have risen by 70% based on the premise that, if both roads and transit were both operated as utilities whose users pay the full cost, there would have been in 2015 a significant increase in utilization of bus, streetcar, light-rail, subway, and regional train service.

- State spending would also have risen by 70%, based on the same premise, but with the state's involvement focused on increased utilization of regional, intrastate, and interstate rail systems.

- Federal spending would have decreased by more than half, reflecting the elimination of federal subsidies and the refocusing of federal transit policy on major interstate rail service.

These spending changes would be accompanied by treating all transit systems as utilities, ending tax subsidies for transit, and requiring riders or other users (e.g., employers and schools) to pay for the full cost of operating the buses and rail systems.

Since low-income workers, persons with disabilities, and retired seniors would have substantially higher incomes under the economic security policies of a New Deal 3.0, they would be able to pay normal fares for the roads and transit they use.

REVENUE CHANGES

The 2015 budget recalculation also rests on numerous revenue changes. The overall approach is to reduce broad taxes, particularly the regressive property tax. Cuts in taxation also have been applied to the other broad taxes—sales, individual income and corporate income—at all levels of government.

A strong case can be made that when reductions in governmental spending create the opportunity to lower taxes, the shrinking of the tax burden should be smaller in magnitude. This allows the buildup of "rainy-day funds" that (if carefully protected from raids) can be used to avoid draconian spending cuts or punishing tax hikes when economic downturns cause revenue to plummet. For the purpose of this 2015 budget recalculation, however, it is important to show that creating a New Deal 3.0 not only avoids increasing taxes but also permits significant reductions in tax burdens, especially for lower-to-middle income filers.

This book's overarching policy of eliminating subsidies for specific types of consumption and investment would mean, however, that tax bases would actually rise for the four major taxes—on property, sales, individual income, and corporate income—as dozens of tax expenditures are deleted from the tax system. Each tax base would be shorn of most of its exclusions, deductions, and special credits. As a result, the total amount of taxable property, sales, and income would jump. Unless action is taken to intentionally lower the burden of property, sales, and income taxation, individuals and firms would unintentionally end up paying higher taxes of each kind.

Since this budget exercise for 2015 aims to show that a New Deal 3.0 is compatible with lowering tax burdens, the simplest and most responsible way to achieve that goal in the context of rising amounts of taxable property and taxable sales would be to lower the tax rates that apply to property and sales. With respect to the rising amount of taxable income, two simple and responsible courses of action would be possible.

One path would be to raise standard deductions, i.e., the per-person or per-corporation amount of income that is exempt from taxation. Another path would be to lower income tax rates, keeping them progressive (i.e., rising with higher increments of income) but lowering each marginal tax rate. The two actions could be combined. This appendix does not recommend specific formulas for reducing tax burdens, with one exception.

A final section of this appendix on the federal individual income tax spells out a proposal for reforming that biggest of all taxes. It does not estimate specific tax base or tax rate changes. Nor does it present numbers. But it does outline the general principles that individual income tax reform should follow.

This 2015 budget recalculation therefore recommends major changes on the revenue side. Table D-9 highlights the major tax and revenue changes for 2015 that would have occurred at each level of government.

At the local level, the fall in taxation and rise in fees are both quite sizeable, with tax cuts significantly greater than fee increases. At the state level, smaller tax cuts are partially offset by yet smaller fee increases. A modest federal tax reduction would be a bit higher than federal fee increases. Overall, governments would see declines in total revenue.

Table D-9 illuminates the fact that the revenue changes included in this New Deal 3.0 budget reconstruction are not random. Rather, several key goals embedded in the redesign of the New Deal settlement provide the logic for why certain revenues fall while others rise:

- The goal of improving economic security — which requires greatly increasing the disposable income of low-to-middle income individuals — is the reason for reducing the broad taxes on property, sales, and individual income. Consistent with that goal, the intent is to ensure that the overwhelming share of these tax cuts accrue to low-income and middle-class Americans.

- The goal of strengthening the market, both by improving the profitability of businesses and by pushing back against cost externalization, is at once the reason for (A) cutting the corporate income tax, (B) raising taxes on alcohol and tobacco, (C) imposing a new carbon tax on CO_2 emissions, and (D) shifting from taxes to user fees as the basis for financing utilities.

Table D-9: 2015 Actual Vs. New Deal 3.0 Proposed Budgets: Estimated Revenue Changes *(amounts in billions)*

	Local	State	Federal	Total
2015 Actual Revenue Total:	$1,206.2	$1,554.9	$3,249.9	$6,011.0
Lower Broad Taxes on People and Firms				
– Cut general property taxes	$ (189.1)			$ (189.1)
– Cut general sales taxes	$ (32.7)			$ (32.7)
– Cut individual income taxes	$ (12.7)	$ (57.2)	$ (102.8)	$ (172.6)
– Cut corporate income taxes	$ (3.4)	$ (8.3)	$ (22.9)	$ (34.6)
Lower Excise Taxes and License Fees				
– Repeal gas tax	$ (1.3)	$ (42.5)		$ (43.8)
– Repeal airway and highway excise taxes			$ (55.1)	$ (55.1)
– Reduce vehicle license fees	$ (1.5)	$ (20.2)		$ (21.7)
"Side-Effect" Tax Increases Due To:				
– Motor fuel sales now covered by sales tax		$ 28.2		$ 28.2
– TJs > higher UI and payroll tax base		$ 0.1	$ 10.9	$ 11.0
Raise Narrow Taxes on Cost-Externalizing Economic Behavior				
– Alcohol tax and Tobacco tax	$ 0.5	$ 12.1	$ 12.0	$ 24.6
– Carbon tax			$ 100.0	$ 100.0
TOTAL TAX CHANGE: Net Change in All Taxes and License Fees	$ (240.2)	$ (87.8)	$ (57.9)	$ (386.0)
Require Users of Utilities to Pay Fees				
– Road utilities	$ 124.7	$ 41.4	$ 9.5	$ 175.6
– Transit utilities	$ 80.4	$ 27.4	$ 5.0	$ 112.8
– Airports and water ports	$ 0.8	$ 0.8	$ 30.0	$ 31.7
– Other utilities	$ 8.6	$ 0.4	$ 10.0	$ 19.0
TOTAL USER FEE CHANGE:	$ 214.5	$ 69.9	$ 54.5	$ 339.0
ALL REVENUE CHANGE: Taxes and Fees	$ (25.70	$ (17.9)	$ (3.4)	$ (47.0)
2015 REVISED REVENUE TOTAL	$ 1,180.5	$ 1,537.0	$3,246.5	$ 5,964

Numbers in rows or columns may not result in totals shown due to rounding.

DETAILS OF MAJOR REVENUE CHANGES

Following is a description of each of the significant revenue changes.

Property Taxes

The biggest revenue change in this budget recalculation is a huge 40% drop in local property taxes. In 2015, local governments collected $472.7 billion in property taxes. The re-estimate would drop that to $283.6 billion, a cut of $189.1 billion.

Because of the sharp drop in local spending due to the combination of three proposed policies—the transfer of the full cost of K12 schools to states, the elimination of means-tested welfare programs, and the shift in financing of roads and transit from taxation to user fees—there is no need for local governments to levy the frequently high levels of property taxes that many now impose. Renters in the long run, and homeowners as well as the owners of commercial and manufacturing property, should see big drops in their property tax bills.

Sales Taxes

The picture for general sales taxes, excise taxes, and license fees is messier. The sharp drop in local spending means that, to the extent local governments rely on these types of taxes, the tax rates they apply should generally be reduced and tax revenues should generally decline. But there is also sound reason to raise some of these taxes and fees as the direct consequence—or an indirect side-effect—of the overarching New Deal 3.0 policy of preventing cost externalization.

The following analysis walks through the 2015 recalculated re-estimates of revenue within the crowded arena of sales taxation for each level of government.

Local Governments: To achieve parity with lowering property taxation, the budget recalculation assumes a 40% reduction in general sales taxes, which some localities rely on heavily. In other words, if local property taxes are to be reduced by 40%, local general sales taxes should be reduced by 40%. In 2015, local governments collected $81.8 billion in general sales taxes. The re-estimate lowers that to $49.1 billion, a cut of $32.7 billion.

State Governments: For states, by contrast, the more modest decline in net spending (and the rationale for using almost all of the savings to cancel states' *de facto* operating deficits) argues against cutting general sales taxes, which represent a major source of spending for almost all states.

At the same time, the elimination of all taxpayer subsidies for roads, and the substitution of user fees to finance the full cost of roads, means that the gas tax should be ended. The gas tax is a special sales tax, labeled an "excise" tax. It is not a true user fee. There has always been a big disparity between the fixed per-gallon gas tax paid by vehicle users vs. the variable number of road miles they drive. The disparity between per-gallon taxes vs. the miles that users actually drive has steadily grown due to fuel efficiency gains and increasing reliance on batteries to propel cars. The dollar savings to drivers due to terminating the gas tax is discussed shortly.

The elimination of the per-gallon gas tax, however, should not spell an end to taxing the sale of petroleum products. Rather, motor fuels should simply be made subject to the same general sales taxes that states apply to other sales, i.e., based on the dollar amount of the sale. This budget recalculation estimates that, in applying their general sales tax rates to motor fuels, state general sales tax revenue would rise from $286.4 billion to $314.6 billion, a $28.2 billion increase. This would be offset, as will shortly be discussed, by the elimination of $42.5 billion in state motor fuel excise taxes.

Excise Taxes and License Fees

We now switch to (1) excise taxes in general, i.e., the special sales taxes that apply to unique products such as gas, alcohol, and tobacco, and (2) license fees related to vehicles that (since almost every adult has a driver's license and owns a car) are functionally the same as a tax.

Local Governments: Consistent with the rationale for ending the gas tax and relying on true user fees to pay the full cost of roads, the budget recalculation assumes the elimination of local governments' gas tax revenue, saving $1.3 billion. Also consistent with the switch from taxes to user fees to pay for roads, the recalculation also assumes a 90% reduction of local motor vehicle license fee revenue, from $1.9 billion to a $0.4 billion, saving $1.5 billion, to reflect the use of these fees to recover only the cost of issuing licenses and enforcing their validity. (If the evidence shows that local governments need more or less than $0.4 billion to perform this licensing function, the amount should be altered).

It is important to recognize, however, that local governments' collections of user fees to finance roads, bridges, and transit will result in a very large increase in that fee revenue. The growth in user fees is taken up later in the overall section on utility fees.

Partially offsetting the end of gas tax revenue and drop in vehicle license fee revenue, the budget recalculation assumes 50% increases in local excise taxes on alcohol and tobacco products, from a combined $1.1 billion to $1.6 billion, a $0.5 billion increase. This is intended to internalize to buyers and sellers of these high-risk products a greater share of the costs that they disproportionately impose on the general public, e.g., lost lives, injured health, and damaged property due to car accidents, building fires, and health expenses in general.

State Governments: As already noted, with the elimination of the state gas tax due to a shift to true user fees to finance roads, states' revenue from their gas taxes would drop by $42.5 billion. In addition, paralleling roughly the 90% proposed reduction in localities' vehicle license fees, states' much larger vehicle license revenue would be reduced by 80%, from $24.5 billion to $4.2 billion, a $20.2 billion decrease. Compared to the 90% cut at the local level, states would need to retain somewhat more of this revenue—thus: the 80% "only" cut—since states have added responsibility in issuing vehicle licenses and enforcing their validity, e.g., state troopers. (As at the local level, however, if the evidence shows that states in fact require more or less than $4.2 billion to perform this licensing function, the amount should be altered).

It is again important to recognize that state governments' collections of user fees to finance state-owned roads, bridges, and transit will result in a large increase in state user fee revenue.

That growth is reviewed later in the overall section on utility fees.

Offsetting in part the states' gas tax and vehicle license fee revenue losses, this budget recalculation assumes a 50% increase in state excise taxes on alcohol and tobacco products. In 2015, states collected a combined $24.1 billion in these taxes. The re-estimate is for $36.2 billion, a $12.1 billion increase in revenue.

Federal Government: Two excise taxes imposed by the federal government—its airway excise tax of $14.3 billion, and its highway excise tax of $40.8 billion—would be eliminated. For 2015, this would have reduced federal revenue by $55.1 billion. The replacement of taxes with user fees explains this policy. To the extent that the federal government owns or leases airports, roads, or transit, it would collect user fees to recoup the full cost of maintenance and operation.

As is true for both localities and states, the federal government imposes alcohol and tobacco taxes. Those excise taxes, too, would be increased by 50%. This would raise the combined sum of federal alcohol and tobacco tax revenue from $24.1 billion to $36.1 billion, a $12.0 billion increase.

Within the sphere of excise taxes, a very big change in proposed federal revenue for 2015 would result from the proposed carbon tax. This 2015 budget recalculation assumes $100.0 billion in carbon tax revenue. The purpose is simple: to decelerate (and in time reverse) global climate change by giving a strong incentive to U.S. emitters of CO_2 and other greenhouse gases to reduce their emissions.

As the discussion of government spending in Chapter Six and this appendix make clear, the $100.0 billion in carbon tax revenue would not be used to pump up government spending. It would instead enable the federal government to lower individual income taxes and corporate income taxes, as discussed in the next section. The money will in this manner be returned to the people and businesses of the United States.

Individual Income Taxes

Three policies—all related to economic security, and with one also related to ending subsidies for politically favored types of consumption and investment—drive this 2015 budget recalculation's approach to the individual income tax:

First: To improve the disposable income—thus, the economic security—of most Americans, the individual income taxes paid by lower-income and middle-class filers would be substantially reduced.

Second: While the focus of reforming the individual income tax should be on raising the disposable incomes of the vast majority of lower-income and middle-class filers, the top marginal top rate should not be set at an excessive level. For 2018, the top federal rate is 37%. Combined with payroll taxes and state income taxes, the combined top marginal rate in some states will approach 50%. It need not go higher (except during national emergencies).

Third: To (A) make sure that raising the disposable income of the vast majority of Americans is not artificially paid for by borrowing and ultimately put at risk; (B) keep the top marginal rate from rising; and (C) eliminate tax subsidies that manipulate consumption and investment, weaken the market's efficiency, and undermine the economy's capacity to build the nation's wealth; the dozens of tax expenditures that tilt the market in favor of politically preferred types of consumption and investment would disappear from the individual income tax.

Consistent with these three policies, the 2015 budget recalculation includes the following reductions in individual income taxes.

Local income taxes would be cut by 40%. This parallels the 40% reductions in local property taxes and sales taxes. In 2015, local income taxes produced $31.6 billion. The budget recalculation reduces that to $19.0 billion, a $12.7 billion decrease.

State income taxes would be cut by 17%. In 2015, states raised $336.2 billion in income tax revenue. The budget recalculation drops that to $279.1 billion, a decrease of $57.2 billion.

Finally, the federal individual income tax would be trimmed by approximately 7%. Actual federal 2015 revenue from this source was $1,540.8 billion. The budget recalculation reduces that to $1,438.0 billion, a $102.8 billion decrease.

Corporate Income Taxes

A central value of the New Deal 3.0 is that businesses should be helped in their struggle to make profits, but not via politically driven subsidies (or other devices) that manipulate the market in favor of particular businesses, economic sectors, or types of consumption and investment. Help that is general in nature and that helps all businesses more-or-less equally — including protection of property and enforcement of valid contracts, an excellent health insurance system, a powerful education system, and an up-to-date infrastructure financed wherever possible by its users in proportion to their use — is needed and appropriate.

But playing games with the market in order to steer consumption and investment in particular directions is harmful.

Consistent with this approach, it makes sense to keep corporate income taxes reasonably low. If they can be lowered in general, fine. To reflect the earnestness of this view, the 2015 budget recalculation replicates the percentage cuts in individual taxation for the corporate income tax. Like individual taxes, corporate taxes are cut by 40% at the local level, 17% at the state level, and 7% at the federal level.

Thus, in 2015, local corporate tax revenue would have fallen from $8.6 billion to $5.1 billion, a $3.4 billion decrease.

State corporate tax revenue would have fallen from $48.7 billion to $40.4 billion, an $8.3 billion decrease.

Finally, federal corporate tax revenue would have fallen from $343.8 billion to $320.9 billion, a $22.9 billion decrease.

Payroll Taxes

It is probable that many of the proposed policy changes that add up a New Deal 3.0 would increase the number of paid workers, thus increase earnings, and thus increase Unemployment Insurance, FICA (Social Security), and Medicare tax revenue. For example:

- Modifying the Unemployment Insurance program and the Social Security Disability Insurance (SSDI) program to enable benefit recipients to voluntarily convert a portion of their cash payments into earnings via Transitional Jobs, by increasing overall U.S. earnings, should increase payroll tax revenue.

- Raising the minimum wage as of 2015 to $10 per hour, and quickly thereafter to $12 per hour, while causing a measure of job loss, is likely to produce more-than-offsetting earnings gains, and thus increase payroll tax revenue.

- More effectively controlling health care costs via YoungMedicare will enable employers to increase the portion of compensation that employees receive as earnings, thus generating higher payroll tax revenue.

Estimating what these (and other) payroll tax revenue increases might have been in 2015 under this recalculated budget for a New Deal 3.0 generally lies beyond the scope of this book.

In one area, however, it is possible to present plausible estimates of a gain in payroll tax revenue. In the 2015 budget recalculation, the proposed nationwide Transitional Jobs program is estimated to cost $78.7 billion. The TJ program would pay $65.6 billion in total wages.

Depending on the state, as of 2017, the state Unemployment Insurance tax (known as SUTA) applies to individual's wages up to between $7,000 and $40,400. SUTA imposes tax rates between 0.1% and 12.0%.[24] Here, a 0.1% rate is assumed. This would add $65.6 million (not billion) in new SUTA revenue to states' 2015 base amount of $52.3 billion. Even if a 1% or 2% tax rate were assumed, which would exceed the minimum tax rate for almost every state, the increase in state governments' total SUTA revenue would be slight.

By contrast, federal FICA (Social Security) and Medicare taxes are easy to calculate. The combined FICA/Medicare tax rate is 7.65% paid by workers and an equal 7.65% paid by their employers. The new revenue due to TJ wages would result in estimated higher federal UI, FICA, and Medicare taxes of $10.9 billion.

Utility Fees

Finally, we come to utility fees. The basic idea is that government utilities—or functions that should be organized as utilities—should have their full costs entirely financed by fee revenue collected by the responsible local, state, or federal government.

In the case of some government utilities, costs are already covered (in whole or in part) by fee revenue. For other government utilities, however, tax subsidies are so large that costs are offset by only small amounts—even no amounts—of fee revenue.

Based on the difference between (A) this 2015 budget recalculation's estimated cost of actual or *de facto* government utilities, less (B) any fee revenue already collected, the following additional fee revenue would have been collected.

Roads, Bridges, and Tunnels: As discussed in the spending section, local spending on the repair and maintenance of existing roads, bridges, and tunnels would have been much higher. This budget recalculation would increase 2015 spending on the local road system from $68.0 billion to $132.3 billion, a $64.3 billion increase. (Note that this is an increase in spending, not fees.)

Taxpayers—mostly local taxpayers, and mostly via property taxes—subsidize local roads more than any other utility. Yet local roads in the U.S. are in bad shape. A substantial increase in spending is needed by local governments to fix streets that are decaying or strewn with potholes, as well as bridges at risk of collapsing. The 2015 budget recalculation more than offsets the elimination of tax subsidies for local roads, bridges, and tunnels by redefining local street grids as public utilities, and then increasing local user fees to pay for the full amount that local governments would spend in maintaining their roads: that is,

$132.3 billion. This would involve raising local user fees from the 2015 actual level of $7.6 billion to $132.3 billion, a $124.7 billion increase in local road fees.

At the state level, road spending would decline sharply because of the lack of need to widen highways and create new lanes. The 2015 budget nonetheless assumes the need for a large amount, $51.0 billion, to maintain existing state highways, including the interstate "I" system. Since states in 2015 already collected $9.7 billion in road fees, the reconstituted state road utilities would raise their fees by an additional $41.4 billion.

Finally, at the federal level, spending on roads would drop most steeply of all. Over a decade ago, in 2006, vehicle ownership peaked and began to fall to the current plateau of minor changes. Even earlier, in 2004, miles driven peaked and began a decline that recently exceeded 5%.[25] In addition, the "I" system is essentially completed. Therefore, the case for the actual 2015 federal budget's allocation of $59.1 billion for roads is weak. The federal government should get out of the road building business. This 2015 budget recalculation drops federal road spending to $9.5 billion. It also proposes the full amount be covered by user fees (perhaps collected at the local or state level, and then remitted the U.S. DOT). Thus, federal utility revenue would increase by $9.5 billion.

Transit: Local spending on transit also should be increased. Our current system of buses, streetcars, light rail, and trains is pathetic at worst, inadequate at best. Poorer countries often do a better job, and developed countries look down on us. With transit fully organized as utilities whose users must pay the full cost, there is likely to be a growing demand for more and better transit. The 2015 budget recalculation raises local transit spending from $54.7 billion to $93.0 billion, $38.3 billion more. (Note that this too is an increase in spending, not fees.)

Accompanying this spending increase, the financing of transit would change. Transit systems are classic public utilities. Under the 2015 proposed budget recalculation, tax subsidies for transit would end. Users—with substantially higher incomes in the lower and middle rungs of the income distribution—would be obliged to pay normal fares to cover the full cost of the bus, streetcar, light rail, and train rides they take. (Employers, universities, and other third parties could of course pick up some of the cost.) In 2015, local user fees for transit came to $12.5 billion. This budget recalculation raises that figure to an amount sufficient to cover the full cost of local transit spending, $93.0 billion, an $80.4 billion local fee increase.

At the state level, transit spending should also increase. In many states, there is an urgent need to create more, better, faster rail links that cut across municipal boundaries to serve entire metropolitan areas. Improved rail service is also needed to connect more distant regions within a state. The end of subsidies for roads and the reliance on user fees to pay for longer road trips will create a demand for these improved rail services.

The 2015 budget recalculation proposes to increase state spending on transit from $18.4 billion to $31.2 billion. With taxes gone as a basis for financing, state transit user fees would thus need to be raised from their 2015 level of $3.9 billion to $31.2 billion, a $27.4 billion increase.

Finally, just as it is appropriate to reduce federal spending on roads, it would be appropriate to reduce federal spending on transit. It is primarily a local, regional, or intra-state concern. In 2015, the federal government gave local and state transit programs a total of $12.1 billion. The budget recalculation lowers federal transit spending to $5.0 billion, which would be devoted to maintaining and expanding interstate rail transit programs such as Amtrak. (Note that these figures are expenditures, not fee revenue.)

Users would finance the entire $5.0 billion. The end of subsidies for roads will raise the cost of driving cars long distances. Some drivers will then be attracted to riding trains. The 2015 budget recalculation thus proposes a $5.0 billion increase in federal transit fees.

Airports and Water Ports: The 2015 budget recalculation proposes no spending changes for airports or water ports. What is required is to modify their revenue sources so that users cover the full cost via fees. (Corporate users in turn would be free to pass on any added cost to their customers or shareholders, although they may find ways to improve the efficiency of their operation so as to avoid or reduce the cost.) The impact of this policy is to raise local user fees by $0.8 billion, state user fees by $0.8 billion, and federal user fees by $30.0 billion.

Other Utilities: Finally, governments operate utilities to provide customers with water, sewerage, and solid waste pickup and disposal. The combined cost in 2015 for all of these was $151.6 billion. No change in spending is proposed here (although the tragic story of the Flint, Michigan, water system suggests that some governments need to better protect public health by investing more in their water utilities). Most of this 2015 cost was already covered by user fees, which totaled $132.7 billion.

Therefore, to raise the total amount of fees collected to the $151.6 billion level, the recalculated budget proposes that users pay an additional $19.0 billion.

DEFICIT REDUCTION

Another important goal of the 2015 budget reconstruction is to lay the fiscal groundwork for improved governmental accountability in general and deficit reduction in particular.

Attentive readers may recall that, in the earlier section on spending, both local governments and state governments were re-estimated to experience net spending decreases of, respectively, $589.4 billion and $99.4 billion. But the previous section's re-estimate of local and state revenues shows net revenue decreases of only $25.7 billion for localities and $17.9 billion for states. What happened to the rest of the spending cuts?

The answer is: this budget reconstruction uses the bulk of the spending cuts to eliminate local and state governments' *de facto* 2015 deficits: for localities, $556.0 billion, and for states, $79.2 billion. This leaves them with small surpluses—for localities, $7.7 billion (as shown in Table D-1), and for states, $2.3 billion (as shown in Table D-2).

Localities and states are not typically seen as running deficits. The common view is that, because of custom and laws (often embedded in state statutes or constitutions), they balance their budgets. Yet for a variety of understandable reason (e.g., holding down poorer communities' tax rates, trying to equalize K12 pupil spending, and letting governments "closer to the people" make fiscal decisions), local and state governments in fact receive giant chunks of their revenue from higher levels of government. In 2015, localities balanced their budgets only because they received $557.2 billion from states and the federal government. The same year, states balanced their budgets only because they got $79.2 billion from Washington, DC. Local and state governments can be viewed as running *de facto* deficits in the sense that the dollars they spend far exceed they revenue they themselves collect ("own-source revenue") from taxes, fees, and charges.

This 2015 budget recalculation ends these *de facto* deficits. In 2015 and future years, local and state governments would "pay their own way." Two major transformations in the economic capacity of localities and states, and in the fiscal pressures they face, would position them to meet the challenge.

First: A dramatic improvement in the economic security of U.S. residents (that is: employment, earnings, income, childcare, health insurance, etc.) will enable them to better afford to pay local and state taxes, user fees, and charges.

Second: Simultaneously, local taxes would be much lower, down by more than 30% in total. State taxes will be lower as well, down by 7% in total. In the proposed design of a New Deal 3.0, local and state taxes would plummet because of:

- The transfer of localities' two most costly tax-supported responsibilities (K12 education and roads) to either states (K12 education) or user fees (roads);

- The elimination of one of the states' biggest, most out-of-control, costs (Medicaid) due to the creation of a new federal health insurance program (YoungMedicare); and

- The shift from states to Washington of most of the cost of financing colleges.

The resulting "sorting out" of different levels of governments' fiscal duties has several purposes. It will result in simpler and more understandable local, state, and federal budgets. It reassigns the financing of several key functions—especially K12 education and health insurance—to the level of government whose resources are better equipped to handle the responsibility.

But two purposes stand out. Requiring local and state governments to "pay their own way" will help to ensure greater accountability, responsibility, and efficiency at every level of government. The other positive outcome will be the reduction—one hopes the elimination—of localities' and states' large *de facto* deficits.

A final important note on deficits. This 2015 budget recalculation would result in reducing the 2015 federal deficit from $450.5 billion to $359.7 billion, a sizeable $90 billion (when rounded) drop.

Tax Expenditure Changes

The proposed redesign of American government does not assume the elimination of all tax expenditures. Ultimately, their total elimination may be desirable. There is a strong case for treating all government allocations of resources as direct spending and situating those allocations "on budget." Doing so would improve the transparency of government activity and help build trust in government institutions. It would also improve policymaking, since the use of the tax system to allocate resources muddles thinking about how much money government really spends, makes it harder to compare spending choices, and confuses us about how much government is dedicating to which purposes.

In the short-to-mid term, however, it would badly distort government budgets if their direct spending totals were augmented by hundreds of billions in tax expenditures, even ones that make sense. There is also a case to be made that some spending is actually better administered through the tax system, particularly if the amounts thus allocated depend on calculations that must be made as part of filing income tax returns. The two tax expenditures proposed in this reform of the New Deal, i.e., the proposed Earnings Supplement Tax credit and the proposed YoungMedicare Tax Credit, may on the merits be better delivered through the tax system.

What matters most is that the tax system no longer serve as a device for subsidizing specific types of consumption or investment.

Using the tax system to help all filers lower their overall tax burden (with the degree and amount of tax relief diminishing as income rises) is appropriate. Thus, the federal individual income tax's standard deductions make sense. Providing a uniform reduction in gross income per person (or per adult, with a lower figure per child), as part of building the filer's taxable income, is simple. It is also fair, if not technically progressive. Standard deductions reduce the final tax burdens of lower-income and middle-class filers' by higher percentages than for high-income filers.

Of equal importance, standard deductions do not manipulate the economy. They provide filers with extra disposable ("after-tax") income that may be used for any purpose. Standard deductions do not involve any attempt by government to induce taxpayers to channel their savings towards any particular type of consumption or investment.

Standard deductions are not the only income tax device that meets the tests of (1) wide application, (2) simplicity, (3) fairness, and (4) economic neutrality. The two following tax expenditures would also do so. Indeed, they are even better in two respects. First, the tax reductions they provide are "refundable," thus providing resources to filers with no or little tax liability. Second, the two following tax expenditures would be calculated so as to provide larger dollar amount reductions to lower-income and middle-class filers, in addition to (as is also true of standard deductions) larger percentage reductions in final tax burdens, compared to high-income filers.

Earnings Supplement Tax Credit

The proposed refundable federal Earnings Supplement Tax Credit would provide all workers, based on their earnings, a simple refundable tax credit. Chapter Five spells out the Earnings Supplement Tax Credit formula. The amounts laid out in Chapter Five, however, are gross credit amounts. The final credit that a filer would receive would be a net amount that reflects a slow tapering of the gross credit in proportion to the filer's highest marginal tax rate.

The following illustration shows how this reduction in the credit would work. Assume three filers qualify for the same

Earnings Supplement Tax Credit of $9,500. Assume their taxable incomes differ: one has $15,000, another $50,000, and the other $100,000. Assume (for the sake of the illustration only) that three different top marginal tax rates apply to their last dollar of taxable income, i.e., 10%, 15%, and 30%. The Earnings Supplement Tax Credit would be different for each of them as follows:

- Filer #1 would have a credit= $9,500 – ($9,500 x 10%) = $8,550

- Filer # 2 would have a credit =$9,500 – ($9,500 x 15%) = $8,075

- Filer #3 would have a credit = $9,500 – ($9,500 x 30%) = $6,650

A problem with the current EITC is that its phase-out imposes very high effective marginal tax rates. The CTC begins to phase out at much higher levels, but at those points it too subjects filers to very high marginal tax rates. As explained in Chapter Five, the impact of these high effective marginal tax rates is to discourage both work and marriage. The idea here is not to subject the new Earnings Supplement Tax Credit to a special phase-out rate that elevates the filer's combined tax rate to punishing levels, but to treat the Earnings Supplement just like all other "last dollar" income and apply whatever the filer's existing top marginal tax rate happens to be.

This approach ensures that the lowest-income filers get almost the full credit, middle-income filers get less but still a lot, and high-income filers get substantially less, but still a significant amount. Some may object to providing high-income filers with any Earnings Supplement Tax Credit. But there are several reasons why they should.

First, under the proposed overall reform of the federal individual income tax system, to be illustrated at the end of this appendix, high-income filers will generally see a higher share of their real income treated as taxable income. Interest, dividends, and capital gains would be fully subject to taxation. No special exclusions or artificially lower tax rates would apply to any form of interest, any type of dividend, capital gains from any source, or any other "special" type of income.

The two new tax credits (i.e., the Earnings Supplement Tax Credit and the YoungMedicare Tax Credit) would be the only tax credits available. Except for standard deductions and legitimate business expense deductions, all other deductions (that is: the ones that aim to promote politically favored types of consumption and investment) would be gone.

Thus eliminating all of the other tax expenditures now embedded in the tax code will result in high-income filers paying a much fairer, more transparent, share of their total income. Generally, that will mean a higher share of their income. Allowing high-income filers to receive a portion of the Earnings Supplement Tax Credit would offset in most cases only a very small portion of the much larger increase in tax liability that high -income filers will typically be obliged to pay.

Second, the other big programs that historically have done the most to help low-income Americans — think of Unemployment Insurance, Social Security, and Medicare — have not been limited to low-income people. They are "universal." You get UI, Social Security, and Medicare whether you are poor, middle-class, or wealthy.

The more broad-based a program is in the U.S., the more popular it is. This powerful precedent argues for also making "universal" the new Earnings Supplement Tax Credit and the YoungMedicare Tax Credit. To lock in popular support for the enormous help these new tax credits will provide the most vulnerable low-income workers and often struggling middle-class families, giving the same credits to wealthy taxpayers is a reasonable price to pay.

What, then, would the proposed Earnings Supplement Tax Credit cost?

According to the Social Security Administration, in 2015, approximately 158,587,600 adults aged 19 to 69 worked in jobs covered by the FICA and Medicare payroll tax system.[26] If we estimate that 95% of them would qualify for the per-worker Earning Supplement Tax Credit, the number of claimants is approximately 150,658,000.

Not all of them, but many of them, would also claim a larger Earning Supplement Tax Credit that varies by the number of their dependent children. According to the Census Bureau, in 2015, if an estimated 90% of all children ages 0-18 were thus claimed, the total number of qualifying children would be approximately 70,080,000.[27] (Some children would, of course, be living with adults with disabilities who do not work, seniors who do not work, and other unemployed adults. Thus, the reduction to 90% in the estimated share of qualifying children.)

Some workers will not earn the $15,000 per year required to obtain the maximum Earnings Supplement Tax Credit. For purposes of this budget exercise, however, let us assume they all do. If so, the total estimated cost of the $3,000 per worker piece of the Earnings Supplement Tax Credit that all wage earners would receive, regardless of the presence or number of qualifying dependent children, would be $452.0 billion.

Some qualifying children may live in the households of workers who earn less than $15,000 per year. Let us again assume, however, that each qualifying dependent child qualifies for the maximum. It is reasonable to estimate that the average dollar amount of the child piece of the proposed Earnings Supplement Tax Credit would be $5,500 per child. (The amount for the 1st child is $1,000 higher; $5,500 is the amount for the 2nd child; the amount for a 3rd child is $1,000 lower; it is lower still for each additional child.) Based on these assumptions, the cost of the child piece of the Earnings Supplement Tax Credit would be $385.4 billion.

Thus, the estimated total gross cost of the Earning Supplement Tax Credit (i.e., the per worker piece plus the child piece) would be $837.4 billion. However, claimants would see the credit reduced by their top marginal tax rate. Assuming an average 20% reduction, the net cost of the tax credit would be $669.9 billion. Here's the math:

- 150,658,000 adults x credit of $3,000 = $452.0 billion gross credit
- 70,080,000 children x credit of $5,500 = $385.4 billion gross credit
- Total credit = $837.4 billion gross credit
- Less 20% reduction = $669.9 billion net credit

YoungMedicare Tax Credit

The YoungMedicare Tax Credit is easier to estimate. It is based on 70% of the employees' share of the cost of the YoungMedicare program.

As the following section will lay out, the estimated cost of the overall YoungMedicare program is $1,326.5 billion. To cover the cost, employers would be required to remit payroll-based premiums, equal to 17.5% of Medicare earnings, to the National YoungMedicare Corporation.

Workers could be charged up to half of that amount—that is: $663.2 billion—by their employers (although a lesser charge, or none at all, would be possible, depending on the employer). Assuming that that the cost is split 50/50, both the workers' share and the employers' share would be $663.2 billion. Thus, the Young Medicare Tax Credit in gross terms would be 70% of the assumed worker's share of $663.2 billion, or $464.2 billion.

Workers, however, would see the credit reduced by their top marginal tax rate. Again assuming an average 20% reduction, the net value of the YoungMedicare Tax Credit would be $371.4 billion.

Under this scenario, workers' true out-of-paycheck cost for their maximum possible $663.2 billon share of their employers' premium obligation would thus be $663.2 billion minus the final $371.4 billion YoungMedicare Tax Credit they receive. In other words, workers' maximum out-of-pocket costs for YoungMedicare would be $291.8 billion.

Summary

This 2015 budget exercise proposes two new federal tax expenditures whose combined net cost—$669.9 billion for the Earnings Supplement Tax Credit plus $371.4 billion for the YoungMedicare Tax Credit—would be $1,041.3 billion. Offsetting these amounts, most existing federal tax expenditures would be eliminated in order to keep the net total of federal tax expenditures close to its current levels, which by 2019 will reach $1.5 trillion.[28] (The joint Urban Institute/Brookings Institution Tax Policy Center indicated it could be 6% higher.)[29]

YOUNG MEDICARE

The 2015 budget recalculation for a New Deal 3.0 proposes the creation of the new national health insurance program, YoungMedicare, as an independent program whose cost and revenue are handled outside the regular structure of the federal government. The reasons for that choice are explained at length in Chapter Six, and will not be repeated here.

A major question, however, remains. How was the estimated cost of the YoungMedicare program—$1,326.5 billion—derived?

Estimated Cost of YoungMedicare

As of July 1, 2015, the Census Bureau estimated that 273,162,326 residents of the United States were less than 65 years of age.[30] For various reasons, not 100% of them would choose to enroll in YoungMedicare. Their reasons for not doing so may include: fear of entanglement in the legal system or dislike of government; personal or religious objections to health insurance; or lack of awareness about how to enroll in a national health insurance program. Several larger sub-groups of the under-65 population that may choose not to enroll in Young Medicare include those enrolled in alternative health insurance programs, such as Medicare, TRICARE, or the VA system.[31] The impact on the cost of YoungMedicare due to several of these non-participating groups is taken into account in the specific estimates of costs that follow.

It would be convenient if one could multiply the total number of potential YoungMedicare enrollees every year by a fixed average per-person health care cost (adjusted for inflation) in order to construct the cost of YoungMedicare from year to year. Unfortunately, the average cost of health care for the entire under-65 population in any "baseline" year is of limited value in constructing the population's total health care costs from year to year.

Health care costs vary widely by age, as well as by sex, between birth and 65. In addition, the number of individuals in each age/sex cohort is far from uniform. The size of each cohort varies by birth rate (i.e., how many boys and girls were born in a specific year) as well as by mortality rate (i.e., how many of the individuals who were born in a specific year survive to a particular age). To determine the aggregate health care cost of the under-65 population from year to year, it is necessary to multiply (A) the changing number of persons in each age cohort in each year, times (B) each cohort's unique and changing average cost of health care. In short, estimating the cost of YoungMedicare is not a simple matter.

Nonetheless, one must start somewhere. A good starting point is a 2017 analysis by the Milliman organization of the projected premiums in 2018 for individual coverage for different age groups at the Affordable Care Act (ACA) benchmark Silver plan level. The Milliman report is particularly useful for our purposes because it provides estimates for what Silver premiums would be for different age groups from 0 to 64, the same population that YoungMedicare would cover. In addition, the Milliman report indicates what Silver premiums would be under both (1) the Congressional requirement that younger enrollees in ACA plans must pay higher premiums than actuarially warranted, so that older enrollees may pay lower premiums than actuarially warranted, in order to hold the premium ratio between 21-year-olds and 64-year-olds at 1:3, and (2) the more actuarially valid ratio of young-to-old premiums of 1:5.[32]

Table D-10 shows the impact of applying the Milliman age-adjusted premium estimates for 2018 ACA individual coverage at the Silver level to the U.S. population in 2015 for (A) the 0-14 age cohort as a group, and (B) each of the next 50 single-age cohorts from 15 to 64. The Milliman estimates apply both of the above-mentioned actuarial ratios between a 21-year-old enrollee and a 64+ enrollee: i.e., the 1:3 ratio and the 1:5 ratio.[33] (To keep Table D-10 on a single page, I combined the results for the single-age cohorts between 15-64 into five-year subtotals (i.e., 15-19, 20-24, etc.)

I explain the adjustments shown in the bottom half of Table D-10 on subsequent pages.

Table D-10: Estimated Cost of YoungMedicare in 2015

Age	Population 2015	Annual Premium 1:3 Age Curve	Annual Premium 1:5 Age Curve	Annual Cost (billions) 1:3 Age Curve	Annual Cost (billions) 1:5 Age Curve
0-14	61,016,787	$3,192	$2,400	$194,766	$146,440
15-19	21,108,903	$3,468 > $3,924	$2,616 > $2,952	$78,019	$58,767
20-24	22,739,313	$4,044 > $4,176	$3,048 > $3,144	$94,359	$71,056
25-29	22,461,554	$4,188 > $4,668	$3,168 > $3,888	$98,975	$78,490
30-34	21,675,648	$4,728 > $5,064	$3,984 > $4,488	$106,436	$92,234
35-39	20,374,585	$5,100 > $5,268	$4,536 > $4,788	$105,328	$94,620
40-44	20,215,198	$5,328 > $5,820	$4,884 > $5,628	$112,219	$105,620
45-49	20,853,844	$6,024 > $7,116	$4,928 > $7,572	$136,484	$140,038
50-54	22,334,317	$7,452 > $8,904	$8,076 > $10,272	$182,141	$204,171
55-59	21,807,942	$9,300 > $10,860	$10,860 > $13,212	$221,028	$264,365
60-64	19,069,877	$11,316 > $12,516	$13,908 > $15,696	$228,535	$284,169
	273,657,968		TOTAL	$1,558,289	$1,539,969

	1:3 Age Curve	1:5 Age Curve
Offset for people under 65 covered by Medicare (-5%)	($77,914.43)	($76,998.47)
Offset for population covered by TRICARE,VA, IHS (- 5%)	($77,914.43)	($76,998.47)
NET after subtracting these two groups:	$1,402,460	$1,385,972
Offset for administrative efficiency and incentive effect (-10%)	($140,246)	($138,597)
NET after subtracting these savings:	$1,262,214	$1,247,375
Offset for premium deflation (to 2015 from 2018)(-20%)	($252,443)	($249,475)
NET after subtracting this reduction:	$1,009,771	$997,900
Increase for enhanced benefit (i.e., Silver to Platinum +) (+30%)	$302,931	$299,370
NET after adding this benefit increase	$1,312,702	$1,297,270
Add preventive pediatric dental and vision care: $8 billion	$1,320,702	$1,305,270
Add YoungMedicare program management costs: $2.5 billion	$1,323,202	$1,307,770

Numbers in rows or columns may not result in totals shown due to rounding.

In order to calculate what YoungMedicare would have cost in 2015, it is necessary to make several adjustments to the result derived from multiplying the entire 2015 population under age 65 by Milliman's projected 2018 costs for the ACA Silver plan. The adjustments, summarized at the bottom of Table D-10, are explained below.

Persons Covered by Medicare: Individuals under 65 who are covered by Medicare would be excluded. Since 1973, Medicare has covered recipients of Social Security Disability Insurance (SSDI) who are under 65. According to a 2016 report by the Kaiser Family Foundation, "Today, Medicare covers 9.1 million people with disabilities who are under age 65."[34] This is approximately 3% of the 2015 under-65 population of 273.2 million. Because this group has high medical needs, the cost reduction is assumed to be 5.0%.

Persons Covered by TRICARE, VA, and Other Health Services: Individuals who are covered by existing (and already funded) programs for active military personnel and veterans should be excluded. Over 1.0 million Americans were active members of the five branches of the military (Army, Navy, Marines, Air Force, Coast Guard).[35] A significant number are stationed overseas.

There were also 20.4 million veterans in 2016, over half of whom were under 65.[36] In addition, many Native Americans receive health care services from the Indian Health Service. Assuming that a combined total 12.0 million military personnel, veterans, and Native Americans under 65 receive their health care from TRICARE, the VA, and the Indian Health Service, they would constitute over 4% of the under-65 population. Given the significant medical needs of this population, the cost reduction is assumed to be 5.0%.

Administrative Efficiencies: The private health insurance system, which generated the ACA premiums that underpin this 2015 cost calculation, spends significant amounts of money on administration—that is, on billing, coordination of benefits, commissions, advertising, marketing, and other administrative costs. Some of these insurance administration cost would be eliminated under YoungMedicare.

According to CMS, of the $1,072.1 billion spent in 2015 for Private Health Insurance, $127.4 billion or over 18% was attributable to what CMS labels the Net Cost of Private Health Insurance, i.e., "the difference between [health care] benefits and total PHI [Private Health Insurance] expenditures" and included "administrative costs" among others.[37] Some of these administrative costs will remain necessary under YoungMedicare. Some relate to insurance that YoungMedicare would not provide, e.g., full dental insurance.

Nonetheless, a reduction in YoungMedicare premiums should be possible due to reducing insurance administrative costs. Young Medicare is simple. There will be little need for an insurer to try to pressure some other insurer into paying medical bills, a process politely called "coordination of benefits" that adds significant expense.

In addition, with virtually everyone covered, no deductibles, and very limited co-pays, hospitals and other providers will be able to cut way back on the cost of hassling patients to pay the uninsured parts of medical bills. Today, these costs are passed along to insurers. Under YoungMedicare, they will largely disappear. The collection process further entangles insurers when they incur costs in verifying or denying their responsibility. These costs, under YoungMedicare, will also largely disappear. Finally, insurance companies under YoungMedicare may be able to cut back on the costs of the commissions they pay to agents and brokers.

Overall, these administrative efficiencies in the operation of the insurance system are assumed to reduce costs by 3%.

Purchasing Pool Size and Incentive Effects: Greater savings will arise because of the combination of YoungMedicare's size and its simple, clear, and strong incentive to enrollees to select the lowest-bidding health care plan.

Under YoungMedicare, enrollees would be obliged to pay the full extra cost of choosing any health care plan that— compared to the lowest bidding health care plan—has bid a higher premium on a risk-adjusted basis. Enrollees' incentive to avoid the extra cost (or at least what they view as "too much" extra cost) will exert enormous and enduring pressure on all the health care plans to hold down their premiums.

The plans will also face a powerful incentive to improve their quality of care. In an environment where only one health care plan is the lowest bidder and thus enrollees must pay extra to join any other plan, but no one knows in advance who the lowest bidder will be, all the plans will want to show potential enrollees that their high quality justifies paying the extra price that most of the plans will be obliged to charge.

It will of course not be easy for health care plans to hold down their premiums and improve their quality. Nonetheless, they will have ample opportunity to do so by squeezing out the errors, waste, and inefficiency that permeate today's health care system.

The capacity of the YoungMedicare model to simultaneously constrain costs and improve quality is not theory. There is ample evidence that when an organization presents the health insurance market with the combination of (1) a very large pool of individual buyers of the same excellent health insurance benefits, and (2) a simple, clear, and strong economic incentive for those buyers to select a low-price, high-quality health care plan from among competing health care plan bidders, the response from the health care plans will be a substantial and ongoing reduction in health care costs together with the maintenance of high quality. Since 1983, the Wisconsin State Employee Health Plan has proved this in Dane County, Wisconsin.

In Dane County, the Wisconsin State Employee Health Plan brings into the health insurance market a very large purchasing pool of state employees that adds up to roughly 25% of the county's non-Medicaid/non-Medicare population. Employees pay the least to enroll in a low-bidding Tier 1 plan, and must pay extra to join the higher bidding Tier 2 or Tier 3 plans. Because (1) the pool of covered lives is such a high share of the county's total population, and (2) employees have such a clear and powerful inducement to save money, the competing HMOs have a very strong incentive to keep down their premiums and maintain high quality. As a result, the state pays much less in Dane County (in 2013, 16% less) than in the average of Wisconsin's other 71 counties, in which the state lacks a large purchasing pool.[38] It is thus reasonable to expect that YoungMedicare's replication of the core feature of this model, but with a purchasing pool of well over 50% of the population of every country in the U.S. and with equally (if not more) powerful incentives, would result in a substantial reduction in premiums compared to the Milliman baseline.

To be conservative, I assume that YoungMedicare's combination of a large purchasing pool and powerful incentives would reduce costs by 7%. (It could be much higher.)

Inflation Adjustment: There will also be major savings because YoungMedicare's premiums in 2015 would be lower than the estimates Milliman developed for 2018. According to a Kaiser Family Foundation report, the average lowest-cost Silver premium for a 40-year old increased by 32% from 2017 to 2018 alone.[39] To deflate the Milliman premium estimates from 2018 to 2015, I have conservatively (I believe) assumed they should be lowered by 20%.

Better Benefit Package: Finally, YoungMedicare's benefit package would be significantly better, thus more costly, than the ACA Silver plan that Milliman modeled. The Silver plan covers an average of 70% of health costs on an actuarial basis. To account for the better benefits provided by YoungMedicare, I assume a final upward adjustment in premiums of 30%. In addition, I have added $8.0 billion to provide additional pediatric dental care benefits (above the ACA level) and a pediatric vision care benefit.

The bottom of Table D-10 shows how these assumptions are used in making a final calculation. The result is an estimate that YoungMedicare in 2015 (using the more realistic 1:5 actuarial ratio of younger to older enrollees) would have cost $1,307.8 billion.

There is a second way to tackle the question of what YoungMedicare would have cost in 2015. It starts by adding the amounts spent in 2015 by the three dominant sources of health insurance for the under-65 population for the same health care services that YoungMedicare would pay for (but excluding, at least initially, the cost of insurance administration).

The Centers for Medicare and Medicaid Services (CMS) annually collects and tabulates data on the following types of insurance that primarily involve the under-65 population:

- Out-of-pocket (in essence, "self-insurance");
- Medicaid and CHIP; and
- Private health insurance

These categories exclude at the outset (thus, do not double-count) other types of insurance or health care coverage that primarily involve smaller, distinct groups of under-65 individuals, e.g., Workers' Compensation, Indian Health Services, Department of Defense (TRICARE), and Department of Veterans Affairs (VA). Also excluded, of course, is the giant program that insures SSDI recipients and the 65-and-older population: Medicare.[40]

The CMS data for each type of insurance identifies the level of spending for over a dozen categories of health care costs, administrative costs (both public and private), public health costs, research costs, and the costs of construction and equipment. The following seven health care services encompass the vast majority of the actual health care costs that YoungMedicare would cover:

- Hospital care;
- Physician and clinical services;
- Other professional services;
- Other health, residential, and personal care;
- Home health care;
- Prescription drugs; and
- Durable medical equipment.

Excluded are health costs that fall under the labels of Nursing Care Facilities and Continuing Care Retirement, Dental Services, Non-Durable Medical Products, Public Health, Research, Structures, and Equipment. Also excluded are the administrative costs of providing health insurance.[41]

According to CMS, in 2015, the three dominant sources of health insurance for the under-65 population — that is: out-of-pocket "self-insurance," Medicaid plus CHIP, and private insurance — spent $1,506.6 billion on the seven categories of health care listed above.[42] YoungMedicare would absorb the responsibility for providing most under-65 individuals now covered by out-of-pocket "self-insurance," Medicaid plus CHIP, and private insurance by guaranteeing them coverage for the same categories of health care from their choice of a private health care plan — either an HMO, PPO, or fee-for-service insurer.

YoungMedicare, however, would have been likely in 2015 to spend significantly less than $1,506.6 billion. There are at least two factors that play into why its 2015 cost would not have been that high.

First, a significant share of the $194.4 million in out-of-pocket ("self-insurance") costs is attributable to the older population enrolled in Medicare. As CMS explains: "Out-of-pocket [OOP] funding is defined as direct spending by consumers for all health care goods and services. This includes the amount paid OOP for services not covered by ... public programs such as Medicare."[43] How much of the $194.4 billion should be attributed to persons who would not be enrolled in YoungMedicare because SSDI eligibility or older age (65 or more) results in their getting Medicare coverage instead? In 2016, the Commonwealth Fund found that an estimated 56,100,007 Medicare beneficiaries spent an average of $1,671 out-of-pocket for inpatient, outpatient, and emergency hospital services, medical providers, and drugs, for a total of $93.7 billion.[44]

Second, the size of the YoungMedicare purchasing pool, combined with the program's clear and powerful incentives for health care plans to lower their premiums and at the same time improve their quality of care, is likely to result in a significant reduction in YoungMedicare's underlying health care cost structure. Based on the State of Wisconsin Employee Health in Dane County, a 7% reduction is again assumed.[45]

Netting out these factors, this second effort to define an estimated 2015 cost for YoungMedicare lowers the total estimated cost of the program from $1,506.6 billion to $1,314.0 billion.

The two-step formula is:

1) Exclude out-of-pocket costs that are unrelated to YoungMedicare. I estimate that this reduction, if occurring in 2015, would likely have been more than the $93.7 billion estimated by the Commonwealth Fund for 2016 due to folding in out-of-pocket costs incurred by the under-65 population for non-medical services, e.g., dental care, incurred by the general U.S. population. I conservatively estimate a decrease of $93.8 billion.

2) Reduce the resulting difference by 7% due to subtracting savings caused by YoungMedicare's purchasing pool size and incentive structure. I estimate that this would have lowered spending by nearly $98.9 billion.

Thus: $1,506.6 billion–($93.8 billion + $98.9 billion) = $1,314.0 billion (rounded). To this, two additional amounts should be added: $10.0 billion to provide YoungMedicare coverage for pediatric dental and vision services, and $2.5 billion to pay for the administration of YoungMedicare. Thus, I estimate that this second way of gauging the cost of YoungMedicare would result in spending of $1,326.5 billion.

Based on the two alternative estimates of what YoungMedicare would have cost in 2015 if the program had then been in effect—that is: $1,307.8 billion and $1,326.5 billion—it seems prudent to use the higher number in proceeding to the challenge of how the program should be financed. The higher number may be too high. I have not subtracted the portion of private health care costs incurred by 65+ Medicare enrollees that are attributable to their Medicare Supplement plans. The curse of American health care policy, however, has been excessive optimism about cost reduction assumptions. Private insurance, Medicaid, and Medicare all ended up costing more than predicted. Better to go with the higher estimate and be overjoyed if it should have been lower.

There are reasons to be hopeful. The powerful incentives that YoungMedicare would put into play might well have reduced the 2015 cost of health care for the under-65 population by more than 7%. A massive degree of error, waste, and inefficiency permeates our health care system. According to several reports published in 2012, the level of waste in the U.S. health system at the time was roughly $700 billion:[46]

> By looking at regional variations in Medicare spending, researchers at the Dartmouth Institute for Health Policy and Clinical Practice have estimated that 30 percent of all Medicare clinical care spending could be avoided without worsening health outcomes. This amount represents about $700 billion in savings when extrapolated to total US health care spending, according to the Congressional Budget Office.

> More recently, an April 2012 study by former Centers for Medicare and Medicaid Services (CMS) administrator Donald M. Berwick and RAND Corporation analyst Andrew D. Hackbarth estimated that five categories of waste consumed $476 billion to $992 billion, or 18 percent to 37 percent of the approximately $2.6 trillion annual total of all health spending in 2011.... Similarly, a panel of the Institute of Medicine (IOM) estimated in a September 2012 report that $690 billion was wasted in US health care annually, not including fraud.

The running room for YoungMedicare to reduce current and future health care costs, without sacrificing quality, is extensive. It is nonetheless wise to be conservative and go with the higher estimate of the program's cost: $1,326.5 billion.

Financing of YoungMedicare: Savings for Workers and Employers

The proposal for financing YoungMedicare is simple. Employers would remit a payroll-based premium to the National Young Medicare Corporation equal to 17.5% of the Medicare Part A taxable earnings of their workers under 65. In 2015, those earnings totaled $7,580.0 billion.[47] Workers could be required to contribute up to half of the employer premium, but no individual worker's deduction could exceed 8.75% of earnings. From year to year, the "split" between worker and employer could be altered based on collective bargaining, individual agreements, or employer discretion. (Self-employed workers would pay the entire 17.5% premium.)

In 2015, the required employer premium would have yielded the necessary $1,326.5 billion. This 2015 budget calculation assumes that all workers would be required by their employers to experience a 8.75% deduction from wages, although in practice the deduction could be less or nothing. Based on this assumption for 2015, however, workers and employers as groups would each have contributed $663.2 billion to finance YoungMedicare.

It is important to repeat and underscore that, in this 2015 budget recalculation, workers would not have actually borne the full cost of the $663.2 billion deduction. They would have been able to claim a refundable YoungMedicare Tax Credit for a large portion of it—up to 70%—when they submitted their federal income tax returns. As with the proposed new Earnings Supplement Tax Credit, most of the YoungMedicare Tax Credit could be made available to workers in installments over the course of the year.

An earlier section described the formula for calculating the specific amount of the YoungMedicare Tax Credit. Based on the assumptions of this section, workers' true cost in 2015 would have been $291.8 billion ($663.2 billion gross assessment - $371.4 billion net credit = $291.8 billion actual cost). This true cost to workers of guaranteeing that virtually all pre-65 Americans have excellent health insurance is $19.0 billion less than the $310.8 billion in "household contributions" to private health insurance premiums that workers actually paid in 2015, typically as deductions from their wages.[48]

The employers' assessment, an estimated $663.2 billion for 2015, would have been treated that year and all future years as a normal business expense for corporate income tax purposes. The amount is also less than what employers actually spent in 2015 for private health insurance premiums, i.e., $692.5 billion.[49] If Young Medicare had been in effect in 2015, employers as a group would have saved $29.3 billion.

For legal reasons, it may be necessary to treat the payroll-based 17.5% employer premium to finance YoungMedicare as a tax.[50] But it is unlike the property, sales, or income tax in that the revenues it generates are not available for general government purposes, but may only be used to finance YoungMedicare. (As explained in Chapter Six, this is one of several reasons why the proposed YoungMedicare program, its costs, and its revenue are placed outside the structure of the regular federal government.) The 17.5% employer premium also differs from a payroll tax in several other respects.

First, it does not require a specific dollar or percentage withholding from a worker's paycheck based on the worker's individual earnings, as the FICA (Social Security) and Medicare tax do. Rather, almost anything goes. All workers may end up paying nothing. Or some workers may pay nothing while others pay something. Or all workers may pay, but pursuant to formulas other than a percent of earnings. If a percent of earnings is used, it need not be the same percent of earnings. The only rules are that no individual worker would be required to pay more than 8.75% of earnings, and no distinctions between what workers pay can be based on a discriminatory factor such as race, sex, age, religion, disability, or sexual orientation.

Second, deductions from workers' paychecks for Young-Medicare may change from paycheck to paycheck, month to month, and year to year. Subject to collective bargaining (where applicable) and individual contracts (where applicable), the employer may alter any worker's contribution from payroll to payroll. Again, the only fixed rules are that no individual worker may be required to pay more than 8.75% of earnings during any pay period, and improper discrimination would not be allowed.

For these reasons, this book's description of YoungMedicare and its financing does not treat the payroll-based employer premium as a tax. It most closely resembles the provision in most states' Workers' Compensation program that mandates employers (of all sizes) to adhere to a legal formula when they remit payroll-based premiums to buy Workers' Comp policies—a mandate that sometimes compels employers to submit their premiums to a single, state-run, Workers' Comp insurer.

To comply with the changing views of the U.S. Supreme Court, it may be necessary to label the mandatory payroll-based employer premium as a tax to the extent that it applies to self-employed individuals and small businesses. This would be necessary if the Court treats the commercial activity of the self-employed and small businesses as immune from Congress's authority to regulate commerce under the Court's narrowing interpretation of the Commerce Clause of the Constitution. Or perhaps the Court will acknowledge that individuals who employ themselves, as well as small firms, can be required to comply with a federal payroll-based premium mandate as a valid regulation of commerce under the Commerce Clause. Certainly (let us hope) the Court will recognize that larger firms can be obliged to remit payroll-based premiums under the Commerce Clause. If not, then formally designating the payroll-based premium as a tax that applies to all earnings—or applying it to all income—may become the best way to finance YoungMedicare.

TAX REFORM

Before concluding, let us again turn to taxes and address the issue of tax reform.

Government costs money. The money has to come from somewhere. American governments raise the greater part of their revenue from taxes and fees.

Yet unfortunately, as critic T. R. Reid declares in the title of his recent book, America's tax system is a fine mess.[51] Our tax system is not merely (as the book's subtitle implies) complex, unfair, and inefficient. The American tax system is also the worst culprit in carrying out government's obsession with manipulating the economy, weakening its productivity, and holding back the nation's capacity to generate wealth.

One of the core tenets of a New Deal 3.0 is the elimination of government's manipulation of the economy by means of subsidies for politically preferred types of consumption and investment. For this to occur, the tax system as a whole must be reformed. The special treatment it confers on favored types of property, sales, and income, via special tax exclusions, deductions, and other loopholes, should end.

This will result in broader tax bases for every major tax: the property tax, the sales tax, and the two income taxes (individual and corporate). If rates remain the same, revenue will rise. The purpose of tax reform, however, is not to collect more tax revenue. Therefore, broadening the tax base should be accompanied by lowering tax burdens, particularly for lower-income and middle-income filers. I conclude this appendix by spelling out the principles that I believe should govern tax reform.

Principles of Taxation

The first principle is that all types of property, sales, earnings, and income should be equally subject to taxation. No category should be exempt. No category should receive unequal treatment. To absolve entirely certain types of property, sales, earnings, or income from taxation—or to tax different categories unequally—is to burden the disfavored types and subsidize the favored types. (This does not mean that higher slices of income should not be subject to progressively higher marginal tax rates. Doing that is not a matter of inequality.) Individuals and firms should be picking the economy's losers and winners, not politicians and governments.

The second principle is that "like" taxpayers — that is: those with property of equal value, sales of equal amounts, and identical combinations of income and personal circumstances (e.g., number of dependent children) — should end up paying the same tax within the same jurisdiction. Americans' resentment of the tax system is rooted, more than anything else, in the belief that some people "like us" manage to get away with paying a lot less, while people a lot better off pay peanuts or zilch.

A third principle is that taxes should only pay for services that users cannot reasonably be expected to finance with user fees. The latter principle may be the trickiest to apply. Reasonable people will differ as to what services users can reasonably be expected to pay for, the calibration of fees, and the practicality of collection. Nonetheless, user fees have many advantages. They are typically paid on an as-you-go basis, avoiding the impact of a big one-time tax bill. User fees are also taxes we can control. Drive less, pay less. User fees also provide an incentive to reduce wasteful costs. A less traveled and more efficiently driven highway, for example, does not require tens of millions of dollars to widen.

Reforming the Federal Individual Income Tax

This book does not delve into the details of tax reform, with one exception.

The federal individual income tax is a special case. At over $1.5 trillion, it dwarfs every other local, state, or federal tax. But it is not size alone that distinguishes the federal individual income tax. Its history and nature do so. It was created for the express purpose of progressing from imposing no taxes on those at the lower end of the income scale, to small tax rates on middle-class individuals, to higher tax rates on the wealthy.

Unfortunately, over the years, the federal individual income tax has degenerated into Congress's most potent tool for manipulating the economy, favoring certain sectors and firms, and thus twisting the American economy into the weaker shape it now exhibits.

The U.S. should reform the federal individual income tax to achieve the following objectives:

- Make the tax dramatically simpler, thus making filing a breeze;

- Restore the tax's fairness, so that filers with the same earnings, income, and family size pay the same final tax;

- Improve the tax's progressivity, so that the gradual rise of real income always results in gradual increases in tax rates (up to a maximum rate);

- Strengthen the tax's capacity as a vehicle for helping Americans to achieve a minimally adequate income and affordable health insurance;

- Remove the tax's current pernicious role in distorting the U.S. economy, and weakening its productivity and wealth, by favoring specific types of consumption and investment; and

- Eliminate, as much as possible, any disincentive to work or wed.

These objectives can be satisfied by replacing today's deeply flawed federal individual income tax with the following model:

1) Each adult would pay taxes, and claim credits, based on her or his individual income. (Married couples could still file jointly, combining their individual tax calculations at the bottom of a single form.)

2) All income would be subject to taxation.

   - All earnings, interest, dividends, capital gains, and other forms of income would be fully subject to taxation.

   - This includes all government benefits that individuals receive as cash, i.e., Workers' Compensation benefits, Unemployment Insurance benefits, SSDI benefits, Social Security payments, Railroad Retirement benefits, etc.

   - Just as no income would be excluded from taxation, no income would be only partially included.

3) Each filer would receive a standard deduction. It could be as low as $5,000 or as high as $10,000. An additional standard deduction would also be provided for each dependent child. If a couple is married and filing jointly, they would decide which adult gets to claim which child.

4) All other existing exemptions, exclusions, deductions, and credits — except for the Earnings Supplement Tax Credit and YoungMedicare Tax Credit — would be eliminated.

5) The full difference between all income and the sum of standard deductions would be taxable income.

6) Taxable income would be subject to a base tax rate, e.g., 10%. Above a specified initial amount of taxable income (e.g., $10,000), each additional increment of $1,000 of taxable income would be taxed at a slightly higher marginal rate, e.g., by adding 0.025% to the immediately preceding marginal rate. Once the tax rate reaches 35%, the rate increases would stop. Thus, 35% would be the highest possible federal marginal tax rate.

(This approach, which modern technology and on-line tax filing of tax returns makes possible, avoids the major pitfall of tax brackets: i.e., the incentive to lie or fudge in order to keep taxable income below the next—significantly higher—tax rate bracket.)

7) The final result would be the filer's gross tax.

8) The filer's preliminary tax payment or refund would equal:

- The gross tax (as calculated above),

- Minus any income tax withheld or otherwise paid.

9) To calculate the final tax or refund, the preliminary tax would be reduced by the sum of:

- The filer's refundable Earnings Supplement Tax Credit (which, as explained earlier, would be diminished by the filer's highest marginal tax rate), less any part of the credit the filer has already received in advance (either periodically or as a "mini-lump"); and

- The filer's refundable YoungMedicare Tax Credit (which, as explained earlier, would also be diminished by the filer's highest marginal tax rate), less any part of the credit the filer has

> already received in advance (either periodical-
> ly or as a "mini-lump").

10) If the amount determined above is a negative
number, the filer would receive a refund of the
amount.

Two of the greatest justices of the U.S. Supreme Court—Justice Oliver Wendell Holmes, Jr., and Chief Justice John Marshall—have both weighed in with famous epigrams on the role of taxes. Their comments have framed our thinking on the subject for over a century.

Taxes, said Holmes, are the price we pay for civilization. Yet the power to tax, Marshall cautioned nearly a century earlier, is the power to destroy.[52]

One should be careful about editing the opinions of Oliver Wendell Holmes and John Marshall. But it may be fitting to end with the following revision: Taxes and fees are prices we must pay in a civilized society to achieve public safety and health, guarantee economic security, and ensure an effective market. They must, however, be simple and fair. And they should only be as high as necessary, always leaving individuals and firms with the greater part of their income. A society with insufficient taxes is no civilization. A society with excessive taxes is not free.

NOTES

CHAPTER 1: "A COMPLETE CHANGE OF CONCEPT"

[1] Franklin D. Roosevelt, *The Public Papers and Addresses of Franklin D. Roosevelt*, Volume Two, "The Year of Crisis: 1933," Inaugural Address, March 4, 1933 (New York: Random House, 1938), 11-12.

[2] Stanley Lebergott, Bureau of Labor Statistics (BLS), "Technical Note: Labor Force, Employment, and Unemployment, 1929-39: Estimating Methods," *Monthly Labor Review*, July 1949, https://www.bls.gov/opub/mlr/1948/article/pdf/labor-force-employment-and-unemployment-1929-39-estimating-methods.pdf. BLS estimated that, in 1932, the labor force was 51,250,000, and the number of unemployed was 12,060,000. For 1933, the BLS's estimate of the total labor force was 51,840,000, and the number of unemployed was 12,830,000. Thus, the 1932 unemployment rate was 23.5%, and the 1933 unemployment rate was 24.7%.

[3] Donald M. Fisk, Bureau of Labor Statistics (BLS), "American Labor in the 20th Century," *Compensation and Working Conditions*, Fall 2001, https://www.bls.gov/opub/mlr/cwc/american-labor-in-the-20th-century.pdf. "The average workweek changed dramatically during the 20th century. In 1900, the average workweek in manufacturing was 53 hours. . . .During the Great Depression, the average number of hours per workweek for production workers in manufacturing dropped as low as 34.6."

[4] Federal Reserve Bank of St. Louis, "National Income: Annual," *FRED (Federal Reserve Economic Data)*, https://fred.stlouisfed.org/series/A032RC1A027NBEA. US National Income in 1929 was $94.181 billion. U.S. National Income in 1933 was $48.925 billion.

[5] Federal Reserve Bank of St. Louis, "Gross Domestic Product: Annual," *FRED (Federal Reserve Economic Data)*, https://alfred.stlouisfed.org/series?seid=GDPA#0. U.S. annual GDP in 1929 was $104.556 billion. U.S. annual GDP in 1933 was $57.154 billion.

[6] Federal Reserve Bank of St. Louis, "Industrial Production Index: Monthly," *FRED (Federal Reserve Economic Data)*, https://alfred.stlouisfed.org/series?seid=INDPRO. The U.S. Industrial Production Index in March of 1929 was 7.7262. By July 1929, it had climbed to 8.1693. By March of 1933, the month

Franklin Roosevelt became President, the Industrial Production Index had fallen to 3.9046.

[7] U.S. Department of Agriculture, Agricultural Marketing Service, Crop Reporting Board, *Agricultural Prices: 1959 Annual Summary*, June 1960, Table 3-Index numbers of prices received by farmers, by commodity groups, United States, 1910-59, 7, https://downloads.usda.library.cornell.edu/usda-esmis/files/pk02c9724/3x816p72b/b5644v185/AgriPricSu-06-00-1960.pdf. In 1929, the index number for "All Crops" was 135. By 1932, it had plunged to 57; and by 1933, it stood at 71. The 1929 index number for "All Livestock" was 159. By 1932, it had fallen to 72; and by 1933 it dipped further to 70. The combined 1929 index number for "Crops and Livestock" was 148. By 1932, it had dropped by well over 50% to 65; and by 1933, it had risen only a little to 70. (Also from 1929 to 1933, the National Farm Product—that is: the total value of farm output—fell in constant dollars by more than 50% from 13,579 million to 6,654 million. John W. Kendrick and Carl E. Jones, "Gross National Farm Product in Constant Dollars, 1910-1950, Survey of Current Business, September 1951, Table 1, 15, https://fraser.stlouisfed.org/files/docs/publications/SCB/pages/1950-1954/4379_1950-1954.pdf).

[8] Federal Reserve Bank of St. Louis, "Number of Banks in the United States: Semiannual, End of Period" *FRED (Federal Reserve Economic Data)*, https://alfred.stlouisfed.org/series?seid=X02NOB. The number of U.S. banks in mid-1929 was 25,113. The number fell by the end of 1932 to 18,394, and by mid-1933 dropped to 14,523.

[9] Federal Reserve Bank of St. Louis, "Dow-Jones Industrial Stock Price Index for United States: Monthly," *FRED (Federal Reserve Economic Data)*, https://fred.stlouisfed.org/series/M1109BUSM293NNBR. Data are based on daily closing prices on the New York Stock Exchange and are averages of the highest and lowest indexes for the month.

[10] Jonathan Alter, *The Defining Moment: FDR's Hundred Days and the Triumph of Hope* (New York: Simon and Schuster, 2006), 2.

[11] Nathan Miller, *FDR: An Intimate Portrait* (New York: Doubleday, 1983), 252.

[12] William E. Leuchtenburg, *Franklin D. Roosevelt and the New Deal* (New York: Harper Torchbooks, 1963), 4.

[13] Franklin D. Roosevelt, *Public Papers and Addresses of Franklin D. Roosevelt*, Volume One, "The Genesis of the New Deal: 1928-1932," Nomination Acceptance Speech, July 2, 1932 (New York: Random House, 1938), 647 ff.

[14] Leuchtenburg, 10.

[15] Roosevelt, *Public Papers*, Volume One, 799, 808.

[16] Leuchtenburg, 12.

[17] Leuchtenburg, 12.

[18] Leuchtenburg, 12.

[19] Leuchtenburg, 33.

[20] Raymond Moley, *After Seven Years* (New York: Harper and Brothers, 1939), 369-370.

[21] Frances Perkins, *The Roosevelt I Knew* (New York: Viking Press, 1946), 166-167.

[22] Perkins, 166-167.

[23] Perkins, 173.

[24] Perkins, 173.

[25] Associated Press story by unnamed reporter with headline "Crowd Mind Read by Mrs. Roosevelt," dated March 4, 1933, published in *The New York Times*, March 5, 1933, 7.

[26] Roosevelt, *Public Papers*, Volume Two, 11-12.

[27] Roosevelt, *Public Papers*, Volume Two, 11-12.

[28] Roosevelt, *Public Papers*, Volume Two, 11-12.

[29] Roosevelt, *Public Papers*, Volume Two, 11-12.

[30] Roosevelt, *Public Papers*, Volume Two, 11-12.

[31] Roosevelt, *Public Papers*, Volume Two, 11-12.

[32] Roosevelt, *Public Papers*, Volume Two, 11-12.

[33] Roosevelt, *Public Papers*, Volume Two, 11-12.

[34] Roosevelt, *Public Papers*, Volume One, 807.

[35] Roosevelt, *Public Papers*, Volume One, 807.

[36] Roosevelt, *Public Papers*, Volume One, 810.

[37] Joseph Lelyveld, *His Final Battle: The Last Months of Franklin Roosevelt* (New York: Alfred A. Knopf, 2016), 92.

[38] Lelyveld, 79.

CHAPTER 2: THE NEW DEAL'S FOUR POLICY CLUSTERS

[1] Alter, 5, 6.

[2] Roosevelt, *Public Papers*, Volume Two, 11-12. "Action in this image and to this end is feasible under the form of government which we have inherited from our ancestors. Our Constitution is so simple and practical that it is possible always to meet extraordinary needs by changes in emphasis and arrangement without loss of essential form. That is why our constitutional system has proved itself the most superbly enduring political mechanism the modern world has produced. It has met every stress of vast expansion of territory, of foreign wars, of bitter internal strife, of world relations."

[3] Roosevelt, *Public Papers*, Volume Two, 11-12.

[4] See Chapter Three ("Success and Failure") for a list, within each broad purpose of government, of the major functions that government performs.

[5] The list does not include the National Industrial Recovery Act of 1933, which included provisions to promote economic security, provide housing for the poor, regulate the market, and intervene in the market. It was struck down in May 1935 by the U.S. Supreme Court, was scheduled to expire in June 1935, and (even if not invalidated) had become so unpopular that it would probably not have been renewed.

[6] See: (A) Roosevelt, Public Papers, Volume Two, 80-84, and (B) Civilian Conservation Corps (CCC) Legacy, 2018, "Camp Roosevelt, NF-1," http://www.ccclegacy.org/Camp_Roosevelt_68B9.php, and "CCC Brief History," http://www.ccclegacy.org/CCC_Brief_History.html.

[7] Arthur E. Burns and Edward A. Williams, *Federal Work, Security, and Relief Programs*," Federal Works Agency, Works Projects Administration, Division of Research, Research Monograph XXIV, 1941, Chapters IV and VII, 31 and 54. The CWA hired as many as 4.2 million workers. At its height, the WPA employed 3.0 million workers.

[8] Chris Carola, The Associated Press, "FDR Insurance Job Desk Coming to Hyde Park," *Newsday*, February 19, 2012, https://www.newsday.com/news/nation/fdr-insurance-job-desk-coming-to-hyde-park-1.3542558. Roosevelt worked from 1921 to 1928 in the New York City office of the Baltimore-based Fidelity and Deposit Company.

[9] Frances Perkins, "The Roots of Social Security," speech delivered at Social Security Administration Headquarters, Baltimore, MD, October 23, 1962, Social Security Administration, *Speeches and Articles*, https://www.ssa.gov/history/perkins5.html.

[10] Burns and Williams, 16-19 and Table 2, 133. In February 1933 — President Hoover's last full month in office, and therefore before Franklin Roosevelt became President — there were 4.4 million cases of individuals receiving federally-funded emergency relief, a number which was cut nearly in half to 2.6 million in December 1935 as a result of the WPA's transfer of unemployed adults from "relief" to wage-paying jobs.

[11] Perkins, "The Roots of Social Security." Former Secretary of Labor Perkins, in her 1962 speech, recalled how intensely FDR hated the dole: "Franklin Roosevelt was greatly opposed to the dole: 'Oh, we don't want the dole; not the dole!'"

[12] Franklin D. Roosevelt, *The Public Papers and Addresses of Franklin D. Roosevelt*, Volume Four, "The Court Disapproves: 1935," Annual Message to the Congress," January 4, 1935 (New York: Random House, 1938), 19-20.

[13] U.S. Department of Health and Human Services, Office of the Assistant Secretary for Planning and Evaluation, *Indicators of Welfare Dependence: Annual Report to Congress*, March 1, 2001, Appendix A, Table TANF 1. "Trends in AFDC/TANF Caseloads, 1962-1999," A-8, https://files.eric.ed.gov/fulltext/ED457288.pdf; and Center on Budget and Policy Priorities, *Chart Book: Temporary Assistance to Needy Families*, August 16, 2017, https://www.cbpp.org/research/family-income- support/chart-book-temporary-assistance-for-needy-families.

[14] U.S. Department of Agriculture, *Supplemental Nutrition Assistance Program (SNAP): A Short History of Snap*, November 28, 2017, https://www.fns.usda.gov/snap/short- history-snap.

[15] John Joseph Wallis, Richard E. Sylla, and Arthur Grinath III, "Sovereign Debt and Repudiation: The Emerging-Market Debt Crisis in the U.S. States, 1839 -1843," *NBER Working Paper Series*, National Bureau of Economic Research, Working Paper 10753, September 2004, 2-3 and Table 2, 33, https://www.nber.org/papers/w10753.pdf. From 1841 to 1843, eight states — Arkansas, Illinois, Indiana, Louisiana, Maryland, Michigan, Mississippi, Pennsylvania — and the territory of Florida defaulted on their debt service payments. Four states — Arkansas, Louisiana, Michigan, and Mississippi — as well as the territory of Florida ultimately repudiated their debits, in part or in whole. Most of the debt was issued to finance infrastructure investments in canals, banks, and railroads.

[16] Encyclopedia Britannica Editors, "Pacific Railways Acts," *Encyclopedia Britannica*, https://www.britannica.com/event/Pacific-Railway-Acts.

[17] Abraham Lincoln, "Order Establishing Gauge of Union Pacific Railroad," *Collected Works of Abraham Lincoln*, Volume 6, January 21, 1863, https://quod.lib.umich.edu/l/lincoln/lincoln6/1:125?rgn=div1;view=fulltext: and

U.S. Congress, 37th Congress, 3rd Session, Chapter 112, "An Act to Establish the Gauge of the Pacific Railroad and Its Branches," Approved March 3, 1863, *Statutes at Large*, Library of Congress, https://www.loc.gov/law/help/statutes-at-large/37th-congress/session-3/c37s3ch112.pdf. President Lincoln, pursuant to the first Pacific Railway Act of 1862, issued an order on January 21, 1863, "that the uniform width of the track of said Rail Road and all its branches which are provided for in the aforesaid Act of Congress, shall be Five (5) feet." Congress objected, enacting a law, approved by Lincoln on March 3, 1863, that reduced the track width to the "standard gauge" of four feet and 8-1/2 inches.

[18] Wayne D. Rasmussert, Gladys L. Bakers, and James S. Ward, U.S. Department of Agriculture, "A Short History of Agricultural Adjustment, 1933-75," *Agricultural Information Bulletin No. 391*, March 1976, http://naldc.nal.usda.gov/download/CAT87210025/PDF.

[19] The resulting array of tax expenditures is summarized in a report by the staff of the U.S. Congress, Joint Committee on Taxation, *Estimates of Federal Tax Expenditures for Fiscal Years 2016-2020*, JCX -3-17, January 30, 2017.

[20] Urban Institute and Brookings Institution, Tax Policy Center, *What Is The Tax Expenditure Budget?* Briefing Book, https://www.taxpolicycenter.org/briefing-book/what-tax-expenditure-budget, citing (A) U.S. Congress, Joint Committee on Taxation, *Estimates of Federal Tax Expenditures For Fiscal Years 2017–2021*," JCX-34-18, 2018, and (B) Eric J. Toder, Daniel Berger, and Yifan Zhang, Urban-Brookings Tax Policy Center, *Distributional Effects of Individual Income Tax Expenditures: An Update, 2016*. According to an analysis by the Tax Policy Center of the Urban Institute and Brookings Institution of the findings of the U.S. Congress's Joint Committee on Taxation (JCT): "JCT's tax expenditures for fiscal 2019 (including outlay effects) added up to just under $1.5 trillion." The Tax Policy Center notes that the actual cost of tax expenditures may be higher: "The combined revenue loss for all provisions does not equal the sum of the losses for each provision because of how the provisions interact. For example, eliminating one exemption from taxable income would push taxpayers into higher-rate brackets, thereby increasing the revenue loss from remaining exemptions. Toder, Berger, and Zhang (2016) estimated that the actual combined revenue loss from all individual tax expenditures in 2015 was about 6 percent larger than the amount computed by summing individual tax expenditures—though for one subcategory, itemized deductions, the total revenue loss is less than the sum of losses from the separate deductions."

[21] Chapter Six ("Running the Numbers") and Appendix D ("How a New Deal 3.0 Changes Government Budgets") provide additional detail on the cost of subsidies.

22 Don Jenkins, "U.S. Cranberry Growers to Seek Volume Control," *Capital Press*, August 25, 2017.

23 *US Cranberries*, 2017, http://www.uscranberries.com/About/.

24 Lenin is given credit for originating the concept of Communist government's central control of "the commanding heights of the economy," and he apparently used the expression or a variant of it. The concept if not the phrase, however, owe much to the work of Yevgeni Preobrazhensky, a Bolshevik economist whom Stalin had arrested in 1935 and murdered in 1937. Lenin's recorded notes for a speech delivered at the Fourth Congress of the Comintern read in part: "What is the plan or idea or essence of NEP [New Economic Policy]? (a) Retention of the land in the hands of the state; (b) the same for all commanding heights in the sphere of means of production (transport, etc.); (c) freedom of trade in the sphere of petty production; (d) state capitalism in the sense of attracting private capital (both concessions and mixed companies)." See: (A) 2000 PBS interview of Anatoly Chubias, https://www.pbs.org/wgbh/commandingheights/ shared/minitext/int_anatoliichubais.html; (B) Biographical Note for Evgenii A. Preobrazhensky, 1898-1937, https://www.marxists.org/ archive/preobrazhensky/1921/fromnep/biog.html; and (C) V.I. Lenin, "Notes for a Report 'Five Years of the Russian Revolution and the Prospects of the World Revolution" at the Fourth Congress of the Comintern," written before November 13, 1922, published in *Pravda* on January 26, 1926, and in, *Lenin's Collected Works*, Vol. 36, 585-587, https:// www.marxists.org/archive/lenin/works/1922/nov/13b.htm.

CHAPTER 3: SUCCESS AND FAILURE

1 Virginia Commonwealth University, *Social Security: Unemployment Insurance*, https://socialwelfare.library.vcu.edu/social-security/social-security-unemployment- insurance/.

2 501(c) Agencies Trust, *Why Unemployment Insurance Exists*, www.501ctrust.org/why- unemployment-insurance-exists/.

3 U.S. Department of Labor, "Monthly Program and Financial Data," *State UI Program Data: U.S. Totals*, https://oui.doleta.gov/ unemploy/5159report.asp, updated 11/30/2017.

4 U.S. Department of Labor, *State UI Program Data*.

5 The Social Security Old Age, Survivors, and Disability Insurance (OASDI) Program also provides benefits to retired workers' dependents (spouses and children), survivors of deceased workers, and disabled workers and dependents (spouses and children).

6 Social Security Administration, *Historical Background and Development of Social Security*, www.ssa.gov/history/briefhistory3.html.

7 Social Security Administration, *Fact Sheet*, www.ssa.gov/news/press/ factsheets/basicfact-alt.pdf.

8 Social Security Administration, *Fast Facts and Figures About Social Security: 2017*, SSA Publication No. 13-11785, September 2017, 15, 18, 20, www.ssa.gov/policy/docs/chartbooks/fast_facts/2017/fast_facts17.pdf.

9 Social Security Administration, *Annual Statistical Supplement: 2018*, Table 4.A.4, 4.8, www.ssa.gov/policy/docs/statcomps/supplement/2018/4a.pdf.

10 Kathleen Romec and Arloc Sherman, Center on Budget and Policy Priorities, *Social Security Keeps 22 Million Americans Out of Poverty: A State-by-State Analysis*, October 15, 2016, Figure 1, www.cbpp.org/research/social-security/social-security-keeps-22- million-americans-out-of-poverty-a-state-by-state.

11 Dave Manuel, *A History of Bank Failures in the United States*, https:// www.davemanuel.com/history-of-bank-failures-in-the-united-states.php.

12 Federal Reserve, "Banking Act of 1933 (Glass-Steagall)," *Federal Reserve History*, 2013, https://www.federalreservehistory.org/essays/ glass_steagall_act.

13 Federal Deposit Insurance Corporation, *Historical Statistics on Banking: Failures and Assistance Transactions: 1934-2017*, www.fdic.gov/bank/ individual/failed/.

14 Centers for Disease Control and Prevention, *CDC 70th Anniversary: 7 Decades of Firsts*, www.cdc.gov/museum/history/7decades.html.

15 Centers for Disease Control and Prevention, American Academy of Family Physicians, and American Academy of Pediatrics, *Diseases and the Vaccines that Prevent Them: Polio*, February 2013, www.cdc.gov/vaccines/parents/ diseases/child/polio-indepth-color.pdf.

16 Federal Highway Administration, *Highway History*, www.fhwa.dot.gov/ interstate/faq.cfm.

17 Infogram, "Share of World GDP Throughout History," https:// infogram.com/Share-of-world-GDP-throughout-history, based on data from the Maddison Project http://www.ggdc.net/maddison/maddison-project/home.htm.

18 U.S. Department of Transportation, "Why did the federal government pay 90 percent of the cost?" *Highway History*, www.fhwa.dot.gov/interstate/ faq.cfm#question7.

[19] Michael Harrington, *The Other America: Poverty in the United States* (New York: Macmillan, 1962).

[20] James Baldwin, "Letter from a Region in My Mind," *The New Yorker* (November 17, 1962), and James Baldwin, *The Fire Next Time* (New York: Dial, 1963).

[21] Rachel Carson, *Silent Spring* (Boston: Houghton Mifflin, 1962).

[22] Ralph Nader, *Unsafe at Any Speed: The Designed-In Dangers of the American Automobile* (New York: Grossman Publishers, 1965).

[23] Kayla Fontenot, Jessica Semega, and Melissa Kolar, U.S. Census Bureau, *Income and Poverty in the United States: 2017*, September 2018, P60-263, Table B-1, 48.

[24] Fontenot *et al.*, Table B-1, 54.

[25] Fontenot *et al.*, Table B-1, 54.

[26] Fontenot *et al.*, Table B-1, 54.

[27] Liana Fox, U.S. Census Bureau, "Number and Percentages of People in Poverty by Different Poverty Measures, 2017," *The Supplemental Poverty Measure: 2017*, September 2018, P60-265, Table A-2, 21.

[28] It is likely that if—as with the "official" poverty rate—the SPM poverty rates were calculated for the years 1959-1966, SPM poverty would have been nearly 30% in the late 1950s and early 1960s. If true, the drop in the SPM rate from a "guesstimate" of roughly 30% in 1959 to the calculated level of 19% in 1973 would be even more dramatic.

[29] Danilo Trisi, Center on Budget and Policy Priorities, *Economic Security Programs Cut Poverty Nearly in Half Over Last 50 Years, New Data Show*, September 14, 2018, Figure 4, 6, https://www.cbpp.org/research/poverty-and-inequality/economic-security-programs-cut-poverty-nearly-in-half-over-last-50. Percentages are approximate, based on CBPP analysis of data from Columbia University Population Research Center and, for 2009 and later, U.S. Census Bureau.

[30] Trisi, *Economic Security Programs.*

[31] Annalyn Kurtz and Tal Yellin, *Minimum Wage Since 1938*, CNN Money/CNN Business, money.cnn.com/interactive/economy/minimum-wage-since-1938/. Source: BLS. Note: Figures adjusted to 2015 dollars using the CPI-U; Updated November 3, 2015. CPI for 2015 uses H1 average. Different inflation-adjusted minimum wage rates occur as a result of applying different methods for calculating inflation (see, e.g., the "US Inflation Calculator" at www.usinflationcalculator.com/) as well as adjusting for

different final years (e.g., here 2015 is used, but data are now available for a few later years). The pattern is nonetheless the same.

32 Kurtz and Yellin, *Minimum Wage.*

33 Kurtz and Yellin, *Minimum Wage.*

34 Drew DeSilver, Pew Research Center, "For Most U.S. Workers, Real Wages Have Barely Budged in Decades," *FactTank*, August 7, 2018, pewresearch.org/fact- tank/2018/08/07/for-most-us-workers-real-wages-have-barely-budged-for-decades/.

35 De Silver, *FactTank.*

36 Fontenot *et al.*, Table A-4, 44.

37 Fontenot *et al.*, Table A-4, 44.

38 Federal Reserve Bank of St. Louis, "Civilian Labor Force Participation Rate: Women," *(FRED) Federal Reserve Economic Data*, https:// fred.stlouisfed.org/series/LNS11300002. Women's participation in the labor market increased from 37.0% in January 1960, to 43.3% in January 1970, to 51.6% in January 1980, to 57.7% in January 1990. It then flattened. After peaking at 60.1% in January 1990, it fell to 56.9% in January 2017.

39 Fontenot *et al.*, Table A-1, 27.

40 Fontenot *et al.*, Table A-1, 27.

41 Fontenot *et al.*, Table A-1, 27.

42 Employee Benefit Research Institute (EBRI), *FAQs About Benefits-Retirement Issues*, using data from the U.S. Department of Labor and U.S. Pension Benefit Guarantee Corporation, https://www.ebri.org/publications/ benfaq/index.cfm?fa=retfaq14.

43 EBRI, *FAQs.*

44 (A) For 1959-2007: Robin A. Cohen, Diane M. Makuc, Amy B. Bernstein, Linda T. Bilheimer, and Eve Powell-Griner, Centers for Disease Control and Prevention, U.S. Department of Health and Human Services, "Health Insurance Coverage Trends, 1959-2007: Estimates from the National Health Interview Survey," *National Health Statistics Reports*, Number 17, July 1, 2009, Table A, 4, and Table 1, 9. (B) For 1972-2011; Robin A. Cohen, Centers for Disease Control and Prevention, U.S. Department of Health and Human Services, *Trends in Health Care Coverage and Insurance for 1968-2011*, Table 1, https://www.cdc.gov/nchs/health_policy/ trends_hc_1968_2011.htm. (C) For 2012-2018: Emily P. Terlizzi, Robin A. Cohen, and Michael E. Martinez, , Centers for Disease Control and Prevention, U.S. Department of Health and Human Services, "Health

Insurance Coverage: Early Release of Estimates From the *National Health Interview Survey, January–September 2018," National Health Interview Survey Early Release Program,"* Released 2/2019, 12, Table I: Percentages (and standard errors) of Persons Who Lacked Health Insurance Coverage at the Time of Interview, For at Least Part of the Past year, and for More than 1 Year, by Age Group and Selected Years: United States, 1997–September 2018, https://www.cdc.gov/nchs/data/nhis/earlyrelease/insur201902.pdf.
(Note: For 1959, 1963, and 1968, percentages are for the under-65 population without hospital insurance. For 2018, the percentage is for January-September.)

45 *Ibid.*

46 *Ibid.*

47 *Ibid.*

48 Edward R. Berchick, Emily Hood, and Jessica C. Barnett, U.S. Census Bureau, "Health Insurance Coverage in the United States: 2017," P60-264, September 2018, 1.

49 Frederic Slade, "Health Care Inflation: What Might Be Behind the Numbers?" *BenefitsPro*, June 21, 2018, https://www.benefitspro.com/2018/06/21/health-care- inflation-what-might-be-behind-the-num/?slreturn=20180926164830.

50 Gary Claxton, Matthew Rae, Larry Levitt, and Cynthia Cox, Kaiser Family Foundation, "How Have Healthcare Prices Grown in the U.S. Over Time?" *Peterson-Kaiser Health System Tracker*, May 8, 2018, https://www.healthsystemtracker.org/chart-collection/how- have-healthcare-prices-grown-in-the-u-s-over-time/#item-start.

51 Centers for Medicare and Medicaid Services (CMS), *National Health Expenditures; Aggregate and Per Capita Amounts, Annual Percent Change and Percent Distribution: Calendar Years 1960-2015*, https://www.cms.gov/Research-Statistics-Data-and-Systems/Statistics- Trends-and-Reports/NationalHealthExpendData/NationalHealthAccountsHistorical.html, extracted 9/26/2017.

52 Bradley Sawyer and Cynthia Cox, Kaiser Family Foundation, "How Does Health Spending in the U.S. Compare to Other Countries?," February 13, 2018, *Peterson-Kaiser Health System Tracker*, https://www.healthsystemtracker.org/chart-collection/health- spending-u-s-compare-countries/#item-start.

53 CMS projected that U.S. health care spending would reach 19.9% of GDP in 2025. See Centers for Medicare and Medicaid Services (CMS), *2016-2025*

Projections of National Health Expenditures Data Released, February 15, 2017, https://www.cms.gov/Newsroom/MediaReleaseDatabase/Press-releases/2017-Press- releases-items/2017-02-15-2.html.

[54] Uwe E. Reinhardt, "Does the Aging of the Population Really Drive the Demand for Health Care?" *Health Affairs*, Volume 22, No. 6, November/December 2003, https://www.healthaffairs.org/doi/full/10.1377/hlthaff.22.6.27.

[55] Olga Khazan,"Why Are So Many Americans Dying Young?" *The Atlantic*, December 13, 2016, https://www.theatlantic.com/health/archive/2016/12/why-are-so-many- americans-dying-young/510455/.

[56] For two excellent contemporary accounts of some of these newer facets of economic insecurity, see: (A) Jonathan Morduch and Rachel Schneider, *The Financial Diaries: How Americans Cope in a World of Uncertainty* (Princeton and Oxford, Princeton University Press, 2017), and (B) Alissa Quart, *Squeezed: Why Our Families Can't Afford America* (New York: Ecco/Harper Collins, 2018).

[57] See, e.g., United Nations, "WMO Report: 2017 Is Set to Be in Top 3 Hottest Years," November 6, 2017, http://www.un.org/sustainabledevelopment/blog/2017/11/wmo- statement-on-state-of-climate-in-2017/.

[58] Fiona Harvey, "Urgent Action Needed to Stop Terrifying Rise in Air Pollution, Warns OECD," *The Guardian*, June 9, 2016, https://www.theguardian.com/environment/2016/jun/09/urgent-action-needed-to-stop- terrifying-rise-in-air-pollution-warns-oecd.

[59] Harvey, *Guardian*.

[60] Harvey, *Guardian*.

[61] Harvey, *Guardian*.

[62] Alison Henderson, "Oak Creek's Coal-Powered Problem?" *Shepherd Express*, December 19, 2017, https://shepherdexpress.com/news/features/oak-creek-s-coal- powered-problem/#/questions.

[63] Henderson, *Shepherd*.

[64] CNN, *Flint Water Crisis Fast Facts*, December 6, 2018, http://www.cnn.com/2016/03/04/us/flint-water-crisis-fast-facts/index.html.

[65] CNN, *Flint Water Crisis*.

[66] Merlin Hearn, Water Benefits Health, "10 Water Pollution Facts for the United States," *20 Water Pollution Facts for the U.S. and the World*, http://www.waterbenefitshealth.com/water-pollution-facts.html.

67 Lee Bergquist, "Conflict Between Neighbors Highlights Limits of Pollution Regulation," *Milwaukee Journal Sentinel*, January 31, 2016, http:// archive.jsonline.com/news/statepolitics/conflict-between-neighbors-highlights- limits-of-pollution-regulation-b99679679z1-371231701.html/.

68 Raquel Rutledge and Rick Barrett, "Burned: Chemicals Left in Barrels Leave Workers and Neighborhoods at Risk," *Milwaukee Journal Sentinel*, February 15, 2017, https://projects.jsonline.com/news/2017/2/15/chemicals-left-in -barrels-leave-many-at- risk.html.

69 Occupational Safety and Health Administration (OSHA), *Commonly Used Statistics*, https://www.osha.gov/oshstats/commonstats.html.

70 OHSA, *Statistics*.

71 OSHA, *Statistics*.

72 Bureau of Labor Statistics (BLS), "Fatal Occupational Injuries for Selected Events or Exposures, 2011-17," *Economic News Release*, December 18, 2018, Table 2, https://www.bls.gov/news.release/cfoi.t02.htm.

73 Brady Meixell and Ross Eisenbrey, Economic Policy Institute, "*An Epidemic of Wage Theft Is Costing Workers Hundreds of Millions of Dollars a Year*," Issue Brief #385, September 11, 2014, http://www.epi.org/files/2014/wage-theft.pdf.

74 Annette Bernhardt, Ruth Milkman, Nik Theodore, Douglas Heckathorn, Mirabai Auer, James DeFilippis, Ana Luz González, Victor Narro, Jason Perelshteyn, Diana Polson, and Michael Spiller, *Broken Laws, Unprotected Workers: Violations of Employment and Labor Laws in America's Cities*, 2-3, http://www.nelp.org/content/uploads/2015/03/ BrokenLawsReport2009.pdf. In addition to the National Employment Law Project, the staff of the UIC Center for Urban Economic Development and UCLA Institute for Research on Labor and Employment provided support for this project.

75 Bernhardt *et al.*, *Broken Laws*.

76 Bernhardt *et al.*, *Broken Laws*, 5.

77 Bernhardt *et al.*, *Broken Laws*, 6.

78 Meixell and Eisenbrey, *Wage Theft*.

79 Meixell and Eisenbrey, *Wage Theft*.

80 Meixell and Eisenbrey, *Wage Theft*.

81 Woody Guthrie, *The Ballad of Pretty Boy Floyd*, 1939.

[82] U.S. Consumer Product Safety Commission (CPSC), *Injury Statistics*, https://www.cpsc.gov/Research--Statistics/Injury-Statistics/.

[83] CPSC, *Injury Statistics*.

[84] John M. Conor, Professor *Emeritus*, Purdue University, *Price Fixing Overcharges*, 3rd Edition, February 2014, http://www.govinplace.org/content/John%20Connor_Price- Fixing%20Overcharges.pdf.

[85] North American Securities Administrators Association (NASAA), *NASAA Announces Top Investor Threats: Investors Reminded to Approach Unsolicited Offers With Caution*, November 31, 2015, http://www.nasaa.org/38470/nasaa-announces-top-investor-threats/.

[86] NASAA, *Top Investor Threats*.

[87] NASAA, *Top Investor Threats*.

[88] Gallup, *Satisfaction With the United States,* http://www.gallup.com/poll/1669/general-mood-country.aspx. Gallup's question was: "In general, are you satisfied or dissatisfied with the way things are going in the United States at this time?"

[89] Pew Research Center, *Public Trust in Government Remains Near Historic Lows*, http://www.people-press.org/2017/05/03/public-trust-in-government-remains-near- historic-lows-as-partisan-attitudes-shift/1-19/. Pew's question was whether respondents "Trust the federal government to do what is right just about always/most of the time...").

[90] Pew Research Center, *Public Trust*.

[91] Pew Research Center, *Public Trust in Government: 1958-2017*, December 14, 2017, http://www.people-press.org/2017/12/14/public-trust-in-government-1958-2017/.

Chapter 4: The New Deal's Shortcomings

[1] The categories and data that underpin the premise that the U.S. generally has a big job shortage are explained in Appendix B, "The U.S. Job Shortage."

[2] Kayla Fontenot, Jessica Semega, and Melissa Kolar, U.S. Census Bureau, *Income and Poverty in the United States: 2017,* September 2018, P60-263, Appendix B, p. 47, and Table B-1, 48. For a four-person family consisting of one adult and three children under 18, the "official" poverty line in 2017 was $24,944.

[3] See Appendix C, "Defining an Adequate Income," for an explanation of the peculiar history of the U.S.'s official poverty line and its insufficiency as a

measure of what Americans really need to maintain a decent living standard.

4 Pauline Bortolone, "When High Deductibles Cause Even Insured Patients to Postpone Care," *CNN Business*, August 5, 2017, https:// money.cnn.com/2017/08/05/news/economy/high-deductibles-insured-health- care/index.html. "Just over half of people with health plans from their employers now have a deductible of $1,000 or more, up from 10% in 2006, according to the Kaiser Family Foundation. ... Another recent study by researchers at the University of California-Berkeley and Harvard University found that people with high-deductible plans spent 42% less on health care before meeting their deductibles, primarily by reducing the amount of health care they received, not by shopping around for a better price. Jonathan Kolstad, associate professor of economics at UC-Berkeley's business school and co-author of the study, said patients dropped both needed care, such as diabetes medication, and potentially unnecessary care, such as imaging for headaches."

5 See Appendix C for a detailed discussion of what should be seen as a minimally adequate income.

6 Christopher Jencks and Kathryn Edin, "The Real Welfare Problem," *The American Prospect*, Spring 1990, http://prospect.org/article/real-welfare-problem.

7 "49% Believe Government Programs Increases Poverty in America," *Rasmussen Reports*, July 30, 2014, http://www.rasmussenreports.com/ public_content/lifestyle/general_lifestyle/july_2014/49 _believe_government_programs_increase_poverty_in_america.

8 The reputation of the welfare system, whether accurate or distorted, has also trapped many in America's middle class and policymaking circles in a mental "prison" of identifying the poor as primarily welfare recipients rather than as unemployed jobseekers or low-wage workers, thus undermining the effort to reduce poverty by creating or expanding work-based economic security guarantees. This is one of the arguments made in David R. Riemer, *The Prisoners of Welfare: Liberating America's Poor from Unemployment and Low Wages* (New York: Praeger, 1988).

9 U.S. Environmental Protection Agency (EPA), *Nutrient Pollution: Sources and Solutions*, https://www.epa.gov/nutrientpollution/sources-and-solutions.

10 U.S. Environmental Protection Agency (EPA), *Nutrient Pollution: The Problem*, https://www.epa.gov/nutrientpollution/problem.

11 Urban Institute/Brookings Institution, *Tax Expenditure Budget*.

[12] Samuel Johnson, lines added to Oliver Goldsmith's *The Traveller, or A Prospect of Society* (1764).

[13] Alexis de Tocqueville, *Democracy in America*, Volume I, Chapter XIII, Part III, "Self-Control of the American Democracy," 1835, http://seas3.elte.hu/coursematerial/LojkoMiklos/Alexis-de-Tocqueville-Democracy-in-America.pdf.

CHAPTER 5: THE NEXT CHANGE OF CONCEPT: A NEW DEAL 3.0

[1] Wisconsin issued the first unemployment check in the amount of $15 to Neils B. Ruud of Madison, Wisconsin on August 17, 1936. *Unemployment Insurance: 75th Anniversary*, https://www.dol.gov/ocia/pdf/75th-anniversary-summary-final.pdf. This was three years and several months before Ida May Fuller of Vermont received the first Social Security retirement check in the amount of $22.54 on January 31, 1940.

[2] UI recipients who elect this option should be free at any time to re-convert back to their guaranteed UI cash benefits.

[3] The federal minimum wage of $7.25/hour x 40 hours/week x 52 weeks/year yields a gross income of $15,080. But according to the Gallup Poll in 2013, "the smallest amount of money a family of four needs to make each year to get by" was $43,600. For a single person, I estimate the corresponding amount for a single person to be $27,500. See Appendix C, "Defining an Adequate Income," for the methodology used to adjust the Gallup findings to families of different size.

[4] See Appendix C, "Defining an Adequate Income," for the methodology used to adjust the Gallup Poll findings to families of different size.

[5] David R. Riemer, "The Marriage Tax on the Poor, *The New York Times*, July 21, 2000. I am indebted to the late Senator Daniel Patrick Moynihan for including the op-ed in his published remarks in the *Congressional Record*, July 21, 2000, 15774.

[6] Center on Budget and Policy Priorities, "2018 Earned Income Tax Credit Parameters," *Policy Basics, The Earned Income Tax Credit*, April 29, 2018, Tables 1 and 2, https://www.cbpp.org/research/federal-tax/policy-basics-the-earned-income-tax-credit.

[7] A response to the concern that the earnings supplement will then be provided to high-income workers who do not need it is to treat the earning supplement as the equivalent of taxable income by reducing it by the tax filer's highest marginal tax rate. Thus, high-income workers would see larger shares of the earnings supplement "clawed back" through the

normal rules of the individual income tax. I discuss this approach further at the end of Appendix D, "How a New Deal 3.0 Changes Government Budgets."

8 See Appendix C.

9 SSDI recipients who elect this option should be free at any time to re-convert back to their guaranteed SSDI cash benefits.

10 See Appendix C.

11 Carbon Tax Center (CTC), *Why a Carbon Tax?* https://www.carbontax.org/why-a-carbon-tax/.

12 CTC, *Why Carbon Tax*.

13 CTC, *Why Carbon Tax*.

14 Charles Komanoff, Carbon Tax Center, "Carbon Tax Center Backs Climate Leadership Council's Carbon Tax Proposal," February 8, 2017, https://www.carbontax.org/blog/2017/02/08/carbon-tax-center-backs-climate-leadership-councils-carbon-tax-proposal/.

15 James A. Baker, III, Martin Feldstein, Ted Halstead, N. Gregory Mankiw, Henry M. Paulson, Jr., George P. Schultz, Thomas Stephenson, and Rob Walton, "The Conservative Case for Carbon Dividends," *Climate Leadership Council*, February 2017, https://www.clcouncil.org/wp-content/uploads/2017/02/TheConservativeCaseforCarbonDividends.pdf.

16 Baker *et al.*, *Conservative Case*.

17 EPA, *Nutrient Pollution Sources*.

18 EPA, *Nutrient Pollution Problem*.

19 ScienceDaily, "TV Drug Ads: The Whole Truth?" September 16, 2013, https://www.sciencedaily.com/releases/2013/09/130916140455.htm.

20 Margaret Farley Steele, HealthDay Reporter, "FDA May Limit 'Risk-Info' in Direct- to-Consumer TV Drug Ads," *U.S. News and World Report*, August 18, 2017, https://health.usnews.com/health-care/articles/2017-08-18/fda-may-limit-risk-info-in- direct-to-consumer-tv-drug-ads.

21 Jayne O'Donnell, "Inspector General Report: FDA Food Recalls Dangerously Slow, Procedures Deeply Flawed," *USA Today*, December 26, 2017, https://www.usatoday.com/story/news/politics/2017/12/26/inspector-general-report-fda- food-recalls-dangerously-slow-procedures-deeply-flawed/975701001/.

22 O'Donnell, *USA Today*.

23 Theresa May, *Speech at the 20th Anniversary of the Independence of the Bank of England,* September 27, 2017, https://www.gov.uk/government/ speeches/pm-speech-at- 20th-anniversary-of-bank-of-england- independence-event.

Chapter 6: Running the Numbers

1 Matthew Sanford, "Worker's Compensation Requirements by State," *OnPay,* https://help.payrollcenter.com/hc/en-us/articles/201846509-Worker-s- Compensation-Requirements-by-State.

2 ISO, "Basis of Premium," *Workers' Compensation/Technical Achievement Program,* Chapter 3, https://www.verisk.com/insurance/products/ premium-audit-advisory-service/technical-achievement-program/ workers-comp/chapter-3/. Primarily, the basis of premium for Workers' Compensation is payroll. Essentially, this means wages, but the Workers' Compensation Manual states: "Premium shall be computed on the basis of the total payroll paid or payable by the insured for services of employees covered by the policy." This has the effect of broadening the premium base by a considerable extent. Payroll means money or substitutes of money.

3 PrimePay, *How Is Your Workers' Comp Rate Calculated?* June 6, 2018, https:// primepay.com/blog/how-your-workers-comp-rate-calculated. "Three factors of workers' comp premium: 1. Size of the employer's payroll. 2. Employee job classifications. 3. Company's claims experience. Premiums for worker's compensation are calculated by the formula below: Payroll (per $100) x Classification x Experience Modifier = Premium. How your payroll affects your workers' comp rate. The basis for an employer's workers' comp insurance premium is your payroll. For each $100 of your payroll, there is a specific rate, which is determined by the classification code of your employer."

4 International Risk Management Institute, Inc. (IRMI), *Competitive State Funds,* https://www.irmi.com/term/insurance-definitions/competitive-state- funds. "State-owned and-operated facilities that compete with commercial insurers in writing workers compensation insurance specific solely to that state. The states with these funds are California, Colorado, Hawaii, Idaho, Kentucky, Louisiana, Maine, Maryland, Minnesota, Missouri, Montana, New Mexico, New York, Oklahoma, Oregon, Pennsylvania, Rhode Island, Texas, and Utah."

5 International Risk Management Institute, Inc. (IRMI), *Monopolistic State Funds*, https://www.irmi.com/term/insurance-definitions/monopolistic-state-funds. "Jurisdictions where an employer must obtain workers compensation insurance from a compulsory state fund or qualify as a self-insurer (as is allowed in two of the jurisdictions). Such insurance is not subject to any of the procedures or programs of the National Council on Compensation Insurance (NCCI). Instead, each jurisdiction has its own rules and regulations that govern the placement and administration of workers compensation insurance. The following states/jurisdictions are monopolistic fund states: North Dakota, Ohio, Washington, Wyoming, Puerto Rico, and the U.S. Virgin Islands."

6 Centers for Medicare and Medicaid Services (CMS), Office of the Actuary, National Health Statistics Group, *NHE Tables*, "Household Contribution to Employer Sponsored Private Health Insurance Premiums (2015)," Table 5-2, https://www.cms.gov/Research- Statistics-Data-and-Systems/Statistics-Trends-and- Reports/NationalHealthExpendData/NationalHealthAccountsHistorical.html.

7 CMS, *NHE Tables*, Private Business Contribution, Table 5-1, Federal Government Contribution Table 5-3, and State and Local Government Contribution, Table 5-4.

8 Kye Lippold, Urban Institute, *Reducing Poverty in the United States: Results of a Microsimulation Analysis of the Community Advocates Public Policy Institute Policy Package*, March 2015, https://www.urban.org/sites/default/files/publication/48586/2000151-reducing-poverty-in-the-united-states.pdf.

CHAPTER 7: THE PATH TO REFORM

1 Douglas Blackmon, *Slavery by Another Name: The Re-Enslavement of Black Americans from the Civil War to World War II* (New York: Anchor Books, 2008).

2 Roosevelt, *Public Papers*, Volume One, 646.

3 Lelyveld, 60.

4 Lelyveld, 68.

5 Lelyveld, 137.

6 Perkins, *The Roosevelt I Knew*, 5.

7 Perkins, 5.

APPENDIX B: THE U.S. JOB SHORTAGE

[1] Perkins, 95.

[2] Bureau of Labor Statistics (BLS), "Who Is Counted as Unemployed?" *How the Government Measures Unemployment*, https://www.bls.gov/cps/cps_htgm.htm#unemployed.

[3] Bureau of Labor Statistics (BLS), "Who Is Not in the Labor Force?" *How the Government Measures Unemployment*, https://www.bls.gov/cps/cps_htgm.htm#unemployed.

[4] Bureau of Labor Statistics (BLS), "How Does JOLTS Define Job Openings, *Job Opening and Labor Turnover Survey*, April 11, 2017, https://www.bls.gov/jlt/jltdef.htm#2. I have slightly modified the quotation's punctuation and addition of emphasis. BLS also notes that a job opening does not include: (1) positions open only to internal transfers, promotions or demotions, or recall from layoffs; (2) openings for positions with start dates more than 30 days in the future; (3) positions for which employees have been hired, but the employees have not yet reported for work; or (4) positions to be filled by employees of temporary help agencies, employee leasing companies, outside contractors, or consultants.

[5] BLS, *Job Survey*.

[6] Bureau of Labor Statistics (BLS), "Unemployment and Other Labor Market Difficulties," *TED: The Economics Daily*, November 18, 2014, https://www.bls.gov/opub/ted/2014/ted_20141118.htm.

[7] For the unemployed, see BLS, Series ID Number LNS13000000, persons 16 years and over, unemployed (no job, currently available for work, actively looked for work in prior 4 weeks), seasonally adjusted, at http://data.bls.gov/cgi-bin/srgate. For job openings, see BLS Series ID Number, JTS 00000000JOL, job openings (total nonfarm, total US). The data are seasonally adjusted at http://data.bls.gov/cgi-bin/srgate.

[8] *Ibid.*

[9] *Ibid.*

[10] *Ibid.*

[11] BLS, *Job Survey*.

[12] These data add (to the group of "officially" unemployed adults previously discussed) the following group of jobseekers reported at BLS, Series ID Number: LNU05026642: persons 16 years and older, not in labor force, want a job now, available to work now, and searched for work during the prior 12 months, http://data.bls.gov/cgi-bin/srgate. The "officially"

unemployed, whom BLS counts as part of the labor force, are not double-counted in this additional group, which BLS has defined as not in the labor force since their job search did not occur within the last four weeks.

13 See BLS, Series ID Number: LNU05026639, persons 16 years and older, not in labor force, want a job now, at http://data.bls.gov/cgi-bin/srgate.

14 See BLS, "Employed persons by class of worker and part-time status," *Economic News Release*, Table A-8, Footnotes 3 and 4, last modified October 6, 2017, https://www.bls.gov/news.release/empsit.t08.htm.

15 *Ibid.*

16 See U.S. Bureau of Labor Statistics in Series ID Number: LNS12032194, persons 16 and older, employed part time (1-34 hours) for economic reasons, http://data.bls.gov/cgi-bin/srgate.

Appendix C: Defining an Adequate Income

1 Mollie Orshansky, "Children of the Poor" *Social Security Bulletin*, Vol. 26, No. 7, July 1963, 8. The economy food plan is subsequently described as costing "about one-fourth less than the low-cost plan." See, also, Mollie Orshansky, "Measuring Poverty," *The Social Welfare Forum*, 1965, Official Proceedings, 92d Annual Forum, National Conference on Social Welfare, Atlantic City, New Jersey, May 23-25, 1965 (Columbia University Press, 1965), 215-216.

2 Orshanky, *Social Welfare Forum*, 216.

3 Pew Charitable Trusts, *Household Expenditures and Income*, Figure 4-6, 5-7, http://www.pewtrusts.org/~/media/assets/2016/03/ household_expenditures_and_income. Pdf.

4 See Gordon M. Fisher, Office of the Assistant Secretary for Planning and Evaluation, U.S. Department of Health and Human Services, "The Development and History of the Poverty Thresholds," January 1, 1997, https://aspe.hhs.gov/history-poverty-thresholds. This is a summary of Fisher, "The Development and History of the Poverty Thresholds," *Social Security Bulletin*, Vol. 55, No. 4, Winter 1992, 3-14, which in turn is a condensed version of Fisher, "The Development of the Orshansky Poverty Thresholds and Their Subsequent History as the Official U.S. Poverty Measure," unpublished paper, https://www.census.gov/content/dam/ Census/library/working- papers/1997/demo/orshansky.pdf.

5 Orshansky, "How Poverty is Measured," *Monthly Labor Review*, Vol. 92, No. 2, February 1969, 38.

[6] See Kathleen Short, U.S. Census Bureau, "The Research Supplemental Poverty Measure: 2012," *Current Population Reports*, P60-247, November 2013, https://www.census.gov/prod/2013pubs/p60-247.pdf.

[7] Liana Fox, U.S. Census Bureau, "The Supplemental Poverty Measure: 2017," *Current Population Reports*, P60-265, September 2018, Figure 1, p. 1, Figure 3, p. 5, and Table A-3, p. 23.

[8] Past surveys worded the question slightly differently. But Gallup views the polls as a consistent series that captures the same essential information.

[9] Lydia Saad, Gallup, "Americans Say Family of Four Needs Nearly $60K to "Get By," May 17, 2013, http://news.gallup.com/poll/162587/americans-say-family-four-needs- nearly-60k.aspx.

APPENDIX D: HOW A NEW DEAL 3.0 CHANGES BUDGETS

[1] "The Federal Reserve does not receive funding through the congressional budgetary process." Federal Reserve Bank of Richmond, "How Is the Federal Reserve Structured?" *Federal Reserve FAQs*, https://www.richmondfed.org/faqs/frs.

[2] See: Bureau of Labor Statistics (BLS): (A) Series ID #: LNS13008516, persons 16 and older, number unemployed for 15 weeks or more, at http://data.bls.gov/pdq/SurveyOutputServlet; (B) Series ID #: LNS13008756, persons 16 and older, number unemployed for 5-14 weeks, at http://data.bls.gov/pdq/SurveyOutputServlet; and (C) Series ID #: LNS13008396, persons 16 and older, number unemployed for less than 5 weeks, at http://data.bls.gov/pdq/SurveyOutputServlet.

[3] See: Bureau of Labor Statistics (BLS) (A) Series ID #: LNU05026645, persons 16 and older, not in labor force, want a job now, available to work now, searched for work, not currently looking for work because they are discouraged (believe no jobs are available for them or there are none for which they would qualify), at http://data.bls.gov/pdq/SurveyOutputServlet; and (B) Series ID #: LNU05026648, persons 16 and older, not in labor force, want a job now, available to work now, searched for work, not currently looking for reasons other than discouragement (e.g., family responsibilities, in School or training, ill health or disability, and other), at http://data.bls.gov/pdq/SurveyOutputServlet.

[4] Bureau of Labor Statistics (BLS), Series ID Number: LNS12032194, persons 16 and older, employed part time 1-34 hours) for economic reasons, at http://data.bls.gov/cgi-bin/srgate.

5 U.S. Census Bureau, Annual Estimates of the Resident Population for Selected Age Groups by Sex for the United States, States, Counties and Puerto Rico Commonwealth and Municipios: April 1, 2010 to July 1, 2016, released June 2017, https://factfinder.census.gov.

6 Kerri Anne Renzulli, "This Is How Much the Average Americans Spends on Childcare," *Money*, August 9, 2016, http://time.com/money/4444034/average-cost-child-care/. The report found that an after-school sitter set the average family back by even more: $214 for 15 hours of work per week.

7 Christopher Chantrill, usgovernmentspending.com, is the source of the figures used in this section for 2015 spending for SSI and SSDI.

8 Christopher Chantrill, usgovernmentspending.com, is the source of the figure used in this section for 2015 actual spending for Social Security.

9 Centers for Medicare & Medicaid Services (CMS), Office of the Actuary, National Health Statistics Group, *National Health Expenditure Accounts: Methodology Paper, 2015*, Exhibit 1, National Health Expenditures by Type of Expenditure and Program: Calendar Year 2015, 4, https://www.cms.gov/research-statistics-data-and-systems/statistics-trends-and-reports/nationalhealthexpenddata/downloads/dsm-15.pdf.

10 CMS, *NHE Accounts*, 11. "The other health, residential, and personal care category includes spending for school health, worksite health care, ... some ambulance services, residential mental health and substance abuse facilities, and other types of health care. Generally, these services are provided in non-traditional settings."

11 Kaiser Family Foundation, "Distribution of Medicaid Services: FY 2016," *State Health Facts*, https://www.kff.org/medicaid/state-indicator/distribution-of-medicaid-spending- by-service/.

12 Christopher Chantrill, usgovernmentspending.com, is the source of the figure used in this section for 2015 actual spending for primary and secondary education.

13 National Center for Education Statistics, *Digest of Education Statistics*, "Enrollment in elementary, secondary, and degree-granting postsecondary institutions, by level and control of institution, enrollment level, and attendance status and sex of student: Selected years, fall 1990 through fall 2025," Table 105-20, https://nces.ed.gov/programs/digest/d15/tables/dt15_105.20.asp.

14 See: (A) Center for Education Reform, "Average Per Pupil Expenditure," K-12 Facts, updated as of February 2016, https://www.edreform.com/2012/04/k-12-facts/#expenditures; and (B) National Center for Education Statistics, "Total and current expenditures per pupil in fall enrollment in public

elementary and secondary schools, by function and state or jurisdiction: 2015-16," *Digest of Education Statistics*, Table 236.75, https://nces.ed.gov/programs/digest/d18/tables/dt18_236.75.asp.

[15] National Center for Education Statistics, "Children 3 to 21 years old served under Individuals with Disabilities Education Act (IDEA), Part B, by type of disability: Selected years, 1976-77 through 2015-16." *Digest of Education Statistics*, Table 204-30, https://nces.ed.gov/programs/digest/d17/tables/dt17_204.30.asp.

[16] Jay G. Chambers, Thomas B. Parrish, and Jenifer J. Harr, *What Are We Spending on Special Education Services in the United States, 1999-2000?* SEEP (Special Education Expenditure Project, submitted to United States Department of Education, Office of Special Education Programs, Report 1, Updated June 2004, v, http://csef.air.org/publications/seep/national/AdvRpt1.PDF.

[17] Based on 2015 Census Bureau data, the (A) total number of 18 year olds and 19 year olds is each assumed to be 4,216,952 (one-fifth of the 15-19 year old official estimate of 21,084,710); (B) total number of 20-24 year olds is 22,693,026; (C) total number of 25-29 year olds is 22,401, 168; and (D) total number of 30-34 year olds is 21,617,533. U.S. Census Bureau, Annual Estimates of the Resident Population by Sex, Age, Race, and Hispanic Origin for the United States and States: April 1, 2010 to July 1, 2016, June 2017, https://factfinder.census.gov/faces/tableservices/jsf/pages/productview.xhtml?src=bkmk.

[18] Bureau of Labor Statistics (BLS), "College Enrollment and Work Activity of 2015 High School Graduates," April 28, 2016, https://www.bls.gov/news.release/archives/hsgec_04282016.pdf. The Bureau of Labor Statistics (BLS) reported in that, October 2015, 69.2% of 2015 high school graduates were enrolled in colleges or universities.

[19] National Center for Education Statistics, "Back to School Statistics," *Fast Facts*, https://nces.ed.gov/fastfacts/display.asp?id=372. "Some 7.0 million students will attend 2-year institutions and 13.4 million will attend 4-year institutions in fall 2017."

[20] College Board, "Average Estimated Undergraduate Budgets, 2017-2018," *Trends in Higher Education*, https://trends.collegeboard.org/college-pricing/figures-tables/average- estimated-undergraduate-budgets-2017-18.

[21] Based on 2015 actual spending figures in Christopher Chantrill, usgovern-mentspending.com, following are the names of the small federal health programs totaling $23.0 billion and each program's cost (in billions of dollars): Abandoned Mine Reclamation Fund, $0.032, and Transfers from

Abandoned Mine Reclamation Fund, ($0.032); Buildings and Facilities, $0.002; Consumer Operated and Oriented Plan Program Account, $0.212; Consumer Operated and Oriented Plan Program Contingency Fund, $0.138; Consumer Operated and Oriented Plan Direct Loan Program, Downward Reestimate of Subsidies, ($0.006); Early Retiree Reinsurance Program, ($0.011); Covered Countermeasure Process Fund, $0.005; General Departmental Management, $0.411; Health Insurance Reform Implementation Fund, $0.076; Health Resources and Services (3 accounts) $7.670); HHS Accrual Contribution to the Uniformed Services Retiree Health Care Fund, $0.028; HHS Service and Supply Fund, ($0.099); Land and Water Conservation Fund, Surplus Property Sales, ($0.001); Maternal, Infant, and Early Childhood Home Visiting Programs, $0.364); Medicaid and CHIP Payment and Access Commission, $0.009; Miscellaneous Trust Funds, $0.113; Nonrecurring Expenses Fund, $0.417; Office of Inspector General, $0.011; Office of Medicare Hearings and Appeals, $0.004; Office of the National Coordinator for Health Information Technology, $0.105; Pre-Existing Condition Insurance Plan Program, $0.013; Pregnancy Assistance Fund, $0.024; Program Management, $0.241; Rate Review Grants, $0.035; Risk Adjustment Program Payments, $1.759; State Grants and Demonstrations, $0.568; Substance Abuse and Mental Health Services Administration (2 accounts), $3.141; Supplemental Payments to UMWA Plans, $0.142; Transitional Reinsurance Program, $7.308; United Mine Workers of America--1992 Benefit Plan, $0.055; United Mine Workers of America 1993 Benefit Plan, $0.060; United Mine Workers of America Combined Benefit Fund, $0.106; United Mine Workers of America Combined Benefit Fund--Federal Payment, ($0.164); World Trade Center Health Program Fund, $0.238.

[22] Christopher Chantrill, usgovernmentspending.com.

[23] Christopher Chantrill, usgovernmentspending.com.

[24] Urban Institute and Brookings Institution, Tax Policy Center, "State Unemployment Tax Rates: 2008 to 2017," *Statistics*, http://www.taxpolicycenter.org/statistics/state- unemployment-tax-rates.

[25] Anisa Jibrell, "Study Shows Rise in U.S. Vehicle Ownership Per Person, Household," *Automotive News*, January 23, 2018, https://www.autonews.com/article/20180123/MOBILITY/180129900/study-shows-rise-in-u-s-vehicle-ownership-per-person-household. Notwithstanding the title, per-person and per-household car ownership peaked in 2006 at 0.79 cars/person and 2.05 cars/household, falling in 2016 to 0.77 cars/person and 1.97 cars/household. In recent years, the rates have ticked up, but the essential story is that U.S. car ownership is on a plateau. Meanwhile, compared to the 2004 peak, there has been a 5.3% drop through 2016

in miles driven per person and a 7% drop in miles driven per household. This trend, too, may tick up, but the overall picture is a plateau.

26 Social Security Administration, "Earnings and Employment Data for Workers Covered Under Social Security and Medicare, By State and County, 2015," SSA Publication No. 13-11784, May 2018, Table 1, "Number of persons with Social Security (OASDI) taxable earnings, amount taxable, and contributions, by state or other area, sex, and type of earnings, 2015," 3, and Table 2,"Number of persons with Social Security (OASDI) taxable earnings, by state or other area, sex, and age, 2015," 7. The calculation assumes that 40% of the under-20 group of workers with taxable earnings consists of 19 years old.

27 U.S. Census Bureau, Annual Estimates of the Resident Population for Selected Age Groups by Sex for the United States, States, Counties and Puerto Rico Commonwealth and Municipios: April 1, 2010 to July 1, 2016, released June 2017, https://factfinder.census.gov. The calculation assumes that 80% of the 15-19 year old age group consists of 15-18 years olds.

28 Urban Institute/Brookings Institution, *Tax Expenditure Budget*, citing Joint Committee on Taxation, *Estimates of Federal Tax Expenditures For Fiscal Years 2017–2021*, JCX-34-18, 2018.

29 Toder *et al,*, *Distributional Effects.*

30 U.S. Census Bureau, Annual Estimates of the Resident Population for Selected Age Groups by Sex for the United States, States, Counties and Puerto Rico Commonwealth and Municipios: April 1, 2010 to July 1, 2016, released June 2017, https://factfinder.census.gov.

31 Medicare currently provides SSDI recipients under 65 with health insurance. This redesign of the New Deal settlement and 2015 budget recalculation do not alter that policy.

32 Joanne Fontana, Thomas Murawski, and Sean Little, Milliman, *Milliman Research Report*, "Impact of Changing ACA Age Rating Structure: An Analysis of Premiums and Enrollment By Age Band," January 31, 2017, and Table A.2: Changes in 2018 Illustrative Monthly Individual Silver Plan Premiums-3:1 Age Curve v. 5:1 Age Curve, 20, http://us.milliman.com/uploadedFiles/insight/2017/MillimanACAAgeBands_0131_Final.pdf.

33 Fontana *et al.*, *Milliman Research Report.*

34 Juliette Kubanski, Tricia Neuman, and Anthony Damico, Kaiser Family Foundation, *Medicare's Role for People Under 65 With Disabilities*, August 12, 2016, https://www.kff.org/medicare/issue-brief/medicares-role-for-people-under-age-65-with-disabilities/.

35 U.S. Department of Defense, *2015 Demographics: Profile of the Military Community*, "Executive Summary: Overview of Military Personnel," iii, http://download.militaryonesource.mil/12038/MOS/Reports/2015-Demographics-Report.pdf.

36 Kristen Bialik, Pew Research Center, "The Changing Face of America's Veteran Population," *FactTank*, November 20, 2017, http://www.pewresearch.org/fact-tank/2017/11/10/the-changing-face-of-americas-veteran-population/.

37 CMS, *Methodology Paper*, 25.

38 Mike Bare, Erik Bakken, John Mullahy, and David Riemer, "The Dane Difference: Why Are Dane County's Exchange Premiums Lower," *Health Affairs*, December 18, 2014, https://www.healthaffairs.org/do/10.1377/hblog20141218.042838/full/.

39 Ashley Semanskee, Gary Claxton, and Larry Levitt, Kaiser Family Foundation, "How Premiums Are Changing In 2018," *Health Costs*, Table 1: Average Change in the Lowest-Cost Premium by Metal Level Before Tax Credit, 2017-2018 for a 40-year-old, November 29, 2017, https://www.kff.org/health-reform/issue-brief/how-premiums-are-changing-in-2018/.

40 CMS, *Methodology Paper*, 4.

41 CMS, *Methodology Paper*, 4.

42 CMS, *Methodology Paper*, 4. Out-of-pocket ("self-insurance") covered total costs of $194.4 billion. Private health insurance covered costs of $876.6 billion. Medicaid and CHIP covered costs, respectively, of $425.3 billion and $10.4 billion.

43 CMS, *Methodology Paper*, 30.

44 Cathy Schoen, Karen Davis, and Amber Willink, The Commonwealth Fund, *Medicare Beneficiaries' High Out-of-Pocket Costs: Cost Burdens by Income and Health Status*, May 12, 2017, Appendix F, "Appendix 5. Out-of-Pocket Spending by Type of Service and Medicare Beneficiary Income, Coverage, and Health Status," http://authoring.commonwealthfund.org/~/media/files/publications/issue-brief/2017/may/schoen_medicare_cost_burden_appendices.pdf.

45 Bare *et al.*, *Health Affairs*.

46 Nicole Cafarella Lallemand, Urban Institute, "Health Policy Brief: Reducing Waste in Health Care," *Health Affairs*, December 13, 2012, 1-2, https://www.healthaffairs.org/do/10.1377/hpb20121213.959735/full/healthpolicybrief_82.pdf.

[47] Workers' 65 and over would not be covered by YoungMedicare. All references in this section to the financing of YoungMedicare refer to under-65 individuals, under-65 workers, and the wages under-65 employees earn from their employers.

[48] CMS, *NHE Tables*, Household Contribution, Table 5-2.

[49] CMS, *NHE Tables*, Private Business Contribution, Table 5-1, Federal Government Contribution, Table 5-3, and State and Local Government Contribution, Table 5-4.

[50] In the U.S. Supreme Court's ruling in one of the Affordable Care Act cases, *National Federation of Independent Business v. Sebelius*, 567 U.S. 519 (2012), the Court per Chief Justice Roberts found that the individual penalty that workers were required to pay, while not a valid exercise of Congress' power under the Commerce Clause, was a constitutionally valid use of Congress' taxing power. The Court's decision to narrow the scope of the Commerce Clause raises questions about whether commercial activity by self-employed individuals and small firms that does not clearly affect interstate commerce may be subjected to other mandates under the Commerce Clause

[51] T. R. Reid, *A Fine Mess: A Global Quest for a Simpler, Fairer, and More Efficient Tax System* (New York: Penguin, 2017).

[52] In a speech in 1904, Justice Oliver Wendell Holmes, Jr., reportedly declared that "taxes are the price we pay for a civilized society." Almost a quarter-century later, in 1927, the Great Dissenter formally stated in a U.S. Supreme Court case: "Taxes are what we pay for civilized society," *Compania General De Tabacos De Filipinas v. Collector of Internal Revenue*, 275 U.S. 87, 100. The first variation appears above the entrance to the Internal Revenue Service headquarters on Constitution Avenue in Washington, D.C. http://en.wikiquote.org/wiki/Oliver_Wendell_Holmes,_Jr. About a century earlier, in 1819, Daniel Webster had argued in the case of *McCulloch v. Maryland* that the State of Maryland could not tax one of the branches of the Second Bank of the United States. Chief Justice John Marshall agreed, writing for a unanimous Supreme Court majority: "That the power to tax involves the power to destroy . . . [is] not to be denied." 17 U.S. 316, 431. https://supreme.justia.com/cases/federal/us/17/316/#tab-opinion-1918127.

ACKNOWLEDGMENTS

As I wrote this book, I received the help and advice of family, friends, and colleagues. Many helped simply by listening. Others offered detailed suggestions. Their candid criticism has been as valuable as their kind encouragement. I list here their names without titles. I am deeply grateful to each and all.

I am above all indebted to my wife, Ellie Graan, to whom this book is dedicated. More than anyone, she has traveled with me on the decades-long journey to its completion—listening, questioning, commenting, suggesting, and steadfastly providing support as the book grew from vague concept to finished text— always candid, always loving.

I also want to thank our children, Daniel Graan Riemer and Joseph Graan Riemer, for patiently hearing me explain my thinking, and for offering practical help along the way. Their wives, Paula Phillips and Tiffany Choe, have been generous with their attention and feedback. I wish to thank as well the following family members for inspiring and assisting me in different ways: my parents, the late Neal Riemer and Ruby Riemer; my brothers, Jeremiah Riemer and Seth Riemer; and Aaron Dropp, Kyle Dropp, Erica Eigenberg, Julie Eigenberg, Steve Itzkowitz, Judy Katz, Jake Nawrocki, Carol Ovadia, Sa'adia Ovadia, Laurie Riemer, and Stephen Riemer. I should add as well my thanks for the unique inspiration that can come only from a new child: grandson Nathaniel Bernardo Phillips Riemer.

For three decades I have belonged to a group of families who meet every Monday night for dinner to share our news, sorrows, and joys, as well as discuss politics and coordinate several campaigns for public office. The Community Dinner Group, over a long stretch of time, has heard me formulate bits and pieces—eventually, a more coherent summary—of the thinking that fed into this book. Along the way, the members of this group have not been shy to challenge or suggest; but they never flagged in their encouragement. I wish to thank (in addition to my wife and my immediate family) these close personal friends: Cynthia Brown, Karen Campbell, Claudio Cortes, John Gardner, Julie Kerksick, Andy Moss, Maggie Moss, Kathy Ronco, and Kevin Ronnie.

It was during my stint as Director of the Community Advocates Public Policy Institute in Milwaukee, and later as Senior Fellow, that the specific form and content of this book took shape. My colleagues often heard me out, and gave me specific assistance, along the way. Thanks to Michael Bare, Rob Cherry, Andi Elliott, Julie Kerksick (again), Lisa Kaiser, Maudwella Kirkendoll, Kari Lerch, and Conor Williams.

In the fall of 2012, I received the extraordinary gift of a residency at the Rockefeller Foundation's Bellagio Center. During the month I overlooked the beauty of Lake Como in northern Italy, I wrote a draft of this book from start to finish. The residents and staff of the Bellagio Center were the first to give me feedback on the outline of what you have now read. I am indebted to the Rockefeller Foundation for this unique opportunity, as well as to my Bellagio colleagues Mehjabeen Abidi–Habib, Gisselle Corbie-Smith, Danya Dewanti, Kim Dovey, Ahmad Fuadi, Sandra Gifford, Susan Henry, Claudio Holzner, Yuen Foong Khong, Pilar Palacia, Michael Peletz, Rina Saeed Khan, Sonali Ojha, Fatima Sadiqi, and Marla Salmon.

Dozens of other friends and colleagues have heard my summaries of pieces — and sometimes the whole — of this book's analysis and argument. Invariably, they gave me useful criticism and practical help along the turns and straightaways of this book's path from concept to completion. I know I will inadvertently leave out the names of some to whom I am indebted. Remembering as best I can the dozens who have helped me, I want to thank: Lynn Adelman, Tammy Baldwin, Mandela Barnes, Tom Barrett, Jeff Bentoff, Lonnie Berger, Laura Berntsen, Bruce Boucher, John Bryson, Jonathan Canter, Abigail Carlton, Bill Christofferson, Dennis Conta, Caroline Cracraft, Barbara Crosby, Sheldon Danziger, Dennis Dresang, Greg Duncan, Indivar Dutta-Gupta, Peter Edelman, Lisa Ellinger, Jon Ellingson, Joe Ellwanger, Alain Enthoven, Kathleen Falk, Cathy Feierstein, Andy Feldman, Alex Field, Enrique Figueroa, Marty Finkler, Nancy Frank, Austin Frerick, Howard Fuller, Anthony Gad, Craig Gannett, Cynthia Gannett, Ken Germanson, Linda Giannarelli, David Gordon, Whitney Gould, Evan Goyke, Bob Greenstreet, Pat Hall, Ron Haskins, Daniel Holland, Gini Holland, Bill Holohan, Steve Holt, June Hopkins, Dan Horowitz, Helen Horowitz, Lone Hummelshoj, Steve Jacquart, David Kamens, Mary Kelly, Walter Kelly, Don Kettl, Ted Kolderie, Zach Komes, Cary Koplin, Nik Kovac, Robert Kraig, Peter Kramer, Steve Lachowicz, Meghan Ladwig, Larry LeBlanc, Lance

Liebman, Kye Lippold, Ted Marmor, David Marsh, Will Marshall, Bill McLaughlin, Diane Michaels, Carl Milofsky, Anne Montgomery, Michael Morgan, Bill Mortimore, Susan Mudd, Brian O'Malley, Susan McGovern, Susan Mudd, Carl Mueller, David Osborne, John Norquist, Shelia Payton, Gillian Peele, Beth Perry, Judith Plotz, Paul Plotz, Sue Potts, Peter Ross Range, Andy Reschovsky, Alasdair Roberts, Joel Rogers, Jim Rowen, George Rowing, Amy Rynell, Warren Sazama, John Schaetzl, Luke Shaefer, Michael Shanahan, Burt Solomon, Gretchen Schuldt, Beth Schulman, Tim Smeeding, Greg Squires, Dean Strang, Anne Summers, Ken Szallai, Beverly Stein, Eugene Steuerle, Jim Tallon, Kima Taylor, Annie Thomas, Moray Thomas, Bruce Thompson, Lynde B. Uihlein, Sebastian Van Oudenallen, Joe Volk, Chris Warland, Dick Weiss, Dan Willett, Valerie Wolk, and Melissa Young.

My website, www.govinplace.org, also titled *Putting Government In Its Place*, preceded this book. About halfway through writing the book, I felt a powerful need to "get something out there." So I paused for several months, designed and launched the website, and then went back to completing the book. This process had a side benefit: shortening the book's length. I use nearly a dozen links to PDF files embedded in the website as unofficial appendices, rather than adding the text of those PDF files as formal appendices at the end of the book.

The appearance and functionality of the website, however, are not my creation. They are the work of Byte Studio in Milwaukee and the innovative, patient, and responsive Byte team that I had the pleasure to work with: founder Michael Diedrick, Samantha Korthof, and Steven Price.

Gwen Moore has generously provided the Foreword to this book. I would like to thank her not only for her kind words, but also for the extraordinary leadership she has provided to Milwaukee, Wisconsin, and the nation during her remarkable career of public service. An unflagging champion for those left out and left behind, Gwen Moore has been a model for all Milwaukeeans who care about justice and understand—as she does—that the fight will not be won unless it is carried to state capitols and Washington, DC.

Finally, I want to express my enormous gratitude to my editor and publisher, Kira Henschel, and HenschelHAUS Publishing. I am indebted to Kira's faith in the value of this book's story and argument, her skill and imagination throughout the editing process, and her dedication in advancing the book from manuscript to proofs to publication. Every author should be as fortunate as I have been in enjoying the support and skill of such an extraordinary editor and publisher. Thank you, Kira.

ABOUT THE AUTHOR

DAVID RIEMER'S CAREER DEFIES stereotypes. A progressive Democrat, he has worked closely with both Democrats and Republicans to create path-breaking public policy at the state level and influence national policy.

Employment and Income

Helping American adults to achieve full-time employment and adequate incomes through work-based policy reform has been an enduring focus. Since 1989, Riemer has played a lead role in Wisconsin in drafting and enacting state legislation—adopted with both Democratic and Republican support—to create Transitional Jobs programs, launch the nation's first refundable Earned Income Tax Credit (EITC) that adjusted for family size, and replace the state's welfare program with a work-focused substitute.

As the founding Director and now Senior Fellow at the Community Advocates Public Policy Institute in Milwaukee, much of Riemer's anti-poverty activity has involved designing a comprehensive work-based policy package to cut the poverty rate in half. According to an independent analysis by the Urban Institute, the policy package would reduce poverty in the U.S. by

50% or more. Based on this work, U.S. Senator Tammy Baldwin, with co-sponsor Senator Cory Booker, introduced in 2016 the "Stronger Way Act." This federal legislation, reintroduced in 2017, would create a national Transitional Jobs Program and substantially increase the federal EITC.

Health Care

Much of Riemer's work has involved health care. At the federal level, Riemer served as staff to Senator Edward Kennedy, where he helped draft bipartisan legislation to improve the nation's mental health policy.

In Wisconsin in the late 1990s, he worked closely with Democratic and Republican legislators, former Wisconsin Republican Governor Tommy Thompson, and the Clinton administration to expand insurance coverage for working families via the BadgerCare program.

From 2004 to 2007, as Director of the Wisconsin Health Project, he helped fashion two pieces of legislation that, if enacted, would have insured all Wisconsinites and controlled costs by creating an incentive-driven statewide health insurance exchange. Following the enactment of the Affordable Care Act in 2010, he co-authored three *amicus* briefs to the U.S. Supreme Court in support of the law's constitutionality

Education

Riemer has also played important roles at the state level in K12 education policy, both in promoting school integration and in defending school choice. His work included submission of *amicus* briefs to the Wisconsin Supreme Court and the

U.S. Supreme Court—on behalf of a variety of liberal and conservative policy-makers—in support of properly constructed school choice program.

Local and State Budgets

Formulating sound governmental budgets has been a central theme in Riemer's work. From 1988 to 2001, he helped prepare over a dozen City of Milwaukee budgets that improved municipal services and kept property taxes under control. He subsequently helped to craft the 2003-3005 State of Wisconsin budget that closed a $3.2 billion deficit without raising taxes.

Additional Background

Since 2008, Riemer has worked at the Community Advocates Public Policy Institute in Milwaukee, Wisconsin, where he is currently a Senior Fellow.

In 2003-2004, Riemer campaigned for Milwaukee County Executive. He received 101,000 votes, or 43% of the votes cast, in a race against County Executive Scott Walker (later Governor of Wisconsin, candidate for President, and recently defeated candidate for governor).

In 2003, Riemer served as Budget Director for Wisconsin Governor Jim Doyle. From 1988 to 2001, he worked in several positions in the administration of Milwaukee Mayor John Norquist, including Budget Director, Administration Director, and Chief of Staff.

From 1975 to 1988, Riemer was legal advisor to Wisconsin Governor Patrick Lucey; worked for Sen. Edward Kennedy's

Subcommittee on Health and Scientific Research; developed health policy options for the Wisconsin Legislative Fiscal Bureau; prepared a report on Wisconsin's uninsured for the state Department of Health and Social Services; and worked on health care cost containment for Time Insurance Company.

Riemer is the author of *The Prisoners of Welfare: Liberating America's Poor from Unemployment and Low Wages* (Praeger: 1988) and numerous articles on reducing unemployment, raising incomes, improving health insurance, and public administration. He is one of the co-founders of The New Hope Project.

Riemer was an Atlantic Fellow in Public Policy in London and Oxford, England, in 2002. His research focused on supplementing low-income workers' earnings through the tax system. He was an Eisenhower Fellow in Hungary in 1999.

As a Rockefeller Foundation resident in Bellagio, Italy, in 2012, Riemer began work on *Putting Government In Its Place: The Case for a New Deal 3.0.*

Riemer graduated from Milwaukee Public Schools' Riverside High School (1966), received an AB degree from Harvard College in History and Literature (1970), and earned a law degree from Harvard Law School (1975). He and his wife live in Milwaukee, Wisconsin.

CONTACT INFORMATION:

Email: DRiemerMil@gmail.com
info@govinplace.com
Website: www.govinplace.org

INDEX

slavery, 254, 260–261; *see also peonage*
Smith, Adam, 164, 166–167, 171, 427
SNAP (Supplemental Nutrition Assistance Program) ; *see means-tested welfare programs*
Social Security Act, program, and pensions; *see economic security guarantees*
Social Security Disability Insurance (SSDI); *see economic security guarantees*
spending; *see budgets and budgeting*
Stein, Gertrude, 218
subsidies; *see market manipulation*
Supplemental Poverty Measure (SPM); *see poverty line*
Supreme Court, U.S. (and federal courts in general), 47, 66, 221, 241, 254, 389, 395
surplus, 66, 313–314, 421
surpluses, 362

T

tax expenditures, 66–67, 155, 216–217, 219–222, 225, 228–229, 242, 245, 259, 316, 319, 340, 345, 355, 364–366, 368, 372; *see also market manipulation* taxes and taxation; *see budgets and budgeting*
technical colleges; *see education*
technology, 5, 74, 94, 100, 108, 110, 127, 141, 155, 174, 205, 213, 394
Temporary Assistance to Needy Families (TANF); *see means-tested welfare programs*
Tennessee Valley Authority (TVA), 28
transit
Amtrak, 361
light rail, 16, 209, 344, 359–360
rail, 66, 344, 360–361
streetcar, 16, 209, 344, 359–360
subway, 16, 344

train, 16, 209, 344, 359–361
transit (in general), 16, 77, 79, 208–209, 216, 230, 232–233, 250, 294, 321, 343–345, 348–349, 352–353, 359–361
Transitional Jobs (TJs); *see economic security guarantees*
Tricare (TRICARE), 238, 373, 375–377, 381
Trump, Donald, 70, 111, 262

U

U.S. Postal Service (USPS), 320, 342
UI, 57, 74–75, 158, 176–177, 322–323, 348, 357, 368, 403, 412
underemployed and underemployment, 5–6, 73, 79, 85, 134, 136–137, 141, 156, 159, 176, 206, 210, 214, 246, 250, 256, 263, 288, 317, 322–324; *see also economic insecurity*
unemployed and unemployment, 2, 4–6, 25, 29, 34, 49–51, 53–55, 57–59, 65, 73–75, 77–79, 83, 85–88, 134, 136–141, 156–157, 159, 162, 175–177, 185, 187, 206, 210, 214–215, 231, 236–237, 246, 250, 255–256, 263, 265, 272, 277–289, 309, 317, 321–324, 329, 356–357, 368–369, 393 ; *see also economic insecurity*
Unemployment Insurance (UI); *see economic security guarantees*
uninsured and underinsurance, 17, 21, 85–86, 103–105, 109, 128, 146, 159, 273, 378; *see also economic insecurity*
unions, 20, 55, 58, 112, 119, 134, 143–144, 157–158, 184, 254, 256
universities; *see education*
user and utility fees; *see budgets and budgeting*